Youth Justice Across the South Pacific

Youth Justice Across the South Pacific integrates youth justice and criminology research, therapeutic literature, and the authors' front-line experience to capture the complexity of youth offending and the ways in which these young people can present in therapeutic settings.

Drawing on the expertise and wisdom of the communities and practitioners across the South Pacific, this book provides a balanced view of therapeutic, clinical, and cultural (Indigenous, First Nations, Pasifika) understandings, research, and practice in youth justice and criminal justice psychology. It outlines a range of strong theoretical backgrounds, including vital indigenous worldviews, and emphasises the importance of community inclusion to promote and integrate the cultural, community, and clinical contexts within which these young people and their families live.

Written by Indigenous and cross-cultural practitioners, academics, and community leaders, *Youth Justice Across the South Pacific* is essential for those serving within youth justice, including students and professionals committed to working authentically for young people and their families in justice.

Julia Ioane is Professor of Clinical and Pacific Psychology at Massey University, Auckland, Aotearoa, New Zealand, and Clinical Psychologist in the Justice Sector.

Karmyn Billing is a Clinical Psychologist in Tāmaki Makaurau, Auckland, Aotearoa, New Zealand.

Patrick Mendes is Senior Māori Cultural Advisor at Tū Māia, Auckland, Aotearoa, New Zealand.

Ashley Morris is Executive Director, First Nations Services at Victoria Legal Aid, Melbourne, Australia.

Ian Lambie is Professor of Clinical Psychology at the University of Auckland, Aotearoa, New Zealand, and Chief Science Advisor for the Justice Sector for the New Zealand Government.

Youth Justice Across the South Pacific

Aotearoa New Zealand, Australia, and the Pacific Islands

Edited by Julia Ioane, Karmyn Billing, Patrick Mendes, Ashley Morris, and Ian Lambie

Routledge
Taylor & Francis Group
LONDON AND NEW YORK

Designed cover image: Jenny Reid Designs

First published 2027
by Routledge
4 Park Square, Milton Park, Abingdon, Oxon OX14 4RN

and by Routledge
605 Third Avenue, New York, NY 10158

Routledge is an imprint of the Taylor & Francis Group, an Informa business

British Library Cataloguing-in-Publication Data
A catalogue record for this book is available from the British Library

ISBN: 978-1-032-28770-6 (hbk)
ISBN: 978-1-032-28767-6 (pbk)
ISBN: 978-1-003-29841-0 (ebk)

DOI: 10.4324/9781003298410

Typeset in Times New Roman
by Apex CoVantage, LLC

Dedication/Acknowledgement

Warm Pasifika greetings to you.

Tēnā koutou, tēnā koutou, tēnā koutou katoa.

We acknowledge Aboriginal and Torres Strait Islander people as the Traditional Owners of the land on which we live. We pay respects to Elders past and present and all other First Peoples.

We acknowledge and dedicate this book to our young people and their families who are impacted by the Justice system.

Contents

Figures

About the Editors

Julia Ioane (Pasifika)
Descendant from the villages of Fasito'outa and Leauva'a, Samoa

Julia is a clinical psychologist in Aotearoa New Zealand and NSW, Australia, with ongoing experience in child and youth justice. She is Professor of Clinical and Pacific Psychology at Massey University and continues to actively promote the inclusion of Indigenous worldviews in clinical psychology research and practice.

Karmyn Billing (Māori)
Descendant from the iwi (tribes) of Ngāti Pikiao, Ngāti Mākino, Ngāi Tai, Ngāi Tūhoe, and Pākehā (NZ European – originally Ingarangi – English)

Karmyn is from Rotorua, Aotearoa New Zealand, currently residing in Tāmaki Makaurau, Auckland, Aotearoa New Zealand. She is a clinical psychologist with extensive experience working with young people who are justice-involved and their families.

Patrick Mendes (Māori)
Descendant from the Iwi (tribes) of Ngāpuhi, Te Rarawa, and Te Aupouri

Patrick is a community leader and senior cultural advisor in child and adolescent mental health in Tāmaki Makaurau, Auckland, Aotearoa New Zealand. He also plays a pivotal role in providing cultural expertise and interventions for justice-involved Māori rangatahi adolescents and their families. Patrick works closely with many practitioners in youth justice in providing cultural and clinical assessments for the Youth Court.

Ashley Morris (First Nations)
Descendant of the Gunditjmara people

Ashley is from Victoria, Australia, and has worked his whole career to improve justice outcomes for Aboriginal communities. He is currently the inaugural Executive Director of First Nations Services for Victoria Legal Aid. Prior to this, Ashley was the manager of Koori Services and Program at the Children's Court of Victoria, leading the development and expansion of Koori services, including Koori Court and Marram-Ngala Ganbu.

Ian Lambie (Scottish)

Descendant from the Highland Scottish Clan of Lamont, Arygyll Scotland (Alba)

Ian is from Ōtepoti Dunedin (the "Edinburgh of the south"), Aotearoa New Zealand, and is Professor of Clinical Psychology at the University of Auckland with over three decades of experience working with young people in the child and youth justice system. Currently, he is Chief Science Advisor for the Justice Sector for the New Zealand government and continues to publish and present justice-related research at local and international levels.

Foreword

This book has been anticipated for a long time.

You hold in your hands a reference work created by Indigenous scholars, practitioners, and community leaders with the expressed purposes of raising Indigenous voices where Indigenous representation has formerly been silent or silenced; claiming cultural and political spaces that have often been relegated to the margins by dominant colonial institutions and systems; and establishing an authoritative and culturally embedded resource that privileges Indigenous knowledge, prioritises community aspirations, and ultimately contributes to positive outcomes for Indigenous young people involved with justice systems in the South Pacific.

The chapters include rich and insightful commentaries across important issues in the youth justice space such as trauma, the impact of colonisation, discrimination, structural oppression, sexual harm, firesetting, as well as identity and gender. The authors offer the fruit of their labours as *taonga*.[1] Indeed, it could be argued that the origins of the chapters that make up this book go back generations and remind us of the rich heritage that each contributor brings with them. The wisdom of their words draws on past traditions and ancient knowledges, reflecting the traumas and resilience of their people – past and present – but always with a view to maintaining hope and positively productive futures in a rapidly changing society.

To be invited to step into Pasifika, Māori, and First Australian spaces is to encounter collective social worlds within a broader, holistic system with the natural world that is often incommensurate with institutions that are intertwined with oppressive histories. When understood in this way, social networks, families, offending behaviour, interactions with the law, research, and clinical practice take on a wholly different significance.

I am reminded of the well-known whakataukī[2]: *Anei tātou nā ko te pō; anā tātou nā he rā ki tua*,[3] which speaks to the light this volume can offer to dispel the dark and the silences from before. In that spirit, the publication of *Youth Justice Across the South Pacific* signals the arrival of an important key reference work for some time to come.

The moment for this book is *now*.

Armon Tamatea
Rongowhakāta; Te Aitanga-a-Māhaki
Clinical Psychologist and Associate Professor
Te Whare Wānanga o Waikato

Notes

1 Reo Māori: treasure.
2 Reo Māori: saying; proverb.
3 'Here we are in the night and the day is yet to come'.

Our Journey

During 2021, early conversations between some of the editorial members began to look at creating a book about youth justice that prioritised views, experiences, and research relevant for working with youth in the justice system in Aotearoa New Zealand. As discussions continued, and a review of existing textbooks in the field was explored, there was a glaring omission in our opinion.

You will all be aware of the ongoing overrepresentation of Indigenous youth in youth justice statistics. However, what we noticed was that there was a paucity of literature prioritising these worldviews or how young people from these communities with offending behaviour are responded to and dealt with by their own communities and within their own traditional practices. Furthermore, much had been written from a Western worldview or by non-Indigenous authors.

We wanted to write a book that prioritised the voices of our own Indigenous communities.

This is a book *By* Indigenous,
For Indigenous,
With Indigenous

In this book, *Indigenous communities include Māori (Aotearoa New Zealand), First Nations (Australia) and Pacific (Pacific Island communities in the Pacific Islands, Aotearoa New Zealand and Australia).*

However, writing such a book meant that we needed to break the traditions of academic writing. We wanted practitioners, clinicians, cultural advisors, and community leaders to write this book alongside academia. We wanted to bring together community and culture, with academia and research. We wanted authors to come from the communities that they were writing about. Further, we wanted authors to write in their own unique style that acknowledges our oral cultures, such as the use of proverbs and traditional sayings. More importantly, we wanted this book to be readable by anyone. We consider that those working within the youth justice system, students, academics, lawyers, and practitioners would find this book helpful. We especially hope that this book will be helpful for our local Indigenous

DOI: 10.4324/9781003298410-1

communities, our families and hopefully for our young people involved with the Justice system. This was our goal.

We first began making sure that we, as Editors, represented the communities that we were writing about. As the process began to recruit potential authors in 2022, we wanted each chapter to represent our prioritised worldviews of Indigenous, Māori, First Nations, and Pasifika communities. We were ambitious.

We were aware as Editors that we also needed to "walk the talk" of maintaining our own cultural practices and protocols as Indigenous and Pākeha European, leading this project. Therefore, we instinctively prioritised our relationships with authors as being fundamental to our journey. This meant giving time and space to developing meaningful and culturally safe and appropriate connections between our authors and us. We held online meetings regularly (to reduce barriers to meeting due to distance and time commitments), and we assigned an editor to each chapter to maintain the relationship. Extensions to book chapters were needed at times as we were aware of the pressures, expectations, and numerous roles that many of our authors were involved in and that were outside of their professional duties.

We were also aware that authors were writing about their own community in relation to youth justice. This process can be painful as we write about some of the tragedies that continue to affect our communities. However, we remained hopeful as efforts were made to explore our traditional practices and solutions within our own communities.

From 2022 to 2025, there were many challenges experienced across our communities. These included, in Australia, the unsuccessful First Nations Voice Referendum (2023) and the change in bail laws that would undoubtedly impact our First Nations youth in Victoria (2025). In Aotearoa New Zealand, findings were released (2024) from the Inquiry into the Abuse in State Care, which further highlighted the harm experienced by young people (along with other vulnerable groups) in state care, considering the overrepresentation of Māori and Pasifika youth, and the Treaty Principles Bill that was unsuccessful (2025), as well as other legislative changes in Aotearoa New Zealand that particularly affect Māori and indigenous rights and self-determination. We would argue that the challenges faced by most authors and editors in this book are generally not experienced by authors who usually write about and conduct research relating to youth justice. Conducting research and writing chapters and articles in youth justice about your own community can be hopeful and painful – all at the same time. However, we also want to emphasise our gratitude and respect to our friends and colleagues who work alongside our Indigenous communities day-to-day and who participated in this journey. We acknowledge their work, contribution, and advocacy within our communities in justice spaces.

As we came to the end of our journey, we were aware of our ambition to have Indigenous worldviews throughout each chapter. It was not an easy task to have our communities write about themselves and their work, while also serving their community at the same time. Even though we did not fully achieve our goal, we did achieve representation of some of our Indigenous worldviews throughout the chapters. It is a start.

We as editors sincerely hope that you can take something away from this book. We thank you and honour you for all your work, contribution and love to our young people who are justice-involved. We also acknowledge our families who walk alongside their young people on a journey that can be painful and hopeful.

If we are to truly commit to the future of our communities, we must always look at our young people in communities that have largely been ignored or overlooked or whose voices are not prioritised. These include our young people and their families in the youth justice system.

Who We Are*

Associate Professor Susan Baidawi (Mandaean Iraqi) – Social Work, Monash University, Melbourne (Narrm) Australia

I was born in the Middle East and have lived most of my life as a settler in the Kulin Nation, Australia. I love Asian food and have a particular obsession with trying every Laksa I can find! One thing I've learned from working as a researcher with justice-involved young people is that not everything is spoken through words. My advice would be to always be curious about what young people are trying to communicate and to listen with our whole selves.

Professor Lorana Bartels (Jewish Australian) – Criminology, Australian National University; Adjunct Professor of Law, University of Canberra; University of Tasmania

I am a second-generation Jewish Australian with ties to the Netherlands, Romania, Hungary, and Germany. I like reading and bushwalking (tramping). I have seen young people in the "justice" system and how they find joy and connection even in the harshest of environments. My advice is to lean into those needs and try to make what you do with young people fun and engaging!

Dr Karmyn Billing (Māori) – Clinical psychologist

I am from Rotorua, Aotearoa New Zealand. My whakapapa (genealogy) is to Ngāti Pikiao, Ngāti Mākino, Ngāi Tai, and Ngāi Tūhoe on my mother's side and Pākehā (NZ European) on my father's side. I currently reside in Tāmaki Makaurau (Auckland) in the rohe (region) of Ngāti Whātua. I am a clinical psychologist with over 17 years of experience working with rangatahi (youth) who are justice-involved and their whānau. I currently work part-time in adult Māori mental health services and complete forensic assessments in my private practice. I am a Fellow of the New Zealand College of Clinical Psychologists and an associate member of EMDRNZ. I enjoy time at home with my beloved ngeru (cat) Kitty, reading, music, travelling, walks and birdwatching. I chose the following whakatauki (proverb), which encapsulates the most important thing I have learnt working with rangatahi:

DOI: 10.4324/9781003298410-2

Tangata ako ana i te kāinga, te tūranga ki te marae, tau ana

A person nurtured in the community contributes strongly to society

Dr John Davis (First Nations) – Director Riteways Wanjaus

(Ngai Cobble ~ Warra ~Barrungam ~ Bunya Burras: Murri dgaguns, Australia (via QLD))

We are revitalising our languages, I love to sing our songs and speak our lingo, "gundamena warras yau. Barrungam dgagunbarras!" Myself and my wifey are "mad hatters" when it comes to books. We are co/creating our own libraries – here, back on Country – Warra and everywhere in between! The base camp library is called, the "Lore House", a collection of literary and ISK-rich texts for sharing. Home camps are our groundings. It's so important our youth know, name, and can see their safe spaces.

"Each one – teach one . . ." Sharing grows that knowledge strength.

Esther Leauanae Earl (Pasifika) – Educational Psychologist

Kia ora and talofa lava, I'm from New Zealand and the proud daughter of immigrant parents from the villages of Iva and Vailele Uta in Western Samoa. My childhood dream was to voice an animated Disney princess, and although this didn't work out, I trained as a music therapist in a previous life. A good day involves family, true crime shows, jazz, and cheese. Working with youth has taught me the importance of "being with" rather than just "doing for" others and ourselves. My advice: Take and create moments to meaningfully engage with youth, remembering that every interaction is an intervention.

Dr Therese Ellis-Smith (Australian) – Forensic Psychologist.

I am based in south-east Queensland Australia, having worked across Victoria and Queensland within the criminal justice system for over 25 years. I have been in private practice for 15 years, working with offenders. I enjoy travelling, reading/learning and attending the ballet/theatre. Over my career, I have learnt that we all seek the same things, only some of us have fewer skills or fewer opportunities to achieve our goals, leading to antisocial behaviours which provide immediate gratification. When assisting young people to break these offending patterns, I've found it helpful to focus on controlling their impulsivity through non-judgemental guidance and upskilling, while also including their family and community connections.

Dr Inez Fainga'a-Manusione (Pasifika) – Community Research Fellow, Griffith University & Village Connect

Mālō e lelei, I live on the lands of the Yaggera and Yugambeh language-speaking peoples. My roots are in the villages of Pea and Vava'u in the Kingdom of Tonga, the Gumatj clan of the Northern Territory, Suva in Fiji and Fasito'o tai in Samoa. I am a professional actress who uses creativity to bring māfana (warmth) and melie (sweetness) to all spaces. Serving my community is my passion. My pearl of wisdom? Connection before content. Nobody cares how much you know unless they know how much you care.

Dr Edmond Fehoko (Pasifika) – Senior Lecturer, Human Nutrition and Associate Dean Pacific, University of Otago

Mālō "e lelei, I am from Aotearoa New Zealand, with ancestral links to Kotu, Mo" unga'one, Nomuka and Ma'ufanga, Tonga. I enjoy socialising and engaging with peoples around the kava bowl. My one advice would be "the greatest good you could do for another is not to share your riches but to reveal to them their own".

Dr Chris Garrod (United Kingdom) – Consultant Clinical Psychologist, Navigate Psychology Ltd.

I live in Auckland/Tamariki Makaurau. I am originally from Yorkshire in the United Kingdom, which was a historic stronghold of the Celtic and then Norse peoples. I love to experience different places and cultures, having been to all the continents bar Antarctica now. If not that, then outside, at the beach, and in the surf.

Something that I always hold in mind is that most of us would be in similar positions with the same environments. We're all the same, just trying to make our way in the world.

Dr Jessica Gerbic (Māori) – Clinical Psychologist

Ko Kopukairora tōku Maunga
Ko Waitao tōku Awa
Ko Tauranga tōku Moana
Ko Mātaatua tōku Waka
Ko Ngāti Pūkenga, ko Ngāti Pikiao ōku iwi
Ko Te Whetū tōku Mārae
Nō Živogošće, Nō Aerana ōku whānau

I'm based in Aotearoa New Zealand. I love making taonga pūoro (traditional Māori healing instruments) with my daughter. Rangatahi have taught me curiosity, to be like Māui, be a haututu (adventurous), try things, don't fear failing. My advice is to be authentically you. They don't need someone shape-shifted, just safety, predictability, and realness. That's how you help them stand in their mana.

Dr Sharynne Hamilton (First Nations) – Senior Research Fellow, The Kids Research Institute Australia, Adjunct Professor, University of Canberra and University of Western Sydney

I am a Ngunnawal, Aboriginal Australian woman. My ancestral links are to Canberra and Yass in NSW. I have two children and love weaving and art, swimming and walking on the beach. Justice-involved kids deserve better than what our systems give them. Keep your demands high, and your hopes even higher. Change is always possible.

Dr Logan Hamley (Māori) – Kaupapa Māori Researcher; Whakauae Research Services Ltd, Whanganui

Tēnā rā koutou, I'm from Aotearoa New Zealand and descend from the nations of Ngāti Rangi and Whanganui in the central and western regions of the North Island. I am learning how to knit and not get injured while playing "social" netball. Outside of that, I love cooking for family and friends. One thing I have learnt from working with youth in the justice system is that being pono (honest, straight up) will get you far, and not trying to seem "cool" will get you further!

My advice would be to see the big picture when working in the system – it is easy to get focused on the immediate issues and lose sight of what could come from looking a little wider.

Dr Glenda Harward-Nalder – Ngugi Elder, Quandamooka Nation

Yura Inez, I am an Australian Quandamooka First Nation. I was a foundation member of the Griffith University Indigenous Research Network, along with my countryman Prof Chris Matthews, from 2009, when I retired from my full-time position with the School of Education and Professional Studies, at Mt. Gravatt and Logan campuses. I have been a cultural advisor to academic research providing expertise as a First Nation perspective. Many Quandamooka families also have Fijian heritage and another cultural connection to our Pasifika community!

Dr Andrew Craig Immelman (South African) – Child and Adolescent Psychiatrist

I was born in South Africa and have lived in Aotearoa New Zealand for over 30 years. I have ancestral ties to an English missionary to the Pacific and a German WWI fighter pilot. I do not think we should be ashamed of dialectics outside of our control. I enjoy cooking and gardening; increasingly, I appreciate how small efforts create cumulative, meaningful change. My advice is tika, pono, aroha: do the right thing fairly; be straight up, speak the truth with empathy. These are aspirational goals, easier said than done. I've been humbled to hear youth reflect my words back years later, reminding me of the power of connection.

Folasaitu Professor Julia Ioane (Pasifika) – Massey University; Clinical Psychologist

Mālō le soifua maua. I was born in Aotearoa New Zealand, with ancestral connections to the villages of Fasito'outa and Leauva'a in Samoa. Family, friends, and running keep me grounded and humble. Working with young people reminds me that we all want to have someone we can trust and feel safe with. My advice to those of us working in the justice system – do our job well and keep finding ways to do our job better.

Amanda Jones (Australian) – Director of Research and Evidence Development, Victorian Aboriginal Legal Service

I am of settler background, from Wurundjeri Country. I love exploring wine regions and talking to wine makers (I could listen to the good ones for hours)!

I have learned that young people need adults to believe in them and care deeply about them (like everyone else), and that they are experts at recognising whether or not you are being authentic. So if you are not feeling authentic in your positive regard, ask yourself if this work is really for you (and it's not just an off day).

Professor Ian Lambie (Scottish) – Clinical Psychology Department, University of Auckland and Chief Science Advisor for the Justice Sector, New Zealand Government

I was born and raised in Ōtepoti (Dunedin – Dùn Èideann ["fort of Edin"], the Scottish Gaelic name for Edinburgh). My Scottish Clan is Lamont from the Cowal peninsula in Argyll, Scotland/Alba. I love tramping and being outdoors with nature. Spending time with my family and friends is really important to me. Nature and people nourish and feed my soul. I have learnt from young people that trust takes time to build, you must truly listen to them and never, never give up. For those working in the justice system – stay motivated, be committed, and have hope.

Patrick Mendes (Māori) – Kaihautū

Ko Ngātokimatawhaorua Te Waka
Ko Nukutawhiti Te Tangata
Ko Hokianga Whakapau Karakia Te Moana
Ko Ngai Tūpoto Te Hapū
Ko Motukaraka, Mitimiti akū Papakainga
Ko Ngāpuhi, Te Rarawa, Te Aupouri ōku Iwi

I have over 22 years of experience in primary and mental health, specialising in child and adolescent mental health. I continue to provide cultural expertise and interventions, particularly for Māori Rangatahi (Adolescent) and their whānau. I also take many of our justice-involved rangatahi into outdoor sports activities and tournaments.

Ashley Morris (First Nations) – Executive Director, First Nations, Services, Victoria Legal Aid

I am currently living in central Victoria, Australia, with connections to Gunditjmara people from southwest districts in Victoria. I love music and enjoy restoring and working on cars. Over the years, working with young people in the justice system, I've learnt that connection to culture and community is a significant protective factor for Koori young people.

My advice would be to recognise Aboriginal expertise and enable transfer of power, resourcing, and decision-making to Aboriginal communities.

Dr Raewyn Mutch (Māori) – Clinical Associate Professor, University of Western Australia, Curtin University; Paediatrician, Perth Children's Hospital; Telethon Kids

I am from Tokorima Aotearoa living on unceded Whadjuk Noongar Boodja.

Ko Kāti Te Atawhiua te Hapū, Ko Tahu Pōtiki te Tangata, Ko Waihopai, Ko Awarua, Ko Kāi Tahu ōku Runaka.

I love being in the mountains, the snow, reading, and yoga. Young people in detention are surviving direct and vicarious harm. They'll inspect you on the first meeting to see if you're trustworthy, their safety, yet also their richness, for they still hope to find good in anyone. Don't fail them. Elevate their voice.

Dr Rochelle Nafatali (Pasifika) – Clinical Psychologist

Talofa lava, I hail from Aotearoa New Zealand, of second-generation Samoan (Luatuānu'u, Lauli'i), and third-generation NZ-European descent. I live in Te Tai-tokerau, Northland, where I am a psychologist with the Ara Poutama Aotearoa Department of Corrections. My other love is autism research with Pacific families, inspired by my son. I am often blown away by the willingness of young people to give me their trust when no one in their lives has proven trustworthy; they deserve my best. I believe in the saying "No one cares how much you know, until they know how much you care" Soifua manuia.

Lamauta Dr Vaoiva Natapu-Ponton (Pasifika) – Senior Research Fellow and Academic Advisor for Māori and Pasifika Engagement Program, Griffith University

My ancestral ties link to Samoa (Moata'a, Apolima, Iva, and Saipipi) and Tonga. I enjoy taking long walks on the beach with my family; the ocean always soothes me. For more than two decades, my experience in working with youth in the Melbourne Justice System and wider Australia has shown that young people take note of others who will show genuine care in knowing their values and beliefs. That is when they are willing to participate in programmes that further their prospects.

Dr Victoria Nazari (Iranian Armenian) – Clinical Psychologist

Kia ora, I was born in Tāmaki Makaurau (Auckland) with connections to Iran and Armenia through my whānau. I love nature, spending time with my pets, and catching up with friends and whānau. While I haven't worked extensively with youth in the justice system, I've learned from colleagues and related roles how vital it is to truly see the person you're working with. So, it's important to build genuine relationships, be consistent, and listen deeply – young people always know when you're being real with them.

Negar Panahi (Iranian) – Principal Managing Lawyer of Balit Ngulu at Victorian Aboriginal Legal Service

I'm Negs, short for Negar, and I'm the Principal Managing Lawyer of Balit Ngulu at the Victorian Aboriginal Legal Service. I'm of Iranian heritage and have lived and worked on Wurundjeri Country for the past 25 years. I enjoy spending time with my family and friends, heading to the beach any opportunity I get, and going on long walks. Working alongside Aboriginal young people has shown me the power of resilience, honesty, and connection to culture. My advice for those in the youth justice system: don't make empty promises, build trust first, as without it, change is just talk.

Dr Nina Papalia (Italian) – Senior Lecturer, Registered Clinical and Forensic Psychologist, Centre for Forensic Behavioural Science, Swinburne University of Technology & Victorian Institute of Forensic Mental Health (Forensicare)

I'm Nina – short for my Italian name, Giovanna – and I'm from Melbourne, Australia, where I live with my husband and our two young children. I grew up on the beautiful Mornington Peninsula and love early mornings, staying active, and a strong Melbourne coffee. Through my work and research with justice-involved young people, I've learned that growth rarely follows a straight line – what seems like a small win is often a big one. My advice to others in this space is simple: be yourself. Young people have an incredible radar for authenticity, and when they see it, they value it deeply.

Kate Perry (Māori) – Doctoral Candidate – Doctor of Clinical Psychology, University of Auckland.

I am from Aotearoa New Zealand and whakapapa to Whakatāne in the Eastern Bay of Plenty and Ngāti Awa. I spent my childhood in Brunei and the United Arab Emirates, I enjoy travelling and love spending time with my partner, family and friends. One thing I have learned while working with youth in the Justice System is to never make assumptions and to always put your best foot forward to provide the best care possible. My advice to people working in the Justice system, or to those who hope to, would be to celebrate the small wins and to keep pushing forward despite the barriers you might face.

Carmen Julie Shelley (First Nations) – Aboriginal Clinical Advisor

I am a proud Kamilaroi woman from the Gunnedah region of New South Wales; I was born on Dharuk land and am respectfully recognised by both communities. I love spending time with my family and community, collecting tea sets, and crocheting. Things I have learnt is that many Aboriginal families are distrustful of government systems due to past negative experiences. My advice would be building trust with families, and in Aboriginal communities, this is essential in counselling, as young people need to feel safe before they will open up, something that requires time and patience.

Dr Yvonne Ualesi (Pasifika) – Program Director AFSE, University of Melbourne

Talofa lava, I am from Aotearoa New Zealand with ancestral ties to Samoa, Tokelau, and Fiji, hailing from the villages of Mulivai Safata, Pu'apu'a, Saipipi, Savalalo, Lotopa, Fakaofo, and Ovalau.

I have four adult children with my husband, and we love group fitness. Things I've learned working with youth in the justice system are that they are our biggest teachers. They're the most strategic, creative, and intelligent minds. My advice when working with tupulaga would be to use every opportunity to show Alofa and extend grace, reminding them their story matters and they get to author their next chapter.

Sean Vartiainen – Intern Psychologist, Doctor of Clinical Psychology Candidate; University of Auckland

Talofa Lava, I'm from Aotearoa New Zealand, with ancestral links to Lepea in Samoa and heritage from Helsinki and Poland. I collect graphic novels and enjoy contemporary literature and film. I've been fortunate to study in Pasifika-specific mental health settings, where I've learnt to look beyond symptom and diagnosis – to see the mana of the person across all areas of life. In youth justice, people are often defined by their greatest moments of weakness. I hope we look further – to their strengths, values, and everything that can carry them into a future with hope.

Notes

* *We asked our book family to share who they are and provide what they have learnt from working with young people, or advice to those working with justice-involved young people.*

Section One

Background to Indigenous Youth Offending

1 Indigenous Worldviews and Knowledge in the Youth Justice Space

Edmond Fehoko, Inez Fainga'a-Manusione, John Davis, and Jessica Gerbic

We thank you and acknowledge:

Associate Professor Damian Scarf's unwavering commitment to equity, compassion, and culturally grounded research has helped illuminate pathways of hope and justice for Indigenous youth, challenging systems to honour their strength, stories, and sovereignty. May you continue to rest in peace.

Introduction

Understanding [Indigenous] worldviews of both the targeted [Indigenous] community and ourselves is imperative if we are going to do more good than harm (Bishop et al., 2002). This opening statement by Indigenous scholars in the field of research and education underpins the importance of this chapter. Here, we ground ourselves with the imperative to create and re-create more good than harm for our Indigenous peoples and communities. Like other areas, the youth justice field has evolved over the years, with more inclusive and engaging practices woven to fit the demographics of the system. Even with these changes, Indigenous peoples continue to face systemic and epistemic injustice, with many practices and processes culturally insensitive or unsafe.

In this light, we present Indigenous worldviews, knowledge, and practices to support practitioners in better engaging with young Indigenous peoples, our families, and communities. We draw on our research, where we have employed Indigenous knowledge and practices when engaging with young Indigenous peoples from the Pacific, Australia, and Aotearoa New Zealand. As a collective, we acknowledge the oppression, marginalisation, and exploitation suffered by Indigenous peoples, the desecration of their cultural and traditional landscapes, and the erosion of their rights to be sovereign in their respective nations. This chapter sets out to speak to practitioners, encouraging them to engage in critical self-reflection so that they may become better equipped to appropriately welcome, respect, believe, validate, centre, and value Indigenous knowledge and contexts. This chapter sets out to outline the following key objectives with case studies to aid understanding:

- Insight and context into Indigenous worldviews and how they can be integrated into supporting and better understanding Indigenous families and communities.

DOI: 10.4324/9781003298410-4

- Explore and understand the diversity within Māori and Pacific worldviews with a case study in Aotearoa New Zealand.
- Explore and understand the importance of Pacific worldviews with a case study in Australia.
- Explore and understand the importance of Aboriginal Australian worldviews.
- Explore and understand the importance of Māori worldviews.

Indigenous Worldviews

The notion of worldviews has been defined as mental lenses through which people often describe and perceive the world. Worldviews are cognitive, perceptual, and affective maps that people continuously use to make sense of the social landscape and to find their way to whatever goals they seek (Kurtz, 2013). They are developed throughout a person's lifetime through socialisation and social interaction. They are encompassing and pervasive in adherence and influence. Yet, they are usually unconsciously and uncritically taken for granted as "the way things are" (Hart, 2010). While they rarely alter significantly, worldviews can change slowly over time. A worldview can hold discrepancies and inconsistencies between beliefs and values within the worldview. Hence, worldviews often contain incongruencies (Harris, 2004).

It also has been suggested that, in any society, most members hold a dominant worldview (Brown and Strega, 2005). In light of this understanding of the notion of worldviews, working with Indigenous peoples will often require practitioners to act outside of the dominant worldview. Brown and Strega (2005) posited that there is no one definition of Indigenous knowledge because it is a holistic perspective in which arts, sciences, religion and philosophies are not separated. Further, it is a "cumulative body of knowledge and beliefs, handed down through generations of cultural transmission, about the relationship of living beings (including humans) with one another and with their environment" (Battiste & Henderson, 2000, p. 42). These vast knowledge systems connect human beings' past, present, and future to other living beings, environments, and the Creator, and maintain the lives of Indigenous peoples (Fainga'a-Manu Sione et al., 2024a). Indigenous peoples and communities have established ways of perceiving, viewing and understanding the world. Yet, until recently, their ways of knowing have been largely invisible.

The following sections of this chapter explore the Pacific, Aboriginal Australian and Māori worldviews, each exploration including case studies on how worldviews are implemented in youth initiatives, and each concludes with calls to action for practitioners.

Pacific Worldviews

Pacific people are both local and global; genealogically, spiritually and culturally connected to the lands, skies and seas of the Pacific, tracing back to the regions of Micronesia, Polynesia and Melanesia. As Hau'ofa (1994) noted, Pacific peoples are from the "sea of islands" that represents the vastness of the Pacific Ocean.

Thus, the term "Pacific" is not definitive but rather encompasses the many vast languages, cultures, practices and ethnicities. Emeritus Professor Albert Wendt (cited in Fehoko, 2014) argued that, for many Pacific peoples and for many Indigenous communities:

> We need to write, paint, sculpt, weave, dance, sing and think ourselves into existence. For too long, other people have done it for us – and they've usually stereotyped us or created versions of us that embody their own hang-ups and beliefs and prejudices about us. So, we have to write our own stories.
>
> (p. 1)

Pacific worldviews centre on values and beliefs that encapsulate how Pacific people view the world (Gegeo & Watson-Gegeo, 2001). Former Head of State of Samoa, Tui Atua Tupua Tamasese Ta'isi Efi (2003), noted three essential elements that make up Pacific worldviews:

> [t]he environment, humans, the animate and inanimate (all natural life) as having its source in the sources in the same divine origin, imbued with the life force, interrelated and genealogically connected.
>
> (p. 6)

Mila-Schaaf (2010) concurred with Tui Atua, referring to Pacific worldviews as:

> The interrelationship between all things (between people, the land, sea, sky, rocks, plants, surroundings) is sacred and cosmologically determined.
>
> (p. 135)

Fairbairn-Dunlop (2013) agreed that every Pacific community's behaviours and expectations aim to ensure a balance and harmony between the above-mentioned dimensions, which have also developed and evolved. Waldegrave et al. (2003) argued that the Samoan worldview ensures that relationships and networks are maintained between peoples, villages, the land, and the spirit world.

A Fijian worldview is considered to be shaped by the traditional Fijian social structures in which roles are prescribed according to a kinship group membership, which is based on the traditional hierarchy (Tuwere et al., 2012). Ravuvu (1987) proposed that traditional Fijian ceremonies, which continue today, are a life model that reflects the Fijian worldview and defines the social and political structures, religious beliefs, values and practices that underpin Fijian communities in everyday life.

The Tongan worldview is captured in the notion of fonua, which encapsulates the importance of spiritual and communal relationships, balance, and harmony (Tu'itahi, 2007). Fonua has two different aspects, each with unique and distinctive definitions. Firstly, fonua can be defined as land, country, territory, or people of the land. Fonua can also be defined as faitoka or grave. Secondly, fonua can be defined as a newborn's placenta or the afterbirth.

Working or conducting ethical research with Pacific peoples requires considering and understanding Pacific knowledge systems and specific conceptual frameworks, philosophical values, and beliefs (Tukuitonga & Finau, 1997). Family and community, rather than the individual, constitute the central element of Pacific worldviews. And while acknowledging the commonalities, we must also consider that there are differences between the Pacific cultures. A Samoan perspective values a spiritual and communal understanding and acknowledges the collective as the source needed to maintain and sustain wellbeing. This is reflected in the words of Tui Atua Tupua Tamasese Ta'isi Efi (2009):

> I am not an individual; I am an integral part of the cosmos. I share divinity with my ancestors, the land, the seas and the skies. I am not an individual, because I share my tofi (an inheritance) with my family, my village and my nation. I belong to my family and my family belongs to me. I belong to my village and my village belongs to me. I belong to my nation and my nation belongs to me. This is the essence of my belonging.
>
> (p. 1)

Furthermore, Pacific worldviews reflect an understanding that incorporates elements combined from the spiritual, social, and natural realms, authenticating important things in life. Du Plessis and Fairbairn-Dunlop (2009) highlighted that:

> what sustains people and what connects them to particular places and spaces is crucial to their identity. Spirituality or the sacred is fundamental, people are carriers of the lifeblood of future generations and have complex responsibilities to their physical environment and other living things. In Pacific communities, knowledge is communally made, sanctioned, shared and used with the aim of achieving the good life for all members.
>
> (p. 111)

Case Study: Faikava – A Cultural Practice and Social Space for Young People

Kava drinking has become commonplace for many Pacific peoples in the region and in several diasporic communities of Pacific peoples, such as in Aotearoa New Zealand, Australia and the United States of America. Traditionally, this cultural practice was used chiefly for ceremonial purposes. Today, the kava drinking practice has become more of an informal and socio-cultural classroom, allowing male elders and youth to socialise. Several studies have explored the role of faikava (kava drinking) as a cultural practice and social space for young Pacific peoples. For example, in Aotearoa New Zealand, Fehoko (2014) conducted a study on the experiences of New Zealand-born Tongan males participating in the faikava. He found that the faikava was an identity marker whereby Tongan male youth, through the informal talanoa, socialisation, and the singing of Tongan music, helped maintain and reinforce a sense of Tongan identity in Aotearoa New Zealand. Furthermore, the faikava space became an alternative to excessive alcohol consumption, drug use and abuse, and youth gang affiliation, among other social pressures. Similarly, in Fiji, Singh (2004) found that when kava is consumed, kava drinkers feel a sense of sociability, peace, harmony, brotherhood, reduced anxiety and stress, and a sense of sedation.

Call to Action

We are proposing the normalisation of the cultural practice of the faikava in the youth justice space to support young people in reinforcing and maintaining a sense of Pacific identity in diasporic communities. Collaboration and the co-designing of understanding and awareness of kava consumption will be needed from Pacific community leaders and cultural experts, especially regarding kava's socio-cultural use and value in the youth justice system. Parallel to this, educating justice stakeholders and professionals will also be an imperative for this movement. We must address two critical influencers in the youth justice space for transformative action to occur: raising awareness of the positives of kava use amongst our community leaders and indigenising decision-makers in the social justice space.

Questions for Consideration

- Do you and your organisation consider the diverse nature of Pacific cultures and communities when engaging with young Pacific people?
- Do you and your organisation apply a holistic and intergenerational approach when engaging with young Pacific peoples and their families?
- Do you have good working relationships with church and community groups, and if not, how would you establish and nurture a positive relationship to support young Pacific peoples and their families?
- How constructive are your initiatives and engagement methods, and do you consider a Pacific worldview when working with young Pacific peoples and their families?

Indigenous Worldviews in Australia

> The directional learning path our Indigenous Knowledge (IK) reveals . . . emerging in a way that is based in our lore and systems. What we refer to here in Australia is over 60,000 years of continuous cultural knowledge connected around 60,000 years' worth of campfires. The pattern which we gather and sit around these campfires is in circle . . . (the) pattern we have gathered around creates a distinct flow of energy and knowledge.
>
> (Davis & Coopes, 2022, p. 85)

Aboriginal worldviews span over 60,000 years of continuous cultural knowledge that is collected and "kinnected" through people and place (Davis & Coopes, 2022, p. 86). The circular pattern in which aboriginal communities gather and sit around campfires create a distinct flow of energy, time, and knowledge transfer, resulting in a process of production, transmission, application, and regeneration of Aboriginal knowledge (Davis & Coopes, 2022, p. 85). Such practices are defined by the Cobble (carpet snake) clan of the western Bunya Mountains plains (Queensland, Australia), as wanjau, meaning embassy in English. Wanjau refers to the relationships of exchange, reciprocation, and responsibility – personal, familial, and tribal (Davis & Coopes, 2022, p. 85).

The Aboriginal worldview as interconnected first and foremost with land as lore. What this means is that the land is sacred, as it defines and guides the sense of a fully cultural-spiritual landscape, within which there is an obligation to preserve the surrounding world, responding relationally. We hear the voices of our people and seeing our people in the field, in situ, within the challenges faced in modern living against a backdrop of very real and raw structural and dominant hegemonical power structures in what constitutes Australian society. The power imbalance presents itself as a real challenge for us/all as a modern Indigenous polity.

In our current politicisation of identity, vis à vis a recent national referendum on enshrining the Indigenous Voice into national constitutional law, the migloo majority voted against more voice. The Indigenous identity profoundly speaks truth to power through structures like Indigenous Community-controlled organisations because of this demographic = the Indigenous majority voted for voice. The truth to power comes in the pattern of First Nations' structural power levers and as brokers – upholding our own governance and Indigenous voices threaded through strategic, board-level structures through to operational, business, and service-delivery models. Indigenous Community-controlled businesses or organisations are not the norm or the loudest voices in social justice spaces like the justice system, education, and health. The voice that Indigenous people speak with, and the truth that is spoken to power, is represented in these liminal spaces in-between – the pattern that was signalled earlier in the campfires.

Case Study: Gunya Meta – First Nations Community-Controlled Voice

Off-Country, this right fire, this right story, is represented in a large southern Indigenous diaspora, Logan City – Yugambeh ngin Yuggera dgagun, in the city's centre, by the warm hearths of the First Nations community-controlled organisation called Gunya Meta.

The following is a reflection of the voices that make Gunya Meta pattern or reveal in relation to challenges faced in modern Australian society – like so-called youth justice. Specifically, this section focuses on Gunya Meta's response to the justice systems of the day and how they have co-created (Fletcher et al., 2023; Davis & Coopes, 2022) a programme and process to shift impacts from their liminal spaces.

The spaces that Gunya Meta occupies are the safest spaces for our First Nations communities and families. Recently, in the heart of our city, an Indigenous man was shot by local constabulary in response to a call-out to a scene. Understandably, hurt and confused, the families sought solace at the "back decks" of Gunya. A circle of safety has been created through making a structural change – developing Gunya Meta organisationally, through elders' leadership in the past and through to the current time, and delivering operational outputs coordinated by an expert First Nations CEO, all of which demonstrates "how" to build Indigenous leadership capacity in the social service and justice fields. Yet, as this case study may show, the re-patterning of these right ways, this right fire, is not yet propagated through dominant Migloo power brokerage and economic investment for scalability. The ongoing challenge for First Nations approaches is to move forward from "pilot" stages of programming.

This case study is a reflection on the richer context and Indigenous community-specific responses to the complex challenge of youth justice. Too often in our Migloo Australian media, political and socio-cultural youth challenges are classed as "problems to solve" – and thus massively oversimplified. To reflect the richness of country, we use our own heuristics to inform the approaches and utilise Indigenous research methods such as the enactment of yarning circles in the gathering and collation of data. The yarning circle as a process is part of the pattern of 60,000 campfires and now refers to a specific research data-gathering and sense-making technique which is First-Nations-led.

As in all research translations – like this chapter within a broader book– there are elements of our Indigenous knowledge which get lost in translation. The yarning circle is one such method which can get "lost in translation". We have sought to best show visually the way yarns build (see Figure 1.1). The circle pattern is important in flow and movement. Within Country, circle patterns remain as very real, tangible sites of references with raw materials juxtaposing landscapes as examples

Figure 1.1 A faikava at the Kalapu Fofo'anga, Grey Lynn, Auckland, New Zealand.

and set structures for the space and time of learning and doing. In a land of massive sense-making, of my people and for large groups across Queensland, and in the song lines which stretch over the nation, Bunya Burras is a great example of the bigger yarning circle and sense-making flows which exist on Country now and have existed since time immemorial. The structures in the cyclic pattern are known as bouls and in Migloo translation have become "bora". There are open – baulan – circle patterns and there are closed – duwur – ceremonial patterns (Davis & Coopes, 2022).

Within bouls there are three distinct, strength-based roles which make up and demonstrate the pattern "in action". That is, there is the importance of "setting" yarns in the form – the structure of circle – and there is just as much importance in listening and responding to local context, not as one form of leadership or way of doing but in translating through more than one, something that is "bigger than me", in principle and in praction (Steffenson, 2020). To that end, in the pattern, three parts of a yarn, of a story, are needed in yarning circle translation to show more deeply and see more definitively what the response to the flows are.

Central to the design flow is knowing and understanding context. And this section is focused on the voices of Logan City – specifically represented in the central circle by Gunya Meta Inc (see Figure 1.2). The strength-based setting of Gunya Meta translates in Aboriginal and Torres Strait languages as a familial house. In Indigenous knowledge archaeology and artefact storying, the netting designed and developed for hunting has been described as "mist nets" (Steffenson, 2020). Gunya Meta's social services act like mist nets. The case study logic flow is represented then by the next most powerful voice, Gunya Meta's CEO, Aunty Faith Green, who is "expert" in her field.

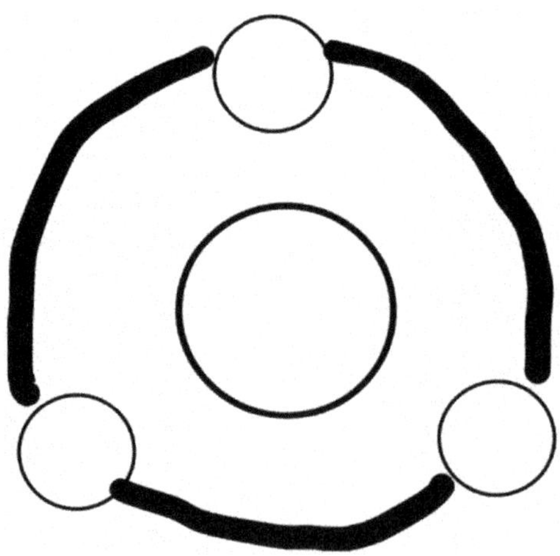

Figure 1.2 Yarning Circle = Case Study Capture

Expert coordination is important in any practice. Aunty Faith, in her dual role as community expert and executive administrator of Gunya Meta, is bringing the mist net, relational and kinnective approach to the fore, making space for First Nations family voices to be heard. The opportunity to pilot a community hub programme for First Nations juvenile justice is a direct output of Faith's leadership – her delivery of the mist net which is known, in Gunya Meta, as a "x3 generations strong" model of First Nations family leadership and support.

Gunya Meta has the expert leadership advice and cultural authority of respected Elder and educator, in Aunty Faith Green. Faith has led sustainable Indigenous education programmes for years in Logan Central. Her school model flagship, the "Bulkari Space" (Davis & Woods, 2019), is still impacting First Nations high school students a decade after she left. What Faith brings is an energy, an experience of the complexities of Logan City life, and knowledge of the impacts of our First Nations' experiences; and she uses these to develop and respond to the social and cultural context of the young people and the families they are kinnected to. Her kinnective mapping is second to none. In the yarning circle methodology and the practice of deep listening, she is able to state, place and brace young people for their experiential learning and for developing and growing within the leadership model. "These are my kids. These are Gunya Meta's families" (Aunty Faith Green, personal communication, 1 September 2023).

Through the organisation Faith administers, she effects further programme opportunities to "be safe" and navigate the juvenile justice system through extra nodular supports. Through enacting the yarning circle methodology and the process of the past in a modernised setting, Gunya Meta is the leading place-based model for change and voice. Gunya Meta's activity across Logan Central and the surrounding districts means that Migloo operators in our space, be they state departments or constabularies or care agencies, need a way to engage and connect with the Gunya Meta programme offerings.

To that end, a *pilot programme* in response to specific First Nations juvenile justice has been created. Aunty Faith seeks to find further, specific youth justice expertise to kolab and ko-design the Gunya Meta-informed juvenile justice pilot. The programme itself, "Stronger Families, Stronger Youth" (SFSY), has been designed to follow the strengths of programmatic responses already achieved in Gunya Meta. To enact the programme, a *Lead Facilitator* (see Figure 1.3) was recruited to actualise and run specific programme supports. This second relational pivot has a clear "line of sight" – this is Dwayne Watson, Senior Team Leader of Gunya Meta.

First Nations leader, Dwayne Watson is a facilitator who brings years of experience in child safety and juvenile justice. Seeking another way, more impactful, Dwayne sought Gunya Meta to work with and alongside his community. The attraction of working with a First Nations first, organisation is the draw card for a leader like Dwayne. The facilitator role is important relationally as the person in that role becomes the regular programme manager who takes any extra load or the pressures of coordination, and is added to the mist nets of support for the families involved.

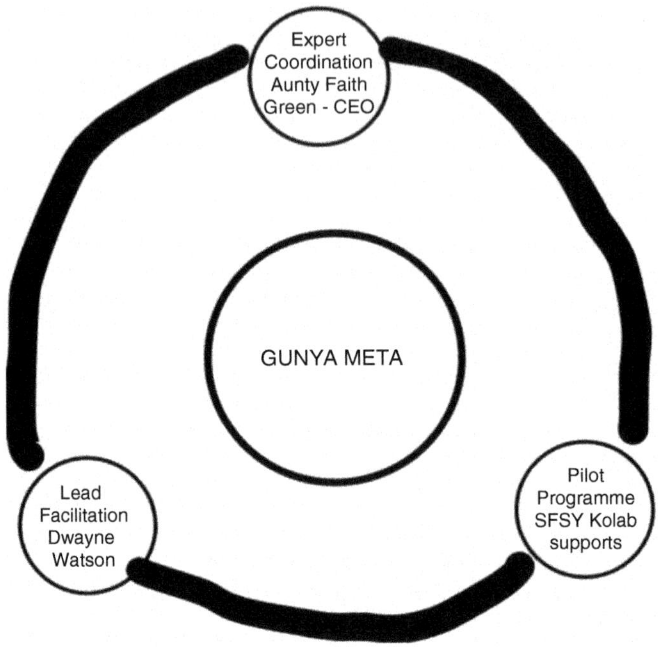

Figure 1.3 Gunya Meta Case Study

The SFSY programme is a pilot based on the strengths of Indigenous community kolab design. The supportive structures, the Migloo power brokers, the state departments and local constabularies, come into a pattern of relationships and connections already regenerated by the community-controlled organisation. The programme is focused on quality relationship support to a specific family group. Not over-subscribing or over-committing outputs, the specific, contextualised, decolonised approach to an Indigenous data response is known as applying "nahra kati" – good numbers (Walters & Anderson, 2013; Walters & Suina, 2018).

The initial responses to Gunya's safe space construction, as shown above, are now moving into the next phase – the expansion of programme. This will be an important step in how the quality assurance and directive flows of a foundational design maintain its integrity and, overall, improve the listening and responsiveness to youth justice challenges, amplifying community-controlled voices so affected families can speak their truths to power.

Call to Action

- Indigenous Knowledge System design and programme logics at the forefront of the design queue.
- Equity partnerships, not pilot projects. Devolve power in the field and invest in First Nations' bases of strength.

- True kolab power lies in the patterning of relationships in the Indigenous Knowledge System based on circles.
- Indigenous research methodology, like the yarning circle, is key to amplifying First Nations' voice.

Hybrid Identities and Worldviews of Māori and Pacific Peoples in Australia

Hau'ofa's declaration of not limiting ourselves to how we as Oceania are defined speaks to the core of the Māori and Pacific context and worldview within the Australian diaspora. It is diverse, differing between generations, with elders born in the islands, parents born and raised in New Zealand, and teenagers born and raised in Australia (Sione, 2023). Furthermore, there is a broader mix of cultural heritage within Māori and Pasifika families that not only spans across the Pacific nations but also includes First Nations Aboriginal, Torres Strait Islanders, Spanish, African, and other migrant communities. These differences result in the marrying of many Indigenous cultures, creating platforms for collaboration and challenges between worlds (Durham et al., 2022). Despite such challenges, there is a strong sense of cultural capital that remains prevalent among Australian-born Pasifika young people who embrace the differences as a strength (Durham et al., 2022). In Logan, Queensland, for example, there are 234 different cultural groups within a population of 363,057 people, and among whom Samoan is the second most spoken language after English (Fainga'a-Manu Sione et al., 2024b).

Emerging from such expansive diversity, six key frameworks are undergirding this multicultural Indigenous and intergenerational worldview that interweaves between the differing cultures and generations. First, spirituality plays a key role across generations and cultural groups. This includes Indigenous, Christian and traditional beliefs which inform our ways of being, knowing, and doing (Fainga'a-Manu Sione et al., 2024b; Fainga'a-Manu Sione et al., 2023). Within the diaspora, Christianity continues to play a prominent role in the lives of Pacific communities, with the Pacific church being the village that four to five generations attend regularly to engage in their culture, community, language, traditional foods, and spiritual/traditional healing methods (Durham et al., 2022; Fainga'a-Manu Sione et al., 2023). Research reveals that services established upon Western frameworks do not resonate with Pacific communities, which are more inclined to seek help, support and advice from their families, churches and community (Akbar et al., 2022; Cruickshank et al., 2019).

Service to others and privileging the collective over the individual is still a strong priority in Pacific communities (Akbar et al., 2021); however, with the younger Australian-born generation, there is a prominent shift to include the importance of the individual and prioritising their needs, as well as the collective, in a collective–individual manner (Fainga'a-Manu Sione et al., 2023). Agency, vision and innovation are key factors that mobilise multicultural communities to thrive and flourish, despite being from different Indigenous lands, after migrating to Australia to establish and build their families within a predominantly Western nation

(Fainga'a-Manu Sione et al., 2023). It is a vision for a better future for themselves and their families that sets the precedent for communities as they uphold their own Indigenous cultural ways of being, knowing, and doing.

How this impacts the ways in which services work with young people within the juvenile justice system, and their families, results in a hybrid approach which embraces a broader, diverse worldview. The KOKO Program is an example of a service being delivered using Māori and Pasifika knowledges and informed by Pasifika worldviews in Queensland, Australia, whilst also tailoring the delivery generationally, culturally and contextually. KOKO weaves together diverse worldviews and cultural fusions.

Case Study: KOKO Program for Māori and Pasifika Youth

Village Connect is Australia's first Pasifika Holistic Health Hub (hereafter, the hub), where a clinical maternity hub and a Pasifika charity are co-located inside a Pasifika church (Fainga'a-Manu Sione et al., 2024b). Numerous programmes, including spiritual, cultural, clinical, communal and individual services, are delivered from this one community-owned location. Pasifika ways of knowing and being are privileged within the hub. The KOKO Program was developed by Village Connect to reduce recidivism by connecting young people, their families/carers and significant others to country, culture and community, using a village approach.

It is a holistic framework that incorporates elders and church and community stakeholders, who are interwoven through the programme, which is facilitated by young Pasifika mentors aged between 18 and 25. This includes a 12-week intensive face-to-face programme. The connection to country, land and sea includes traditional fishing methods and cultural cooking practices and foods. Pathways into earning or learning ensure that family and individual-centred support engages the young person, their family/carer or significant others in the country, culture and community. Practical support, food parcels where appropriate, home visits to build relationships with the families or carers and a graduation ceremony are significant cultural practices in the village approach.

In 12 months of the pilot programme, referrals for 37 young people were received. Of the participants, 18 were listed on the serial repeat offenders list, meaning they are the state's most frequent repeat offenders. After their engagement in the KOKO Program, 11 young people were removed from the repeat offenders list, and 16 of the 27 young people who were engaged in the programme did not reoffend within 12 months. In an evaluation conducted by Griffith University (McDermid & Wren, 2023), one of the Pacific parents shared the following: "I felt that my child was more at ease in the programme, and that the Māori/Pacific workers were understanding to our family and situation. We were happier to engage and felt we were not looked down on". The capacity to reconnect young people to their country, community and culture in a holistic, intergenerational manner has been instrumental to the success.

Call to Action

We advocate for the youth justice sector to recognise that Western-centric systems and punitive detention centres are failing our Māori and Pasifika young people and their families. Authentic relationships need to be forged with Māori and Pasifika elders, faith leaders and community leaders, families, young people and their peers, to develop a village approach to working alongside both the youth justice system and the young offenders in a way that reconnects them back to country, culture and community. The inclusion of multicultural Indigenous perspectives centred upon spirituality, service, agency, vision and innovation is a significant way of working in a culturally grounded manner (Fainga'a-Manu Sione et al., 2023).

Questions for Consideration

- How can you diversify your support of the young person who acknowledges their cultural heritage? Consider the engagement of elders, community and connection to country strategies that KOKO includes.
- Representation matters. Do you have diversity in the workforce and service delivery that reflects the same cultural heritage groups of your young people and their families?
- Have you built networks and relationships into the local community and context in terms of elders, parents and young people?

Māori Worldviews

For Māori peoples, Te Ao Māori, or a Māori worldview, is a traditional belief system and way of understanding the world. It is not a static concept, but one that continues to evolve and reflect the realities of the spaces Māori occupy while maintaining core principles and values (Patterson, 1992). It encompasses various aspects of life, holding the belief that there is a continuous interconnection from the past, present and into the future for tangata (people) and the taiao (environment/whenua) as outlined in a well-known whakataukī (proverb)

> Kia whakatōmuri te haere whakamua:
> "I walk backwards into the future with my eyes fixed on my past"

Walker (1996), a prominent Māori academic, stated the past and present are knowable, reflected in the enduring collective strength Māori hold, carrying with them their Tīpuna (ancestors), Māoritanga (actioning of culture), and intrinsic connections to the whenua (land) existing both within the spiritual realm and in the physical (Patterson, 1992; Walker, 1996). This relationship is both unquantifiable and inseverable in the sense that it existed before someone was born and will continue once someone passes, for future generations. A Te Ao Māori worldview is best thought of as an intrinsic and holistic worldview, one that is grounded in Mātauranga Māori (Māori knowledge forms) and tikanga (customs and protocols).

Mātuaranga Māori does not refer explicitly to any particular methodology or a set of explicit actions or goals, as is the case with Kaupapa Māori theory. Instead, Mātauranga Māori is a phrase used to describe a body or a continuum of knowledge. Emerging from intergenerational and scientific observation, Mātauranga Māori is embedded in, and communicated through stories, traditions, practices (e.g. raranga (weaving)), and rituals (Smith et al., 2016; Hikuroa, 2016). It is comprised of traditional knowledge that traversed the Pacific as Māori migrated, along with distinct knowledge forming through time and isolation as a direct response to the environment Māori occupied upon their arrival to Aotearoa New Zealand (Mercier, 2018). Mātuaranga Māori is its own unique knowledge base as outlined by the concept of tūrangawaewae, with roots to the wider Pacific as reflected in shared concepts like "tapu".

Mātauranga Māori plays a crucial role in preserving and transmitting knowledge across generations. The embodiment and expression of Mātauranga Māori is seen within tikanga, with some viewing tikanga as a segment or expression of Mātauranga Māori. Tikanga takes many faces depending on the lens applied to it and the space it operates within; for example, in the justice system, it has been conceptualised as a framework and means of rehabilitation (Mead, 2016; Mikaere, 2005). Mead (2016) noted that tikanga Māori is a form of social control and expression:

> Tikanga Māori cannot be understood without making use of Mātauranga Māori. While Mātauranga Māori might be carried in the minds, tikanga Māori puts the knowledge into practice and adds the aspects of correctness. People then see tikanga in action, and they do it, feel it, understand it, accept it and feel empowered through experience. Tikanga Māori might be described as Māori philosophy in practice and as the practical face of Māori knowledge.
>
> (p. 1)

Consequently, Mātauranga Māori and tikanga cannot be separated from the collective they emerge from and exist in, remaining a central and enduring aspect of Māori identity – Māoritanga. Both concepts act as a framework of accumulated intergenerational collective wisdom and experience. There are noted differences from one tribal region to another in the way Mātauranga Māori and Tikanga are applied, interpreted, shared, and carried out. This is a direct response to historical, cultural, environmental, and contemporary factors that vary across Aotearoa New Zealand and abroad for Māori (Hudson et al., 2020; Kukutai & Pawar, 2013). For example, tikanga may reflect adaptations made in response to the taiao, such as the steps taken to gather and prepare kai from the taiao (environment) in coastal versus inland areas. Similarly, tikanga may feel foreign in nature to those who were not raised in the boundaries of their iwi, or in whānau or environments where they were practised but their relevance was not explained. This highlights a need to explore and contextualise tikanga Māori within a person's lived experience, as it provides valuable information about a person's journey and lens of the world.

The targeted attack on Māori through attempted genocide and settler colonialism led to a period where Māori were forced to put aside, dampen, or hide their tikanga Māori practices (Durie, 1994). This simultaneously disrupted the continuation and sharing of Mātauranga Māori and tikanga practices between generations – a pivotal component of the shaping of Mātauranga Māori and Tikanga. Today, we find Māori operating on a continuum of proximity to Mātauranga Māori and tikanga, on one end, Māori sit between revitalisation and renaissance, where people feel well versed, confident, and have access to Mātauranga Māori and Tikanga, which serve as a cultural resource (Durie, 1994, Hoskins, 2007, Houkamau & Sibley, 2010). The other end of the spectrum are experiences of distance or unknowing of their own Māori culture and foundational knowledge. This can be most notable when exploring with Māori what their tūrangawaewae comprises.

Tūranga, being "standing place" and waewae meaning "feet", Tūrangawaewae literally means a place to stand (Irwin, 2019): a powerful Māori concept referring to a spiritual and physical place where one feels connected, empowered, and sustained. Tūrangawaewae exists as the source and nurturance of one's Māoritanga, providing a place of belonging. Traditionally, the Marae played a key role in one's tūrangawaewae, outlining and strengthening one's whakapapa links to people and surrounding landscapes and elements of the taiao such as mountain, river, lake, ocean and so on. This is reflected in the tikanga Māori practice of one sharing their pēpēha, where Māori introduce themselves in proximity to key features of their whakapapa before introducing who they are. This is a practice not all Māori continue to use, which reflects the colonised reality where Māori have varying ability, knowledge, and comfortability in being able to locate themselves within their whakapapa and then express this in traditional practices. Remembering comfortability and ability reflects not only a personal experience, but also entails their whānau, hapu and iwi experiences, along with socio-political influences.

The disruption to the transmission of culture has created a separation between individuals and whānau to the collective they are intrinsically linked to. This experience has increasingly been referred to as "disconnection", however, this very term itself infers a severing, which is at odds with the beliefs outlined in this section. Regardless of the mental knowing of foundational knowledge bases and practices, there remains an unbreakable relationship for every Māori to Te Ao Māori. If you whakapapa Māori, as in you are born Māori, you are Māori; therefore, you are intrinsically an extension of Te Ao Māori. There has been a failure to reconcile this variability for Māori, which is particularly seen within the youth justice space (Te Uepū Hāpai i te Ora, 2019; Gluckman, 2017), with a tendency for Māori rangatahi to be pathologised as an individual "deviant" or whānau issue, as opposed to responding to broader societal failures and outcomes of colonisation that have led to accumulated intergenerational issues (Jackson, 1987; Tauri, 1999; McIntosh & Workman, 2017). This has often left whānau feeling responsible for reconciling generations of distance and oppression in accessing their cultural needs (Stanley & de Froideville, 2020).

It is necessary to frame Māori experiences broadly, with compassion and curiosity, to move towards a process of reconciliation of past and present experiences which should be firmly rooted in tūrangawaewae, allowing whānau, hapū and iwi to be supported, resourced, and allowed to whakamana (uplift) their people (Hoskins, 2007, Mikahere-Hall, 2019). Therefore, acknowledging all approaches for healing should be grounded upon Mātauranga Māori and tikanga as a direct response to both the personal and collective trauma experienced (Pihama et al., 2020; Te Uepū Hāpai i te Ora, 2019), preventing further perpetuation of intergenerational cycles of distance from Te Ao Māori.

Case Study

Wānanga are multifaceted and a unique practice for Māori. In the context of youth justice, I will draw on its role as a traditional forum where Māori can safely come together to learn, discuss thoughts, opinions, and experiences. Traditionally, this custom has origins from pūrākau (storytelling) around our atua (deities), for instance, when Tāne Māhuta sought to gather the baskets of knowledge. In modern times, they have come to play a crucial role in the revitalisation and transmission of Māori culture, particularly Mātauranga Māori including tikanga. Usually, people gather for wānanga based on a pre-set Kaupapa (idea/focus) where mutual participation and open dialogue allow for people to contribute to a model of teaching and learning from one another. Pare Hauraki is an iwi-led initiative which serves as an example of a consistent, well-functioning series of ongoing wānanga for rangatahi and their whānau to strengthen their Māoritanga. The wānanga are held on their local whenua, often under the shadow of their tūpuna maunga Moehau. These wānanga are open to all who whakapapa to Hauraki iwi, serving as a space to revitalise Mātauranga and tikanga specific to their area and identity. This enhances the cultural resourcing, capabilities, confidence and understanding of who their descendants are as individuals amongst the collective.

Allowing their people the opportunity to experience a breadth and depth of Mātauranga Māori and tikanga in an intimate manner, their iwi members can solidify their tūrangawaewae. Some Kaupapa they have focused on include tākaro (play), Rongoa (healing system), mahi kōwhatu (hand carving), raranga (weaving), waka ama (kayaking), tā moko (tattooing), traditional trapping, mahi aute (tapa), uku (diving), earth dying, net making and maramataka (knowledge making) and more. The extensive range of topics covered occur over weekends, with most having 30 people in attendance and more symposium styled wānanga where they had 300 people register. These wānanga allow their iwi members who live on their whenua, along with those who live away from home, an opportunity to return to their tūrangawaewae, solidify and practice traditional knowledge forms and rituals in a way their Tīpuna would have. Most importantly, the ongoing nature of these wānanga provides ample opportunities for the continuation of relationships, knowledge sharing and rituals together, the very epitome of Mātauranga Māori and Tikanga. Demonstrating how mana Motuhake occurs when iwi is resourced and able to serve their own people in an enduring manner.

Call to Action

We are proposing the need to locate Māori rangatahi within the concept of tūrangawaewae by supporting them and their whānau to gain Mātauranga Māori, tikanga and strengthen meaningful connections. Understanding rangatahi and whānau can never be disconnected as they are born connected and remain connected regardless of whether they know the names of people or places. This strengths-based approach has the aim of supporting whānau to step into the mana of their Māoritanga and express who they are within the spaces they choose to locate themselves. Whether it be within the confines of their marae, whenua, or urban locations. Prioritising mana Motuhake, would include collaboration and sufficient resourcing of rangatahi, whānau, hapū, and iwi within wānanga, promoting Mātauranga Māori and tikanga. These wānanga would allow rangatahi alongside whānau to experience a range of activities, roles, and responsibilities to find their place within Te Ao Māori in an authentic manner. This in turn provides an internal working system as a foundation for rangatahi Māori and their whānau to self-actualise within a collective. Therefore, directly contributing to the breaking of intergenerational cycles that impact wellbeing out of the recognition of the disenfranchisement caused by colonisation.

Questions for Consideration

- Do you and your organisation take into consideration Mātauranga Māori and tikanga Māori when engaging with a Māori whānau?
- Do you and your organisation actively invest in the cultural responsivity of staff to have awareness of the practices needed to make a Māori whānau feel safe?
- Do you and your organisation consider a person and whānau whakapapa (genealogy), relationship to the taiao, proximity to cultural resources and interpretation and expression of their Māoritanga?

Reflections

Non-Indigenous practitioners in the youth justice space must understand that Indigenous youth, their families and communities have different cultural orientations or worldviews. It is also clear that the needs and rights of Aboriginal Australians, Māori and Pacific children, adolescents, families and communities need an integrated, coordinated approach to legislative provision, policy and programme development rather than a one-size-fits-all approach.

References

Akbar, H., Chow, I., Nuimata, W., Kani, T., Wynn, A., Langan, A. V., & Gallegos, D. (2021, May). *Development of a Pasifika Women's diabetes wellness program: From the perspective of Māori and Pasifika women living in Queensland*. Queensland Women's Heath Forum.

Akbar, H., Gallegos, D., Anderson, D., & Windsor, C. (2022). Deconstructing type 2 diabetes selfmanagement of Australian Pacific Islander women: Using a community participatory research and talanoa approach. *Health and Social Care in the Community*, 30(5), 1988–1999. https://doi.org/10.1111/hsc.13580

Battiste, M., & Henderson, J. Y. (2000). *Protecting indigenous knowledge and heritage*. Purich Publishing Ltd.

Bishop, R., Berryman, M., & Richardson, C. (2002). Te Toi Huarewa: Effective teaching and learning in total immersion Maori language educational settings. *Canadian Journal of Native Education*, 26(1), 44–61.

Brown, L., & Strega, S. (2005). *Research as resistance: Critical, Indigenous, and anti-oppressive approaches*. Canadian Scholars' Press.

Cruickshank, A. H., Lilley, T. S., Radcliffe, B., Nosa, V., & Fenwick, J. (2019). Māori and Pasifika perceptions of their local maternity care in Logan, Australia. *Women and Birth*, 32(3), e359–e365.

Davis, J., & Coopes, R. (2022). Our fire stories – Emergence through the circle work-process at the indigenous knowledge systems lab. *Journal of Awareness-Based Systems Change*, 2(2), 85–108. https://doi.org/10.47061/jasc.v2i2.3892

Davis, J., & Woods, A. (2019). Durithunga boul: A pattern of respectful relationships, reciprocity and socially just literacy education in one urban school. In J. Rennie & H. Harper (Eds.), *Literacy education and indigenous Australians: Theory, research and practice* (pp. 51–69). Springer.

Du Plessis, R., & Fairbairn-Dunlop, P. (2009). The ethics of knowledge production. *Pacific Challenges International Social Science Journal*, 60(195), 109–114.

Durham, J., Tafa, S., Etuale, J., Nosa, V., Fa'avale, A., Malama, E.,. . . Fa'avale, N. (2022). Belonging in multiple places: Pasifika young peoples' experiences of living in Logan. *Journal of Youth Studies*, 26(2), 196–212. https://doi.org/10.1080/13676261.2021.1994130

Durie, M. (1994). Maori perspectives on health and illness. In *Social dimensions of health and disease: New Zealand perspectives* (pp. 194–203). Oxford University Press.

Fainga'a-Manu Sione, I., Faleolo, R., & Hafu-Fetokai, C. (2024a). Finding harmony between decolonization and Christianity in academia. *Art/Research International*, 8(2), 519–546.

Fainga'a-Manu Sione, I., Harvey, A., Stuart, J., Statham, M., Pelite, N., Aloalii, F., & Aloalii, R. (2024b). Enhancing equitable inclusion for the Pasifika diaspora in mainstream Australia, using Pasifika methodologies within higher education and community settings. *Equality, Diversity and Inclusion*, 43(6), 910–925. https://doi.org/10.1108/EDI-11-2022-0313

Fainga'a-Manu Sione, I., Stanley, G., & Enari, D. (2023). Collective or individual- why not both. *Waka Kuaka: The Journal of the Polynesian Society*, 132(1/2), 165–180.

Fairbairn-Dunlop, P. (2013). The interface of Pacific and other knowledge's in a supplementary education site. *Compare: A Journal of Comparative and International Education*, 1–21.

Fehoko, E. (2014). *Pukepuke fonua: An exploratory study on the faikava as an identity marker for New Zealand-born Tongan males* (Unpublished MA Thesis). Auckland University of Technology, Auckland, New Zealand.

Fletcher, G., Waters, J., Yunkaporta, T., Marshall, C., Davis, J., & Manning Bancroft, J. (2023). Indigenous systems knowledge applied to protocols for governance and inquiry. *Systems Research and Behavioral Science*, 40(4), 757–760. https://doi.org/10.1002/sres.2932

Gegeo, D. W., & Watson-Gegeo, K. A. (2001). "How we know": Kwara'ae rural villagers doing indigenous epistemology. *The Contemporary Pacific*, 13(1), 55–88.

Gluckman, P. D. (2017). *Youth suicide in New Zealand: A discussion paper*. Office of the Prime Minister's Chief Science Advisor.

Harris, H. (2004). Indigenous worldviews and ways of knowing as theoretical and methodological foundations for archaeological research. In C. Smith & H. Wobst (Eds.), *Indigenous archaeologies decolonising theory and practice*. Routledge.

Hart, M. A. (2010). Indigenous worldviews, knowledge, and research: The development of an indigenous research paradigm. *Journal of Indigenous Voices in Social Work*, 1(1).

Hau'ofa, E. (1994). Our sea of islands. *The Contemporary Pacifc*, 6(1), 147–162.

Hikuroa, Dan. (2016). Mātauranga Māori – The Ūkaipō of Knowledge in New Zealand. *Journal of the Royal Society of New Zealand*, 47(1), 5–10.
Hoskins, J. (2007). Whanau transformation through tribal reconnection. *MAI Review LW*, 1(2), 8.
Houkamau, C. A., & Sibley, C. G. (2010). The multi-dimensional model of Māori identity and cultural engagement. *New Zealand Journal of Psychology*, 39(1), 8–28.
Hudson, M., Whaanga, H., Waiti, J., Maxwell, H., Davis, K., Arahanga, T. A.,. . . & Taitoko, M. (2020). Visualising Mātauranga Māori for iwi outcomes. *New Zealand Science Review*, 76(1–2).
Irwin, R. (2019). Decolonising technological futures: A dialogical tryptich between Te Haumoana White, Ruth Irwin, and Tegmark's artificial intelligence. *Futures*, 112, 102431.
Jackson, A. M., Hakopa, H., Phillips, C., Parr-Brownlie, P. B., Russell, P., Hulbe, C.,. . .& Elder, H. (2019). Towards building an indigenous science tertiary curriculum. *New Zealand Science Review*, 75(4), 69–73.
Kukutai, T., & Pawar, S. (2013). *A socio-demographic profile of Māori living in Australia*. University of Waikato. Available at SSRN 2463653.
Kurtz, D. (2013). Indigenous methodologies: Traversing Indigenous and Western worldviews in research. *AlterNative: An International Journal of Indigenous Peoples*, 9(3), 217–229.
McDermid, L., & Wren, R. (2023). *Keep our kids out (KOKO) Pasifika holistic youth hub: An analysis of program effectiveness*. Logan, Australia: Pathways in Place, Griffith University. https://doi.org/10.25904/6DSK-B026
McIntosh, T., & Workman, K. (2017). Māori and prison. In *The Palgrave handbook of Australian and New Zealand criminology, crime and justice* (pp. 725–735). Palgrave Macmillan.
Mead, H. M. (2016). *Tikanga Maori (revised edition): Living by Maori values*. Huia Publishers.
Mercier, O. (2018). Mātauranga and science. *New Zealand Science Review*, 74(4), 83–90.
Mikaere, A. (2005). Cultural invasion continued: The ongoing colonisation of Tikanga Maori. *Yearbook of New Zealand Jurisprudence*, 8(2), 134–172.
Mikahere-Hall, A. (2019). Tūhono Māori: Promoting secure attachments for indigenous Māori children. A conceptual paper. *Ata: Journal of Psychotherapy Aotearoa New Zealand*, 23(1), 49–59.
Mila-Schaaf, K. (2010). Pacific health research guidelines: The cartography of an ethical relationship. *International Social Science Journal*, 60(195), 132–143.
Patterson, J. (1992). *Exploring Māori values*. Palmerston North, New Zealand: Dunmore Press.
Pihama, L., Smith, L. T., Cameron, N., Te Nana, R., Morgan, H. R. K., Skipper, H., & Mataki, T. (2020). *He Oranga Ngākau*. Te Kotahi Research Institute.
Ravuvu, A. (1987). *The Fijian ethos*. Institute of Pacific, University of the South Pacific.
Singh, Y. (2004). *Kava: From ethnology to pharmacology*. London, United Kingdom: CRC Press.
Sione, I. F. A. M. (2023). The Fala methodology. *Waka Kuaka: The Journal of the Polynesian Society*, 132(1/2), 237–256.
Smith, L. T., Maxwell, T. K., Puke, H., & Temara, P. (2016). Indigenous knowledge, methodology and mayhem: What is the role of methodology in producing indigenous insights? A discussion from Mātauranga Māori. *Knowledge Cultures*, 4(3), 131–156.
Stanley, E., & de Froideville, S. M. (2020). From vulnerability to risk: Consolidating state interventions towards Māori children and young people in New Zealand. *Critical Social Policy*, 40(4), 526–545.
Steffenson, V. (2020). *Fire country – How indigenous fire management could help save Australia*. Hardie Grant Publishing.

Tauri, J. (1999). Explaining recent innovations in New Zealand's criminal justice system: Empowering Maori or biculturalising the state? *Australian & New Zealand Journal of Criminology*, 32(2), 153–167.

Te Uepū Hāpai i te Ora. (2019). *The safe and effective justice advisory group*. Retrieved from https://maorilawreview.co.nz/2019/06/criminal-justice-te-uepu-hapai-i-te-ora-he-waka-roimata/

Tu'itahi, S. (2007). *Fonua: A model for Pacific health promotion.* Paper presented at the meeting of the Health Promotion Forum in New Zealand, January 2007.

Tui Atua, T. T. E. (2003). In search of nuance and metaphor in social policy. *Social Policy Journal of New Zealand*, 20, 49–63.

Tui Atua, T. T. E. (2009). *O le e lave i tiga, ole ivi, le toto, ma le aano: He who rallies in my hour of need is my kin.* Paper presented at the New Zealand Families Commission Pasifika Families' Fono, Auckland, New Zealand, November 2009.

Tukuitonga, C., & Finau, S. (1997). The health of Pacific peoples in New Zealand up to the early 1990's. *Pacific Health Dialog,* 45(2), 59–67.

Tuwere, I., Ligalevu, A., NcNicholas, T., Moala, M., & Tuifagaletele, K. (2012). *Vuvale doka sautu: A cultural framework for addressing violence in Fijian families in Aotearoa New Zealand.* Ministry of Social Development.

Waldegrave, C., Tamasese, K., Tuhaka, F., & Campbell, W. (2003). *Just therapy – A journey: A collection of papers from the just therapy team.* Dulwich Publications.

Walker, R. (1996). *Ngā Pepa a Ranginui: The Walker papers.* Auckland, New Zealand: Penguin.

Walter, M., & Andersen, C. (2013). *Indigenous statistics: A quantitative methodology.* New York, NY: Routledge.

Walter, M., & Suina, M. (2018). Indigenous data, indigenous methodology and indigenous data sovereignty. *International Journal of Social Research Methodology*, 22(3), 233–243.

2 Pasifika Youth – Identity and Belonging

Sean Vartiainen

Pasifika peoples are inherently diasporic, with heritage lines and migration pathways stretching far beyond the islands where these cultures were formed. Our communities span the Pacific Islands, Aotearoa New Zealand, Australia, the United States, and beyond (Anae, 1998; Hau'ofa, 1994).

Importantly, across these contexts, Pasifika youth make up a distinctly young and growing demographic. In Aotearoa New Zealand, the median age for Pasifika peoples is 24.9 years (Statistics New Zealand, 2024b), and similar trends are reflected across other diasporic communities – highlighting a population whose future is disproportionately shaped by the experiences of its youth.

But what does it mean to identify as Pasifika? Pacific cultures are historically collectivist – structured around kinship, obligation, and shared identity – yet many Pasifika young people are raised within Western societies that are, by contrast, deeply individualistic (Pulotu-Endemann, 2001; Tiatia-Seath, 2014). On top of this, Pasifika peoples exist as a racialised category – marked as distinct from the white majority and often framed through deficit-based narratives. These overlapping conditions create a contested, liminal space in which identity and belonging are constantly navigated, negotiated, and, at times, resisted.

Pasifika youth often experience both cultural strength and systemic adversity. Many report strong ties to family, community, and cultural or religious life, yet also face higher rates of mental distress, discrimination, and socio-economic hardship (Veukiso-Ulugia et al., 2024). Crucially, Pasifika youth are not cultural replicas of their elders – they are shaped by a rapidly shifting, globalised world. Their identities draw not only on ancestral knowledge but also on peer cultures, digital spaces, and transnational influences, producing new and evolving forms of cultural expression (Mila-Schaaf, 2010; Katavake-McGrath, 2021).

This chapter explores the author's own positionality, key features of Pasifika identity and cultural self-understanding, and how these are experienced and interpreted within the context of youth justice.

Author's Positionality – A Personal Reflection on Inherited Identity

My family's story begins with my grandmother, born in Upolu and raised in Savai'i. She came to Aotearoa New Zealand at 16 – the first of her family to emigrate.

DOI: 10.4324/9781003298410-5

It was a decision made to preserve her life through essential medical treatment for a heart condition that couldn't be treated in Samoa. What began as a medical necessity became permanent when she married a Finnish man who had migrated to Aotearoa New Zealand through industrialisation pathways.

Her life in Aotearoa New Zealand was deeply shaped by the era of the Dawn Raids – a time when Pacific Islanders were targeted, vilified, and marginalised. The pressures of entering a white-dominated society weighed heavily on her. My grandmother did her best to assimilate, to "fit in" to the new world she saw around her. Through all of this, her faith remained central to her identity as a Samoan woman.

Her need for survival in new social landscapes came with sacrifices. My father and his siblings were never taught Gagana Samoa. Though they identified as Samoan, they were distanced from the traditions and deeper nuances of Samoan life in the hope that this would advantage them in Aotearoa New Zealand society.

Dad grew up in Tokoroa, then a budding town with a booming economy – at the time thought of as a potential new city. And in this predicted metropolis, my dad grew up poor. At times, they often went without food or undergarments. As children, they were left alone and worked odd jobs to earn their grandfather's beer money. In these jobs in forestry, as only a young teenager, my father told me about his experiences of racism – of adult white men throwing away his lunches because he was Samoan and they were white.

Despite his claims of run-ins with the Hells Angels and his stories of an old dusty Harley Davidson, my dad has always been a big old nerd. He told me about his love for maths, for computers and science – of being the only brown boy in the advanced class of white students. He left school as soon as he could, becoming an electrician, but always harbouring a passion for computers. Through loss, adversity, and difficulty, my father built himself an IT business. Now semi-retired, he spends his days building databases and playing golf.

My uncle – his best friend through childhood, his little brother – experienced a different pathway. There are photos of me as a three-year-old, sitting on uncle's bike, his arms around me. His black leather jacket decorated with the insignia of his gang, tattoos covering his arms and his glass eye hidden behind black sunglasses.

As a child, my uncle didn't get selected for any advanced classes, wasn't encouraged to become a computer technician or an athlete. His story went somewhere else. I remember, as a little boy, being called into my dad's office so he could tell me that my uncle would be going to prison for a long time. He'd been involved in serious offending, and we wouldn't be seeing him for a few years. I remember asking if Dad was okay.

I remember visiting the prison after travelling to Australia. I wonder what was going through my father's mind then. My dad and his brother – one in a polo with the logo for his IT company, the other in a green jumpsuit, proudly claiming that here, in this building surrounded by barbed wire, he was the leader.

Years later, after my uncle's release, we were all sitting down for a family dinner. My uncle proudly declared that one of my cousins – a "quarter Samoan," just like me, fairer-skinned with blond hair and blue eyes – was going to become an

All Black and then work in an office. When we asked about my cousin's younger brother – the story was different. He laughed to himself: No, this brother would join the gang like him. He had brown skin, dark hair and eyes – like my father, like my uncle, like my grandmother. He was visibly Samoan.

Through this story, I see the echoes of three generations of Pasifika youth:

- My grandmother's migration – as a young Samoan girl, navigating survival in a hostile society during the Dawn Raids, prioritising assimilation to protect her family.
- My father and uncle's experiences – growing up in poverty and facing systemic racism, charting radically different paths shaped by opportunity, or the lack of it.
- My cousins' futures – the legacy of migration, racialisation, and fractured identity continues. For one, whiteness grants opportunity; for the other, brownness signals struggle.

My father raised me to be proud – of being Samoan, of our family's story, of our identity. It has always been a struggle for me; my fair skin and lack of cultural knowledge meant I've often felt like I'm on the outside looking in. Claiming something that doesn't always feel right to say is mine.

In my life, I know I have been privileged – afforded opportunities my father and the "brown sides" of my family never had. I think about the sacrifices my family has made – the things my grandmother experienced, the things my father experienced. How I have benefited from what they struggled through and fought for. How the fruits of their labour have shaped me and made me who I am today.

I ask myself: what does it mean to inherit both the trauma of colonialism, diaspora, and racism, and yet also the benefits of whiteness simultaneously? For me, my identity is not something I passively experience; rather, it is something I must actively negotiate. I must walk this tension. My culture is a relationship – to my past, my family, my geography, my social conscience, and the wider world. In no other aspect of my heritage do I feel as politicised, as powerfully significant, as through my Pasifika identity. In no other way has my heritage shaped my values of community, of connection, of respect. It is for this reason that being Pasifika is important to me – to think about, and to actively give back towards.

Pasifika Identity – Definitions, Debates, Lived Realities

Pasifika identity is commonly defined in policy and demographic contexts as referring to individuals of Polynesian, Melanesian, or Micronesian descent, typically linked through genealogical ancestry to the Pacific Islands (Anae, 1998; Statistics New Zealand, 2023). This ethnic framing aligns with what Phinney (1990) describes as "ethnic identity": a paradigm grounded in Western thinking that emphasises group membership based on common ancestry, language, or national origin. While genealogy is deeply meaningful to many Pasifika peoples, this model risks reducing identity to a static, biologically derived category, insufficient for capturing its lived, social, and relational aspects.

For Pasifika communities, identity is not only inherited but also constituted through cultural obligations, social roles, and reciprocal relationships. As Tamasese et al. (2005) articulate, identity in Pacific cultures is fundamentally relational, often enacted through one's place within fanau (family), village, and spiritual life. These cultural expectations create an identity deeply embedded in collective well-being and interdependence – values that stand in contrast to the individualism of Euro-centric identity frameworks.

To address the limits of ethnic categorisation, cultural theorists such as Stuart Hall (1990) have reframed identity as historically contingent and discursively produced. Hall argues that identity is shaped by positioning within cultural narratives, not fixed essence. This concept resonates with Anae's (1998) insights into the Samoan diaspora, where identity is understood as a negotiation between inherited cultural markers and evolving lived experience. Anae's work shows how Samoan youth in Aotearoa New Zealand construct belonging through both ancestral ties and contemporary social contexts, including education, peer networks, and language use.

This theoretical framing helps make sense of the plural and hybrid identities of Pasifika youth today. Individuals of mixed heritage, those who do not speak an ancestral language, or those raised outside traditional cultural structures, may not meet rigid expectations of ethnic authenticity. As Mila-Schaaf (2010) notes, Pasifika youth often navigate "cultural hybridity" – synthesising ancestral identity with contemporary, globalised influences. These hybrid identities challenge essentialist assumptions and affirm that Pasifika identity is both contextual and generative.

The tension between ethnic and cultural identity thus reveals Pasifika identity as a complex and negotiated phenomenon. Rather than privileging one framework over another, it is more accurate to understand identity as a dynamic cultural practice – rooted in genealogy, shaped by social history, and lived through community engagement.

Living and Inherited Identity

In many ways, trying to capture the entirety of a cultural identity in a single definition is like catching rain with a sieve. Something is bound to slip through the cracks. When we are eager to define something, we often look for something tangible – a consistent thread that can reliably point to an answer each time. But cultural identity isn't a solid entity; it is a dynamic, fluid concept that shifts and transforms with its environmental context and over time. This is especially true for Pasifika peoples (Anae, 1998; Hau'ofa, 1994).

Consider this: is the Pasifika identity of Tongans living in their islands during the 1980s the same as that of Samoans growing up in Māngere, Aotearoa New Zealand in the 1990s? Will it be the same for generations born in 2040 in their home islands? Or for those growing up in Aotearoa today? Pasifika people draw their identities from the great diaspora of the Pacific Islands – across Polynesia, Micronesia, and Melanesia – through a vast array of different immigration pathways. The nuances of intersecting identity and mixed cultural heritage mean that Pasifika young people today form an enormously diverse population (Mila-Schaaf, 2010). In other words, it is not a single thread but more like a siapo (traditional woven cloth) made of many different threads – woven in the past, added to over time, and still being woven today. This metaphor evokes a living cultural fabric that reflects both continuity and transformation.

This complexity doesn't make cultural identity meaningless or so fluid that it can't be distinguished from one person to the next. Instead, it calls for a nuanced approach – one that acknowledges flexibility while seeking to understand the different forms it can take (Tupuola, 2004). This is especially important when examining Pasifika youth identities. These young people are navigating a world where their cultural heritage intersects with dominant Eurocentric norms, often outside their ancestral homelands. They are continually generating their own interpretations of what it means to be Pasifika, based on their unique experiences (Mila-Schaaf & Hudson, 2009).

When thinking about youth, it is important to recognise them not only as the receivers of cultural identity but as its active contributors (Tupuola, 2004). They inherit the traditions of their ancestors, but they also hold the responsibility of creating new meanings. This dynamic process should be celebrated – it shows that Pasifika cultural identities are living, evolving, and resilient (Mila-Schaaf, 2010). Colonial narratives have often framed Indigenous and non-European cultures as static, archaic, or incompatible with modern life – contributing to their marginalisation in contemporary discourse (Smith, 1999; Hau'ofa, 1994).

Yet, as reported by the Youth19 Pacific Cohort Report, around 70% of Pasifika young people in Aotearoa are actively engaged in cultural activities (Veukiso-Ulugia et al., 2024). At the same time, innovation across social media, television, and online platforms continues to shape the ways Pasifika youth perform and interpret their identities, creating diasporic cultural spaces that are locally grounded yet globally connected (Mila-Schaaf, 2010).

The ongoing evolution of Pasifika identities – through language, art, and communal practices – challenges the stereotype of culture as something static or outdated. Instead, it affirms culture's vibrancy and relevance. This way of viewing culture – as a complex, fluid construct – aligns closely with Pacific worldviews. Pasifika perspectives often emphasise relationships and interconnectedness over individual autonomy, viewing identity as part of a living ecosystem maintained through reciprocal ties (Pulotu-Endemann, 2001; Suaalii-Sauni & Fulu-Aiolupotea, 2014).

This is embodied in models like the Fonofale, developed by Fuimaono Karl Pulotu-Endemann, which places fanau (family) at its foundation and emphasises the importance of community life (Pulotu-Endemann, 2001). Concepts such as va – the sacred relational space between people, drawn from multiple Pasifika cultures – highlight the deeply interconnected nature of Pasifika identity (Suaalii-Sauni & Fulu-Aiolupotea, 2014). These values stand in contrast to Western ideals of self-sufficiency and instead emphasise belonging, reciprocity, and collective responsibility. For Pasifika peoples, we belong to our families, our communities, and our ancestors – just as they belong to us (Tamasese et al., 2005).

Strengths of Pasifika Youth

Pasifika youth in Aotearoa New Zealand demonstrate enduring strengths across cultural, social, and educational domains. Cultural identity remains a central protective factor for many – shaped through church, language, performing arts, and family networks (Veukiso-Ulugia et al., 2023). These cultural ties foster belonging, identity stability, and resilience through collective connection and engagement (Veukiso-Ulugia et al., 2023).

Pasifika young people also express strong future aspirations. The Youth19 Pacific report found that over two-thirds of Pacific students planned to pursue tertiary education, reflecting high internal motivation and future orientation (Veukiso-Ulugia et al., 2023). Despite ongoing socio-economic challenges, educational ambition remains strong.

Events such as Polyfest – the largest Polynesian youth festival in the world – showcase not only cultural performance but also youth leadership, logistical coordination, and collective pride (Ministry for Pacific Peoples, 2022).

Leadership extends beyond traditional spaces. Pasifika youth are active in church and family systems, and are increasingly involved in digital innovation and creative industries. Platforms like The Coconet provide digital content grounded in Pasifika identity, humour, and politics – a powerful example of culturally grounded media created by and for youth. Similarly, initiatives such as Fibre Fale offer culturally embedded pathways into tech industries, highlighting how Pasifika youth innovate while remaining anchored in collective values. Across these domains, Pasifika youth demonstrate adaptability, relational intelligence, and a deep commitment to community wellbeing.

Challenges for Pasifika Youth

While Pasifika youth demonstrate resilience and leadership, these strengths often emerge in the context of structural adversity. Across education, health, and socio-economic measures, Pasifika peoples continue to face significant inequities – shaped by colonisation, systemic racism, and the demands of diaspora (Ioane, 2023; Veukiso-Ulugia et al., 2023).

In Aotearoa New Zealand, 29.9% of Pasifika children experience food insecurity, and 25.8% live in material hardship – rates significantly higher than national averages (Ministry of Social Development, 2023). Median household income for Pasifika sits at $42,424, compared to the national $50,369 (Stats NZ, 2024). Health disparities include high obesity and diabetes rates – often double the national averages – and 16% report severe psychological distress (Veukiso-Ulugia et al., 2023). Despite this, Pasifika peoples remain underrepresented in mental health service access (Veukiso-Ulugia et al., 2023).

Educationally, attendance for Pasifika students was 80% in 2022, compared to 92% for NZ European students. They also remain overrepresented in school suspensions and stand-downs (Ministry of Education, 2022). These outcomes are often shaped by the misreading of cultural behaviours – such as collective expression or assertiveness – as disruption or defiance (Marriott & Sim, 2015).

Pasifika youth also navigate cultural tension. Raised in collectivist communities that value service and humility, they operate within systems that reward self-promotion and independence (Tiatia-Seath, 2014). Practices like fa'alavelave can reflect cultural strength, yet become financially burdensome under economic stress and institutional misunderstanding (Vaioleti, 2006; Ministry for Pacific Peoples, 2022).

Cultural identity is further constrained by racialisation. Pasifika youth are often framed in deficit terms – as "at risk," underachieving, or disengaged – or exoticised through surface-level celebrations like Polyfest, while facing everyday exclusion. These dynamics reduce complex identities to stereotypes, shaping how youth are seen and how they see themselves (Marriott & Sim, 2015).

Identity and Belonging in a Youth Justice Context

The challenges and strengths held by Pasifika youth take on new significance in the context of youth justice – particularly because Pasifika youth remain disproportionately represented in youth justice systems across Aotearoa New Zealand and other diasporic contexts (Ioane & Lambie, 2016). Structural inequities and racialised assumptions often converge in harmful ways. For example, behaviours such as group solidarity, collective movement, and assertive body language – normative within many Pasifika cultures – are frequently misinterpreted by authorities as defiance or aggression (Ioane & Lambie, 2016). These misreadings are not merely procedural errors; they reflect deeper institutional biases that fail to recognise or respect Pasifika relational norms.

The *Youth Justice Indicators Summary Report* (Ministry of Justice, 2023) further outlines the disproportionate contact Pasifika young people have with the police and the justice system – highlighting the enduring impact of systemic bias. As a result, Pasifika youth are more likely to be policed, excluded, and criminalised – not because they are inherently more disruptive, but because their cultural expressions are filtered through a deficit lens.

To understand these dynamics more fully, we must turn to the youth justice system itself. Here, identity, belonging, and behaviour are often interpreted through frameworks that exclude or misrepresent Pasifika worldviews. What follows is an exploration of how Pasifika cultural identity functions within youth justice contexts – as a protective factor, a site of misrecognition, and, at times, a terrain of resistance and repair.

Historically, cultural dimensions of wellbeing were largely ignored within youth justice systems, in favour of frameworks centred on individual responsibility and risk. However, recent research increasingly recognises that access to strong cultural resources – including church involvement, cultural activities, and family ties – can offer significant protection against antisocial behaviour, substance use, and reoffending (Ioane, 2023). These resources are not merely peripheral supports; they are central to a young person's social world and identity.

In light of this, youth justice systems are beginning to incorporate culturally grounded assessments and programmes. These approaches are most effective when co-designed with communities and rooted in meaningful cultural knowledge (Ioane, 2023). They aim not only to reduce risk but also to foster belonging and cultural pride.

A key cultural framework for understanding harm and repair is the concept of *va* – a relational space found across multiple Pasifika cultures (Pulotu-Endemann, 2001). *Va* refers to the sacred and social relationships that bind individuals and communities. Within this worldview, offending can be understood as a rupture of the *va*, or *soli le va* – a trampling of the relational space (Ioane, 2023). This reframes harm as not only individual but also relational, affecting the broader community fabric.

Culturally grounded care that draws on the *va* has shown promise in helping young people restore relationships with family, community, and self (Ioane, 2023). In this sense, Pasifika cultural identity becomes not only a source of meaning but a pathway toward accountability, healing, and reintegration.

Offending as Relational Dislocation

Offending among Pasifika youth is too often explained through narratives of cultural absence or individual failure. Yet research suggests a more complex picture – one in which cultural belonging is not missing but disrupted, distorted, or overdetermined, shaped by trauma, marginalisation, and relational rupture. Offending becomes an act tied to identity and context – not simply a rejection of culture, but a response to the breakdown of the relational systems that support wellbeing. These systems – family, church, culture, and community – anchor identity and guide moral decision-making, and their rupture often precedes harmful behaviours (Tamasese et al., 2005; Ioane, 2023; Tiatia-Seath, 2014).

Some youth act within a culturally coherent but ethically problematic moral logic. For instance, values such as *fa'aaloalo* (respect) and *tautua* (service) can be enacted through violence when youth feel their family's honour is at stake. A high-achieving Samoan student I worked with was expelled and charged with assault after retaliating against a peer who had bullied her younger brother. Her father had encouraged her to act in defence of the family's integrity. Though this response was criminalised by the school and justice system, it was aligned with her family's cultural framework of duty and protection.

It is tempting to label such actions as distortions of culture. However, this risks oversimplifying the complex realities of cultural interpretation. As scholars like Mila-Schaaf (2010) and Suaalii-Sauni (2006) argue, cultural expectations are not fixed scripts but dynamic and negotiated – yet when treated as rigid protocols, youth are left with little room to adapt in morally ambiguous situations. Culture, in these cases, may function more as a protocol than a dynamic ethic, limiting young people's capacity for reflective agency in the face of competing responsibilities.

In parallel, other youth engage in offending through external substitutions for cultural belonging. As Ioane and Lambie (2016) describe, gang affiliation often provides a surrogate space for dislocated Pasifika youth. These young people – though disconnected from formal cultural institutions – continue to seek identity, status, and connection. Gangs may offer ritual, hierarchy, and loyalty that function as symbolic replacements for lost or inaccessible cultural spaces, especially when traditional collectives like churches have withdrawn support following transgressions (Ioane & Lambie, 2016).

Though these pathways differ in mechanism – one grounded in rigid adherence to traditional norms, the other in improvised belonging – they both reflect the consequences of relational rupture. In the first case, relationality is preserved in form but strained in function: values like honour are enacted without the flexibility to question or recontextualise them. In the second, youth turn to new communities when established ones are no longer safe or available. This may be due to rejection, punishment, or unmet needs in traditional spaces.

In both instances, what is missing is not culture itself, but a safe, responsive environment where culture can be lived and interpreted meaningfully. As Tiatia-Seath (2014) highlight, colonisation, racism, and intergenerational trauma continue to destabilise the relational ecosystems through which Pasifika youth typically construct and maintain identity.

In recognising these dynamics, we must resist both the romanticisation of culture and the urge to protect it from critique. As Mila-Schaaf and Hudson (2009) and Suaalii-Sauni (2006) argue, true cultural accountability includes the ability to identify internal contradictions, critically reflect on inherited norms, and transform practices in ways that honour both ancestral values and contemporary wellbeing. For Pasifika youth navigating violence, discipline, and belonging, this critical negotiation is not an abandonment of culture – it is its living renewal.

Reweaving Identity: Cultural Programmes and Community Responses

As Ioane (2023) and Tiatia-Seath (2014) show, cultural programmes that embed talanoa, metaphor, and communal learning offer promising pathways – but only when they treat culture as a dynamic site of repair and meaning-making, not a static intervention tool. These programmes succeed not because they “deliver culture” but because they invite youth into a co-creative process of identity reconstruction, allowing for fluidity, agency, and relational healing (Ioane et al., 2021).

Belonging, then, is not a switch to be turned on through the introduction of cultural programming. It is cultivated through relationship, recognition, and the co-creation of cultural meaning. Offending must be re-conceptualised not as individual deviance, but as relational rupture – a sign that the pathways for identity, agency, and participation have been blocked.

Conclusion: Complexity Over Correction

Pasifika youth in justice settings are often starved of the possibility to imagine new forms of identity and belonging. Essentialist and neoliberal understandings of culture reduce their sense of what is possible. Their identity may have been decided for them – flattened into boxes, whether pathologised or idealised. What they consider culturally valid, desirable, or even survivable may be profoundly limited.

Addressing offending, then, requires more than cultural inclusion. It requires cultural complexity – an approach that acknowledges contradiction, resists idealisation, and restores the capacity for Pasifika youth to navigate, challenge, and reweave their sense of belonging on their own terms (Tiatia-Seath, 2014; Ioane, 2023).

References

Anae, M. (1998). *Fofoa-i-vao-'ese: The identity journeys of NZ-born Samoans* (Doctoral Dissertation). University of Auckland.

Hall, S. (1990). Cultural identity and diaspora. In J. Rutherford (Ed.), *Identity: Community, culture, difference* (pp. 222–237). Lawrence & Wishart.

Hau'ofa, E. (1994). Our sea of islands. In E. Waddell, V. Naidu, & E. Hau'ofa (Eds.), *A new Oceania: Rediscovering our sea of islands* (pp. 2–16). University of the South Pacific.

Ioane, J. (2023). *You've just got to think about your family and what type of person you want to be: Listening to young Pasifika people in the youth justice system and their families – Research and recommendations* [Research report]. Health Research Council of New Zealand & Massey University School of Psychology.

Ioane, J., & Lambie, I. (2016). Pacific youth and violent offending in Aotearoa New Zealand. *New Zealand Journal of Psychology*, 45(3), 23–29.

Ioane, J., Tofaeono, R., & Lambie, I. (2021). Pasifika youth with harmful sexual behaviour differ from other young people and need a different response. *New Zealand Journal of Psychology*, 50(3), 17–28.

Katavake-McGrath, F. (2021). *Our way to home: An exploratory study of Pasifika gay men in New Zealand, their lived experience, and their navigation of sexual orientation-related legislative change* (Doctoral Dissertation). Auckland University of Technology.

Marriott, L., & Sim, D. (2015). Indicators of inequality for Māori and Pacific people. *Journal of New Zealand Studies*, (20), 24–50. https://search.informit.org/doi/10.3316/informit.276927349255099

Mila-Schaaf, K. (2010). *Polycultural capital and the Pasifika second generation: Negotiating identities in diasporic spaces* (Doctoral Dissertation). Massey University.

Mila-Schaaf, K., & Hudson, M. (2009). The interface between cultural understandings: Negotiating new spaces for Pacific mental health. *Pacific Health Dialog*, 15(1), 113–119.

Ministry of Education. (2024). *Action plan for Pacific education: Progress report 2020–2022*. Wellington, NZ: Author.

Ministry of Justice. (2023). *Youth Justice Indicators Summary Report April 2023*. New Zealand Ministry of Justice. https://www.justice.govt.nz/assets/Documents/Publications/Youth-Justice-Indicators-Summary-Report-April-2023.pdf

Ministry for Pacific Peoples. (2023). *Annual report 2022–2023*. Wellington, NZ: Author. https://www.mpp.govt.nz/assets/Reports/MPP-Annual-Report-2022-2023.pdf

Ministry of Social Development. (2023). *Annual report 2022–2023*. Wellington, NZ: Author.

Phinney, J. S. (1990). Ethnic identity in adolescents and adults: Review of research. *Psychological Bulletin*, 108(3), 499–514. https://doi.org/10.1037/0033-2909.108.3.499

Pulotu-Endemann, F. K. (2001). *Fonofale model of health* [Model description]. https://www.health.govt.nz/our-work/populations/pacific-health/pacific-health-models/pacific-health-models-fonofale

Smith, L. T. (1999). *Decolonizing methodologies: Research and indigenous peoples*. Zed Books.

Statistics New Zealand. (2023). *2023 Census population counts*. Wellington, NZ: Author. https://www.stats.govt.nz/information-releases/2023-census-population-counts

Statistics New Zealand. (2024a). *Household income and housing-cost statistics: Year ended June 2023*. Statistics New Zealand. https://www.stats.govt.nz/information-releases/household-income-and-housing-cost-statistics-year-ended-june-2023/

Statistics New Zealand. (2024b). *Pacific peoples ethnic group summary: 2023 census.* Wellington, NZ: Author. https://www.stats.govt.nz/tools/2023-census-ethnic-group-summaries/pacific-peoples

Suaalii-Sauni, T. (2006). *Le Matuamoepo: Competing 'spirits of governing' and the management of New Zealand-based Samoan youth offender cases* (Doctoral Thesis). University of Auckland.

Suaalii-Sauni, T., & Fulu-Aiolupotea, S. M. (2014). Decolonising Pacific research, building Pacific research communities, and developing Pacific research tools: The case of the Talanoa and the faafaletui in Samoa. *Pacific-Asian Education*, 26(1), 5–19.

Tamasese, K., Peteru, C., Waldegrave, C., & Bush, A. (2005). Ole taeao afua: A qualitative investigation into Samoan perspectives on mental health and culturally appropriate services. *Australian and New Zealand Journal of Psychiatry*, 39(4), 300–309. https://doi.org/10.1111/j.1440-1614.2005.01572.x

Tiatia-Seath, J. (2014). Pacific peoples, mental health service engagement and suicide prevention in Aotearoa New Zealand. *Ethnicity and Inequalities in Health and Social Care*, 7(3), 111–121.

Tupuola, A. M. (2004). Pasifika edge-walkers: Complicating the achieved identity status in youth research. *Journal of Intercultural Studies*, 25(1), 87–100. https://doi.org/10.1080/0725686041000168704

Vaioleti, T. M. (2006). Talanoa research methodology: A developing position on Pacific research. *Waikato Journal of Education*, 12, 21–34. https://doi.org/10.15663/wje.v12i1.296

Veukiso-Ulugia, A., McLean-Orsborn, S., Clark, T. C., Yao, E., Kuresa, B., Drayton, B., & Fleming, T. (2024). *Talavou o le Moana: The health and wellbeing of Pacific secondary school students in Aotearoa New Zealand. A Youth19 report.* Youth19 Research Group, the University of Auckland and Victoria University of Wellington.

Veukiso-Ulugia, A., Shepherd, M., & Bullen, P. (2023). *Youth19 – Pacific youth voices: Home & family life* [Youth19 report]. Youth19 Research Group, University of Auckland & Victoria University of Wellington.

3 Theories of Youth Offending

Patrick Mendes and Andrew Craig Immelman

Introduction

Although the past two decades have seen a substantial decline in youth offending rates nationally in Aotearoa New Zealand (NZ) (Stats NZ, 2023), Māori and Pasifika youth continue to be disproportionately represented in the justice system (Ioane et al., 2016). Pasifika young people experience distinct sociocultural realities compared to their Pākehā (New Zealand European) peers (Leafe, 2017). Collective identity, obligations to family and community (aiga/whānau), strong cultural ties, and experiences of migration, displacement, and marginalisation are key influences on Pasifika youth trajectories (Enari et al., 2024)

Conventional theories of offending, largely developed through Western paradigms, often inadequately account for these sociocultural frameworks. Instead, they risk individualising problems that are deeply collective and systemic in nature (Ioane, 2017).

On the other hand, one size does not fit all; each case of youth offending needs to be understood as best we can in order to maximise the positive impact of mental health professionals. In order to do this, meaningful engagement needs to occur, and this in turn requires the right attitude, knowledge and skills, both culturally and clinically. It mandates the need for having the collective and systemic constantly in mind, as well as discovering the individual issues.

The dialectic of individual vs collective is a recurrent theme not only in how the history of youth offending has been viewed, but also more broadly. In practical terms, both in Aotearoa and abroad, we are seeing this being enacted politically. It may be difficult to argue that individualist short-term material gains have not shown a global resurgence over collective world views, favouring unempathic immediate profit (often equated with progress) over long-term sustainability and collective well-being (often equated with stagnation and weakness).

Moreover, the growing proportion of New Zealanders identifying with mixed Māori and Pasifika heritage adds further complexity to cultural identity, belonging, and the ways young people experience the justice system (Lambie, 2018). Cultural fluidity, multiple community affiliations, and layered experiences of discrimination and belonging are shaping a new generation whose needs cannot be neatly categorised by conventional ethnic labels (Leafe, 2017).

DOI: 10.4324/9781003298410-6

This chapter explores the dominant theories traditionally used to explain youth offending and critically evaluates their relevance for Māori and Pasifika youth. It examines indigenous and culturally grounded approaches for understanding and addressing offending behaviours.

A Short History of Legislation and Theoretical Impacts

The history of youth justice legislation in New Zealand reflects broader socio-political transformations, particularly in relation to Māori and Pasifika communities. While these legislative developments provide vital context, their impact must be understood within the framework of youth offending theories. This section highlights key legislative milestones alongside both mainstream and culturally grounded theories of youth offending, as discussed in Indigenous criminology literature.

Youth offending in New Zealand has historically been defined and shaped by legislation that institutionalised systemic responses to young people deemed "neglected" or "criminal." The definitions embedded within these laws directly reflect societal attitudes toward childhood and deviance – and, importantly, colonial biases.

We believe it is very important to examine how youth offending has been defined, and by whom, if we are to consider any theory of youth offending. In any debate, and especially a legal debate, the definition of terms and which facts can, and cannot be referred to ("admissibility") is vital. This is to prevent confusion and to achieve clarity and fairness, by establishing what is meant by key terms.

One theory of youth offending reflects the criminalisation of poverty by a dominant culture, which then is able to frame issues of poverty as personal failings or moral shortcomings, rather than recognising and addressing the systemic factors – such as unequal access to resources, education, or employment opportunities – that generate and perpetuate poverty. As a result, it is quite possible that the underlying social machinery responsible for these behaviours remains unscrutinised, while the individuals affected are scrutinised, labelled and punished.

There are multiple difficulties in undertaking this approach.

First, human behaviour in general is complex, and considering theories of youth offending behaviour is no exception. Seeing it as a binary "either/or" debate misses the point in our view. Attempts to look at contextual factors could be seen as trying to rationalise or otherwise "to explain away" offending behaviour as a consequence of being a "victim of an unfair system".

Second, it is less than convenient – if data supporting this premise were found – to the dominant culture. Objections could be mounted that there is no relevance, suggesting the absence of a logical connection between poverty and offending. The argument then is effectively won, even before any consideration of probative value (the requisite ability to prove or to disprove the theory) regarding the matter at hand, in this instance, the offending.

If we examine these laws through the lens of theories such as labelling theory and strain theory, would we find any indication that the definitions have reinforced marginalisation and systemic inequities?

The Neglected and Criminal Children Act 1867 marked New Zealand's first legislative intervention into youth offending. It established industrial schools and granted the state sweeping authority to apprehend children deemed "neglected" or "criminal", conflating two quite different terms by having the same potential outcomes (Tuimavave, 2017).

The definition of neglect was heavily influenced by social conditions, including poverty and homelessness – the systemic inequities that disproportionately affected Māori youth during this period. This act appeared to operationalise structural barriers faced by indigenous families, ultimately exacerbating offending trajectories by criminalising poverty and vulnerability (Beals, 2006).

Labelling theory suggests that the way society labels individuals can play a significant role in shaping their self-identity and subsequent behaviour. When poverty is criminalised, individuals experiencing hardship are not just economically disadvantaged – they are also marked by society as deviant or morally lacking. This label, once applied, imposes a social stigma that influences how these individuals are perceived, treated, and even how they come to view themselves. Rather than seeing poverty as a consequence of structural inequality, society frames it as a reflection of personal failure, reinforcing stereotypes that associate poor individuals with criminality or moral inferiority (Becker, 1963).

The consequences of this labelling extend beyond social perception. Legal and social responses – such as increased police surveillance in low-income communities, harsher penalties for offences linked to poverty (like unpaid fines or vagrancy), or barriers to employment for those formerly convicted – perpetuate marginalisation. Individuals who are repeatedly labelled as offenders or morally suspect may internalise these identities, leading to a self-fulfilling prophecy where their opportunities for lawful, norm-abiding participation in society are further reduced. The cycle of stigma and exclusion thus becomes difficult to break, entrenching poverty and deviance. It is difficult to quantify the magnitude of the intergenerational effects, although it is almost certainly unavoidable.

Labelling theory therefore helps explain why efforts that criminalise poverty fail to address systemic causes. By focusing on the individual and assigning blame, society avoids confronting the broader social machinery that generates disadvantage in the first place.

The act of labelling poor people as deviants both distracts from and legitimises the status quo – redirecting attention away from needed structural reforms, and further embedding the link between poverty and criminality in public consciousness.

Strain theory, originally formulated by sociologist Robert Merton, posits that deviant behaviour arises when individuals face a disconnect between culturally valued goals and the legitimate means available for achieving them (Merton, 1938). In societies where financial success and social status are highly valued – but economic opportunities are unevenly distributed – those who find themselves excluded may experience intense pressure, or "strain," to attain these goals through alternative, sometimes unlawful routes.

When poverty is criminalised, the gap between societal expectations and accessible means grows wider. Legal sanctions and social marginalisation erode access to education, stable employment, and civic participation – the very tools theoretically provided to lift oneself out of poverty. Individuals faced with repeated and institutionalised barriers may resort to survival strategies deemed criminal: subsistence theft, unlicensed street vending, or sleeping rough. Rather than being the result of inherent moral failings, these actions emerge as rational responses to social and economic strain.

Strain theory therefore challenges the narrative that criminality among the poor is simply a matter of bad choices or flawed character. It underscores how structural inequalities create environments where traditional, lawful paths to societal goals are closed off for many. By criminalising poverty, society not only compounds individual suffering but also reproduces the conditions that encourage rule-breaking. Instead of focusing exclusively on policing poor individuals, strain theory calls for remedies that target social machinery – by expanding opportunity, reducing inequality, and reshaping policies that punish the disadvantaged rather than supporting them.

Similarly, labelling theory highlights the role of societal reactions, including police apprehensions without warrants under the 1867 Act, in amplifying stigma and marginalisation faced by Māori youth. The overemphasis on targeting "criminal traits" ignored relational dynamics central to Māori and Pasifika worldviews and led to punitive, rather than rehabilitative, responses.

At the same time, during the late 19th century, colonisation created devastating ripple effects for Māori communities. By the 1890s, over 95% of Māori land had been lost due to confiscation, dubious purchases, and systemic manipulation (Came et al., 2021). By 1926, only 5% of Māori lived in urban areas, but this figure rose to 20% by 1945. The resulting cultural dislocation and exposure to new forms of policing in the cities meant that Māori youth were increasingly vulnerable to state intervention and criminalisation. Such losses eroded communal relationships central to Māori socio-cultural identities and forced young Māori into urban environments fraught with socio-economic deprivation (Moewaka Barnes & McCreanor, 2019). Again, strain theory provides insight into how systemic barriers to culturally sanctioned goals – such as the loss of land and whānau networks – contributed to youth offending challenges.

The Industrial Schools Act 1882 (Industrial Schools Act 1882, 1882) expanded state guardianship, replacing familial care structures with institutional management. Indigenous criminology is critical of this legislation for its role in enforcing colonial dominance. By uprooting whānau systems and imposing Eurocentric models of discipline, the Act perpetuated cycles of cultural disconnection and individualisation – features antithetical to Indigenous worldviews emphasising relational accountability (Selvaraj, 2016).

New Zealand's relationship with Pasifika communities also evolved significantly during the late 19th and early 20th centuries, as seen in the annexation of the Cook Islands in 1888 and Niue in 1901. These events encouraged Pasifika migration, setting the foundation for urban labour exploitation that disproportionately involved young people. The historical context of the Dawn Raids and the political activism surrounding them further highlight the systemic discrimination faced by Pasifika peoples (Etherington, 2022).

This has persisted over time; 2018 research indicates that Pasifika youth are often subject to racial profiling, media stereotyping, and discriminatory policing practices (Deckert et al., 2023). Such external labelling can shape self-perceptions, reduce opportunities for positive identity formation, and entrench self-fulfilling prophecies of cycles of marginalisation and reoffending (Faleolo, 2014).

Dominant Theories of Youth Offending

Mainstream theories of youth offending have been developed within Western paradigms, focusing heavily on individual pathology, cognitive development, and socio-environmental deficits. While these theories offer useful insights into some general patterns of adolescent behaviour, they have significant limitations when applied to the lived realities of Māori and Pasifika youth in Aotearoa.

For Māori and Pasifika youth, identity formation occurs not only at the level of the individual but is deeply embedded within collective familial, spiritual, and cultural obligations. Western psychological models, by focusing primarily on individual deficits, risk overlooking the profound importance of family (aiga), community, and intergenerational relationships that shape behaviour and life choices for Pasifika young people.

Psychological models, particularly those grounded in developmental psychology, often focus on risk factors such as poor impulse control, deficits in moral reasoning, or attachment disruptions.

Rolf Loeber was a highly influential criminologist whose most important contributions centred on developmental and life-course criminology, especially through pioneering longitudinal studies such as the Pittsburgh Youth Study, which systematically tracked young people to understand the developmental pathways leading to antisocial and criminal behaviour. He helped define key concepts such as overt and covert pathways of externalising behaviours, demonstrated how persistent and escalating conduct problems could lead to serious offending, and emphasised the critical role of early intervention and prevention in reducing juvenile delinquency. Loeber's research bridged psychology, psychiatry, and criminology, producing empirical findings that linked the trajectories of youth offending to practical recommendations for justice policy and violence prevention, profoundly shaping both academic research and real-world juvenile justice policies (Loeber & Burke, 2011).

David Farrington's main contribution to the theory of youth offending is rooted in his extensive longitudinal research, notably the Cambridge Study in Delinquent Development, which tracked 411 boys over several decades to identify the developmental pathways, risk factors, and life events that predict criminal behaviour. Farrington's work demonstrated that youth offending often peaks in the teenage years and is closely linked to factors such as impulsivity, risk-taking, family history of offending, poor child-rearing practices, and socio-economic deprivation. He emphasised that both individual traits and environmental conditions interact to produce differences in "criminal potential," and later developed the Integrated Cognitive Antisocial Potential (ICAP) theory to explain how antisocial potential is shaped and triggered by life circumstances, cognitive processes, and opportunities. Overall, Farrington's approach highlights the importance of early intervention and the interplay between personal and social factors in explaining and preventing youth crime (Basto-Pereira & Farrington, 2022).

Other models, such as the RNR model and The Good Lives Model also have strengths and weaknesses.

The Risk-Need-Responsivity (RNR) model is an evidence-based framework for reducing recidivism, built around three principles: matching intervention intensity to offender risk (Risk), targeting criminogenic needs (Need), and tailoring programmes to individual characteristics (Responsivity). Widely adaptable across populations and settings, it increasingly incorporates strengths-based elements to enhance engagement while maintaining its structured, theoretically rigorous focus on outcomes and public safety. However, it has been criticised for its deficit focus on risks over personal strengths, an underdeveloped Responsivity Principle lacking detailed guidance, complexity in implementation, and a tendency toward over-manualised "cookie-cutter" programmes. It also gives limited attention to offender motivation, agency, and identity – factors seen as key to long-term desistance and personal growth (Loeber & Le Blanc, 1990).

The model has been implemented in various settings for youth offenders, including probation, residential programmes, and community-based services. Specific assessment tools, such as the Youth Level of Service/Case Management Inventory (YLS/CMI), are designed to operationalise RNR principles for this age group, guiding both judicial decisions and targeted interventions that reduce recidivism. Research indicates that when interventions for adolescents are matched to their risk levels and needs – and delivered in a responsive, strengths-based, and engaging manner – they are more likely to be effective (Hoge & Andrews, 2016).

The Good Lives Model (GLM) is a strengths-based rehabilitation framework that aims to help offenders create purposeful, prosocial, and personally fulfilling lives that naturally reduce the likelihood of reoffending. It prioritises developing personal capabilities, pursuing meaningful goals, and enhancing well-being through collaborative, individualised plans that also address criminogenic needs. Particularly effective for youth offenders aged 14–17 when adapted for developmental needs and family involvement, the GLM promotes engagement, motivation, and positive identity formation. However, it has a smaller empirical evidence base than the Risk-Need-Responsivity model and can be challenging to implement as a practical, measurable protocol. Balancing its emphasis on personal fulfilment with effective risk management remains a key consideration for its application (Ward & Willis, 2014).

Irrespective, theories like Moffitt's dual taxonomy model – distinguishing between the very large "adolescent-limited" group of offenders, and much smaller "life-course-persistent" offenders – remain highly influential (Moffitt, 1993).

This is because a life-course approach to youth offending is increasingly recognised as central to effective prevention and intervention, drawing on Lambie (2018). Research and policy analysis in New Zealand highlight the critical interplay between early severe behavioural problems – especially when accompanied by callous-unemotional (CU) traits – and persistent trajectories into adult criminality, including theories regarding the development of antisocial personality disorder.

To state the obvious, not all youth offending is the same. It should be acknowledged that these studies have low numbers of Māori and Pasifika with limited generalisability and applicability, although the notion of traits as enduring qualities which can be identified early does not appear to be culture specific. While the identification and naming of enduring traits is universal, each culture defines, values, and expresses these traits differently. In Māori, Samoan, and Tongan contexts, terms like āhua, momo, uiga, anga reflect how enduring qualities – both observable and moral – are integral to personal and social identity. The specific cultural values attached to traits may differ, but the underlying concept is widespread and does not appear to be unique to any one culture.

Evidence from New Zealand's Christchurch (Fergusson & Horwood, 1995) and Dunedin (Poulton et al., 2015) longitudinal studies, as well as global research, supports this taxonomy distinguishing "life-course-persistent" (LCP) from "adolescent-limited" (AL) offenders.

The Dunedin Study can be described as under-representative of Māori and Pasifika compared to the New Zealand population because, although the percentage of Māori (about 7.5–8.6%) and Pasifika (1.5%) in these studies is roughly comparable to census figures for the South Island in the 1970s, these proportions are lower than the national average of young people in the same era, and particularly much lower than today's NZ proportions. The smaller absolute numbers of Māori and Pasifika in Dunedin mean that findings about health or social outcomes should not be assumed to generalise to all Māori and Pasifika across New Zealand, especially given possible regional and cultural variation (Poulton et al., 2015)

LCP (life-course-persistent) offenders show early-onset, severe antisocial behaviour that persists into adulthood, while AL offenders display antisocial acts mainly during adolescence, often in the context of peer influence and developmentally typical risk-taking.

LCP youth are more likely to experience neurocognitive problems; display under-controlled temperament and CU (callous unemotional) traits; exhibit behaviours such as aggression before age 10; and have histories of trauma, maltreatment, and family dysfunction.

The presence of CU traits in LCP youth exacerbates risk, indicating emotional deficits such as lack of empathy, shallow affect, and diminished responsiveness to others' distress. But it is more than 50 years ago that the extension of these traits – naming them either as antisocial personality disorder or psychopathy or both, depending on what nosology or classification system on which we rely – was disputed as representing a discrete circumscribed psychiatric disorder. Instead, Lewis elegantly referred to it as being shaped more by social judgement rather than clear clinical boundaries, referring to it as a "most elusive category".

This is because children with early-onset conduct issues and pronounced CU traits show demonstrable differences including biological and social from their peers. Their neurophysiology is not the same, often exhibiting atypical amygdala responses to fear, reduced autonomic reactivity, and a reward-dominant decision-making style that weakens punishment cues. Genetic influences also appear to be particularly strong in the CU subgroup (heritability estimates 0.50–0.70), with epigenetic and contextual factors – including consistent and positive caregiving, exposure to trauma, and social deprivation – thought to play moderating roles.

Whether or not callous unemotionality is really present, it is particularly significant that many LCP youth have histories of extreme adversity. This presents with poverty and disadvantage, family stress and trauma. Early-life deprivation increases risk for externalising behaviours, especially among those already contending with other adversities. Dysfunctional family dynamics, parental mental illness/substance abuse, inconsistent parenting, and exposure to violence compound risk for both conduct disorder and continued offending. In New Zealand, up to 80% of youth offenders report exposure to family violence, with high rates of sexual and physical abuse among those in youth justice facilities.

However, as Lambie (2018) emphasised accurate and early assessment is vital for effective intervention. Many young people who display severe conduct problems do so because of potentially modifiable factors such as trauma, Attention Deficit Hyperactivity Disorder, cognitive and learning difficulties, Fetal Alcohol Spectrum Disorder, environmental stressors, as examples. Once correctly identified, these can be targeted through interventions including the family, school, and professionals. There is evidence supporting the effectiveness of parent management training and early childhood education programmes; teacher-management and school-wide emotional learning strategies; trauma-focused cognitive behavioural therapies and wraparound services; and a range of interventions for cognitive impairments including FASD and ADHD.

These interventions are especially effective when begun early, are culturally informed, and address the full ecology around the child (Becker, 1963), but there is the existence of a small (~10%) subgroup with a different kind of entrenched neurodevelopmental deficit – those with severe CU traits and early-onset conduct disorder – who are much less responsive even to high-quality, well-targeted interventions.

For these young people, the theory is that there is a persistent moral-emotional impairment (a "neurodevelopmental disorder of morals") that underlies such trajectories, setting the stage for a diagnosis of Antisocial Personality Disorder in later years (Lewis, 1974). The risks of reification deserve to be repeated, namely the professional reliance on observable behavioural criteria such as impulsivity, irresponsibility, and repeated criminal acts, rather than on the underlying cognitive or affective dimensions which can simply reflect the outcome of disadvantage and marginalisation in already stigmatised groups, disproportionally qualifying them for a diagnosis.

Labelling theory also highlights the role of societal reactions in perpetuating offending behaviour. Pasifika youth are often subject to racial profiling, media stereotyping, and discriminatory policing practices. Such external labelling can shape self-perceptions, reduce opportunities for positive identity formation, and entrench self-fulfilling prophecies of cycles of marginalisation and reoffending.

Sociological theories have offered more systemic understandings of youth offending, particularly through concepts such as strain theory, labelling theory, and social disorganisation theory. Strain theory, for example, suggests that individuals turn to crime when they are unable to achieve culturally sanctioned goals through legitimate means. In the context of Māori and Pasifika youth, socio-economic marginalisation, educational inequities, and labour market discrimination create real structural barriers that make such strain acute.

However, even sociological theories often universalise experiences and fail to fully capture the specific colonial histories, migration patterns, and cultural frameworks that inform the experiences of Māori and Pasifika young people.

Criminological perspectives, particularly those rooted in critical criminology, have increasingly emphasised the impact of systemic power structures, racism, and colonisation on crime patterns. Indigenous criminology, as advanced by scholars such as Tauri and others (Cunneen & Tauri, 2016), explicitly challenges the Eurocentric assumptions of mainstream criminology and calls for culturally grounded, community-led alternatives (Webb et al., 2022).

This approach aligns more closely with the realities faced by Māori and Pasifika youth. Recognising that offending behaviour often emerges from systemic injustice rather than only individual pathology is critical. However, indigenous criminology is still a developing field and, to date, much of the scholarship has focused more heavily on Māori experiences than on the specific realities of Pasifika youth. There remains an urgent need to expand indigenous criminology to better reflect Pasifika epistemologies and cultural contexts.

While dominant theories offer valuable partial insights, they consistently fall short in explaining the offending patterns of Pasifika youth for several reasons:

- Cultural Specificity: Theories often generalise across cultures, failing to recognise the distinctive values, norms, and relational practices that influence Pasifika behaviour.
- Collectivism versus Individualism: Many frameworks assume an individualistic orientation toward goals, success, and accountability, ignoring the collectivist ethos that defines Pasifika identity.
- Migration Histories: The experiences of dislocation, diaspora, and settlement in New Zealand have profound impacts on Pasifika youth that are only beginning to be integrated into dominant theoretical model.
- Colonisation and Structural Racism: Without explicit attention to the historical and ongoing impacts of colonisation and systemic racism, theories risk pathologising Pasifika youth rather than addressing root causes.

Indigenous and Culturally Grounded Theories

In response to the limitations of dominant Western models, indigenous and culturally grounded theories of youth offending offer alternative frameworks that better resonate with the lived realities of Māori and Pasifika youth. These approaches prioritise relationality, collective wellbeing, historical context, and the centrality of culture in shaping human behaviour.

Indigenous theories recognise that offending behaviour cannot be separated from the historical processes of colonisation, displacement, and cultural marginalisation. For Māori and Pasifika youth, these processes have disrupted traditional forms of social organisation, knowledge transmission, and identity development. The erosion of cultural anchors has been linked to higher rates of disconnection, alienation, and engagement with the criminal justice system (Ioane et al., 2013; Lambie, 2018; Polglase & Lambie, 2024).

Both Māori and Pasifika stress the interconnectedness of people, land, ancestors, and future generations. Healing interventions, therefore, must attend not only to the young person but to the web of relationships that surround them.

Wairua, or spiritual connection, is also fundamental in both traditions. Addressing youth offending must encompass not just physical and psychological dimensions but also spiritual and relational restoration. Applying these concepts in therapeutic and justice settings involves reimagining conventional models to prioritise relational, culturally grounded practices. Innovations such as Family Group Conferences (FGCs), which originated in New Zealand, draw on indigenous traditions of collective decision-making and restorative justice.

Pasifika Youth Courts and Rangatahi Courts further embody this approach by holding proceedings on marae or in culturally significant spaces, incorporating community elders and traditional practices to strengthen cultural identity and engagement (Tuimavave, 2017).

Culturally specific programmes, such as Le Va's "Flo Pasifika" initiatives, provide targeted mental health and suicide prevention support for Pasifika youth through frameworks that emphasise connection, respect, and shared responsibility.

Ranga Tū is a practical outdoor programme that that meets all aspects of Whakawhanaungatanga, Kāwanatanga, Tino Rangatiratanga, Ōritetanga and Wairuatanga through learning, sharing, karakia, tikanga Māori, whakapapa and Te Taiao (natural environment). Ranga Tū is mana-enhancing with a strength-based approach, addresses inequities and offers improvements in health outcomes for Māori. The Māori concept of Tuakana – Teina, that is, "student one week becomes the teacher the next week" provides immediate restoration of mana and integrity through prosocial learning. Ranga Tū, by drawing on a kaupapa Māori approach, integrates indigenous values, community leadership, and cultural identity to promote wellbeing and resilience for rangatahi Māori and Pasifika youth facing mental health challenges.

These practices align closely with the principles of therapeutic jurisprudence, which recognises the law's potential to function as a therapeutic agent, thereby acknowledging that it is not possible to undertake an assessment without having some change occur (Brookbanks, 2015). By placing relational harmony and cultural belonging in the centre, such approaches enhance the psychological and emotional wellbeing of those involved in justice processes.

Practical Approaches to the Theories of Youth Offending

We believe the ultimate value of any theory lies in its practical application to effectively engage with whānau, including young people themselves, to identify and to address potentially reversible factors in their offending trajectories. We think that cultural advisors and mental health clinicians can complement each other's skills to create meaningful change in the lives of young offenders and their families, and at the same time meet the legislative and clinical requirements. And if there is a reduction and preferably a cessation in repeat offending, this is also in the public interest. Simply stated, it is good for everyone.

Effective youth justice intervention requires a synthesis of cultural understanding and clinical expertise. The demographic shifts in New Zealand, particularly the emergence of dual ethnicity Māori and Pacific populations between 2018 and 2023, reflect even more complex cultural identities that practitioners must navigate. This demographic evolution correlates with an audit of findings from Cultural Reports in the Tāmaki Makaurau region authored between 2023 and 2024, where 50% of cases involved Māori and Pacific ethnicity, highlighting the intricate dynamics of whānau and aiga systems that practitioners must understand and respect.

We think that the collaboration between cultural advisors and mental health clinicians represents a unique approach to youth justice intervention. We have found that wearing the hat of an academic and a researcher contributes a valuable theoretical framework, but the practical reality of being prepared to undertake effective and meaningful assessments in the community with "hard to reach" young people and their families, using the principles of therapeutic jurisprudence as well as setting the scene for strategic interventions is our ultimate goal.

Linking to the above theories on youth offending, for instance, labelling theory, although we are providing reports to the Court, we believe we cannot measure something without acknowledging that our presence is already having an impact on the whānau and the young person. This means that while the reports need to be objective and defensible, the process of putting them together also needs to be done in a way that is not harmful to the young person or their whānau (Brookbanks, 2017).

There is a window of opportunity for the process to become a positive experience, using the principles of restorative justice and therapeutic jurisprudence. This is how we started going through the recommendations with the whānau and young people, even when – and especially when – some of the recommendations are about things that the whānau may know they should do, but really do not want to do. It means that we are not ducking the issues.

It means arriving at homes, gang pads, or emergency housing, and other places, which requires a different skill set – one that combines vigilance and awareness of surroundings, safety, cultural observations, and the working hard to present (wherever possible) the culturally and clinically informed formulation and recommendations – upfront and in an honest and compassionate way – that is intended to enhance whānau mana while providing tangible hope for the future. We see this as tika, pono and aroha; and using the cards which we have been dealt.

Although heavily anonymised, certain cases serve as powerful reminders of what works in youth justice intervention when cultural and clinical perspectives are truly integrated.

Take the case of Z, for instance. Z's situation underscores the critical importance of culturally grounded practices in engaging young people. Living on a remote peninsula, Z's circumstances required an initial cultural assessment before any clinical intervention could even hope to make a meaningful impact. Recognising this, the mental health clinician joined the cultural advisor on the second visit to Z's whānau – a move that exemplifies the kind of teamwork needed for effective intervention. This visit was thoughtfully crafted, blending culture with practicality. Bringing kai (food) showed respect for cultural protocols and acted as a relational bridge to the family. This was a very humbling stand-out moment because the young people, although hungry, showed immense cultural respect and restraint, waiting to eat until later and offering the food to us as manuhiri. The cultural advisor and clinician were greatly moved; as materially impoverished as they were, they were not impoverished in manaakitanga at all. The clinician and cultural advisor prioritised connecting with Z and his siblings first, with permission from Z's mother and his whāngai father, whose initial non-participation reflected the need for trust to develop gradually throughout the family. This collaboration highlights how cultural and clinical expertise complement each other. The cultural advisor brought essential insights about local relationships, protocols, and context, while the clinician provided the sharp tools of assessment and intervention planning. Together, they built an understanding of Z's situation that neither could have achieved alone.

P's case further demonstrates the transformative potential of an integrated cultural-clinical approach. Like many young people in the youth justice system, P's journey involved confronting systemic injustices, racial profiling, and a tangled web of factors that fuelled his pathway into offending. What stands out in P's story is how the partnership between culture and clinical work empowered him and his whānau to challenge these injustices and begin carving out a new trajectory, considering he also had an intellectual disability. This meant that it was even more important to engage and to both delicately explain things in a way which P would understand, but also to ensure total consistency so that he had no reason to doubt the good intentions despite his bad experiences with authority figures in the past.

The Role of Cultural Safety and Reciprocal Respect

At the heart of effective youth justice intervention lies the principle of cultural safety and reciprocal respect. This concept is beautifully expressed in the Māori values of "Tika, Pono, and Aroha" (doing what is right, acting with honesty, and nurturing with love). For practitioners, it means moving beyond surface-level cultural competence toward genuinely honouring the dignity and mana of whānau and rangatahi. Trust isn't built through professional titles or qualifications; it is earned through actions – consistent communication, meaningful engagement, and authentic care.

The metaphor of the kūmara (sweet potato) serves as a reminder here. The kūmara doesn't proclaim its own sweetness (Kāore te kūmara e kōrero ana mō tōna ake reka). Its value is revealed through experience. Similarly, youth justice practice is not about self-promotion nor rigid frameworks; it is about earning trust through humility and a demonstrated commitment to whānau wellbeing.

One critical element is acknowledging the dialectics between individual identity and collective identity. Western approaches tend to focus on the individual, while Māori and Pacific worldviews emphasise interconnected relationships and collective dynamics. Addressing youth offending effectively means working within these relational systems and not getting stuck on individual pathology alone.

Cornerstones of Meaningful Engagement

For us, effective cultural-clinical intervention involves several intentional steps:

- **Relationship Building**: Establishing trust through a consistent presence that demonstrates genuine care and respect for whānau wellbeing.
- **Cultural Assessment**: Mapping out the young person's cultural roots, including connections to iwi or a broader cultural community, alongside the important roles of extended family.
- **Collaborative Planning**: Empowering whānau to identify their own solutions while supporting these plans with accessible resources.
- **Sustained Support**: Maintaining connections well beyond the assessment and intervention period to help ensure lasting, meaningful change.

But it doesn't stop there – systemic factors must also be confronted. Many youth justice cases reveal entrenched barriers that need dismantling, from systemic inequities to institutional bias.

Practitioners should strive to:

- Speak up in Court or school situations while maintaining independence in reporting – not shying away from calling out harmful attitudes while staying constructive and fair in their involvement.
- Assist whānau in navigating service systems, which often require translation for both families and professionals.
- Remove practical obstacles like transportation challenges, childcare needs, and housing instability to enable engagement.
- Actively challenge discriminatory practices and push for policy reform within their own organisations and systems.

Providing the Koha of Hope

A cornerstone of effective intervention is offering hope – not as a distant ideal, but as an actionable pathway forward. The "koha of hope", as one cultural advisor calls it, is about showing whānau and rangatahi what's possible beyond their current circumstances.

This involves building mana and dignity, even amidst adversity.

This hope-driven practice includes:

- **Strengths-Based Approach**: Identifying existing capacities within the whānau and building upon them.
- **Future Planning**: Helping rangatahi set goals that are aspirational yet achievable.
- **Celebration of Progress**: Acknowledging every step forward, no matter how small it may seem.
- **Peer Support Connections**: Linking young people with mentors or role models who reflect positive pathways.

Naturally, practitioners must balance this holistic engagement with fulfilling legal or institutional expectations. Documentation, for instance, must reflect both cultural and clinical perspectives while prioritising transparency. Reports should be shared with whānau whenever possible, except in cases that risk harm. This openness can deepen trust and ensure whānau understand the recommendations being made and feel actively involved in the process.

The willingness of whānau to disclose personal information often hinges on their ability to see light at the end of the tunnel. When families can envision a future where recommendations are practical, actionable, and genuinely helpful, openness becomes a natural response. Specialised reports that lay out the issues clearly, coupled with realistic solutions, help foster hopefulness and collaboration.

Challenges of Integration

While the promise of integrated cultural-clinical practice is transformational, it is not without its challenges:

- **Resource Demands**: This work takes time, emotional investment, and specialised skills.
- **Institutional Resistance**: Some systems struggle to embrace the flexibility required for culturally responsive practice.
- **Training Gaps**: Practitioners need ongoing development in cultural competence and collaborative methodologies.
- **Sustainability Concerns**: Long-term relationships with whānau require institutional willpower and support structures.

Toward Empowering Whānau Wellbeing

In this chapter, the cases of Z and P reveal what is possible when cultural wisdom and clinical expertise come together. Although adhering to theoretical practice, these examples show how grounded, relational practices can spark meaningful change in the lives of rangatahi and their whānau.

With patience, humility, and respect at the core, the cultural-clinical approach not only addresses youth offending but helps weave a foundation for hope, dignity, and justice – with mana enhancing every step along the way.

Conclusion

In an attempt to bring these perspectives together, it is clear that understanding Māori and Pasifika youth offending in Aotearoa New Zealand demands an approach that recognises the interplay between individual circumstances and collective, systemic forces. The persistence of historical inequities, the centrality of cultural identity and community obligations, and the realities of migration, displacement, and marginalisation mean that imported, individualised Western theories often miss the mark. Meaningful engagement with young people requires cultural competence, clinical insight, and a willingness to navigate the fluid and evolving nature of identity in our current and diverse society. By holding the collective and the personal in constant balance, and by resisting one-size-fits-all assumptions, we believe that policymakers, practitioners, and communities can better support youth towards pathways that respect both their individual potential and freedom, as well as their collective belonging and need for public safety.

References

Basto-Pereira, M., & Farrington, D. P. (2022). Developmental predictors of offending and persistence in crime: A systematic review of meta-analyses. *Aggression and Violent Behavior*, 65, 101761. https://doi.org/10.1016/j.avb.2022.101761

Beals, F. (2006). *Reading between the lines: Representations and constructions of youth and crime in Aotearoa/New Zealand* (Ph.D Thesis). Victoria University of Wellington.

Becker, H. S. (1963). *Outsiders: Studies in the sociology of deviance*. Free Press.

Brookbanks, W. (2015). Therapeutic jurisprudence – Moving forward. *LawNews ADLSI*, 20, 2–10.

Brookbanks, W. (2017). Therapeutic jurisprudence. *ReSolution*, May, 15–18.

Came, H., O'Sullivan, D., Kidd, J., & McCreanor, T. (2021). The Waitangi Tribunal's WAI 2575 report: Implications for decolonizing health systems. *Health and Human Rights*, 23(2), 223–236.

Cunneen, C., & Tauri, J. (2016). *Indigenous criminology* (1st ed.). Bristol University Press. https://doi.org/10.2307/j.ctt1t893kz

Deckert, A., Busby-Pukeiti, W. T. G., & Tauri, J. (2023). "Young brown men being Brutish": How police Ten 7 portrays māori and pacifica people as violent and criminal in Aotearoa New Zealand. *Journal of Global Indigeneity*, 7(1). https://doi.org/10.54760/001c.77757

Enari, D., Vaka, S., & The University of Waikato. (2024). Pacific youth well-being – Diaspora perspectives. *MAI Journal: A New Zealand Journal of Indigenous Scholarship*, 13(1), 151–155. https://doi.org/10.20507/MAIJournal.2024.13.1.13

Etherington, B. (2022). "I think I beleive in civil rights": Re-remembering trans-indigenous political activism in pauline Vaeluaga Smith's dawn raid. *Studies in the Novel*, 54(3), 293–311. https://doi.org/10.1353/sdn.2022.0024

Faleolo, M. M. (2014). *Hard-hard-solid! Life histories of Samoans in bloods youth gangs in New Zealand*. Massey University.

Fergusson, D. M., & Horwood, L. J. (1995). The Christchurch health and development study: An overview. *Australian and New Zealand Journal of Psychiatry*, 29(2), 199–208.

Hoge, R. D., & Andrews, D. A. (2016). *The youth level of service/case management inventory (YLS/CMI): User's manual*. Multi-Health Systems.

Industrial Schools Act 1882 (1882).

Ioane, J. (2017). Talanoa with Pasifika youth and their families. *New Zealand Journal of Psychology*, 46(3), 40–46.

Ioane, J., Lambie, I., & Percival, T. (2013). A review of the literature on Pacific Island youth offending in New Zealand. *Journal of Pacific Rim Psychology*, 7(2), 428–439.

Ioane, J., Lambie, I., & Percival, T. (2016). A comparison of Pacific, Māori, and European violent youth offenders in New Zealand. *International Journal of Offender Therapy and Comparative Criminology*, 60(6), 657–674. https://doi.org/10.1177/0306624X14560725

Lambie, I. (2018). *It's never too early, never too late: A discussion paper on preventing youth offending in New Zealand.* Office of the Prime Minister's Chief Science Advisor. https://www.pmcsa.ac.nz

Leafe, R. V. (2017). *The influence of shifting Pacific identities in learning: The experience of parents raising children of mixed Pacific ethnicities*. Massey University.

Lewis, A. (1974). Psychopathic personality: A most elusive category. *Psychological Medicine*, 4(2), 133–140. https://doi.org/10.1017/S0033291700041969

Loeber, R., & Burke, J. D. (2011). Developmental pathways in juvenile externalizing and internalizing problems. *Journal of Research on Adolescence*, 21(1), 34–46. https://doi.org/10.1111/j.1532-7795.2010.00713.x

Loeber, R., & Le Blanc, M. (1990). Toward a developmental criminology. *Crime and Justice*, 12, 375–473. https://doi.org/10.1086/449169

Merton, R. K. (1938). Social structure and anomie. *American Sociological Review*, 3(5), 672–682.

Moewaka Barnes, H., & McCreanor, T. (2019). Colonisation, hauora and whenua in Aotearoa. *Journal of the Royal Society of New Zealand*, 49(sup1), 1–13.

Moffitt, T. E. (1993). Adolescence-limited and life-course-persistent antisocial behavior: A developmental taxonomy. *Psychological Review*, 100(4), 674–701.

Polglase, L., & Lambie, I. (2024). A sharp decline in youth crime: Reviewing trends in New Zealand's youth offending rates between 1998 and 2019. *Current Issues in Criminal Justice*, 36(1), 42–62. https://doi.org/10.1080/10345329.2023.2236730

Poulton, R., Moffitt, T. E., & Silva, P. A. (2015). The Dunedin multidisciplinary health and development study: An overview. *Journal of the Royal Society of New Zealand*, 45(1), 1–13.

Selvaraj, J. A. (2016). Inclusive education in New Zealand: Rhetoric and reality. *History of Education Review*, 45(1), 54–68. https://doi.org/10.1108/HER-04-2014-0029

Stats NZ. (2023). *2023 Census population counts by ethnic group*. https://www.stats.govt.nz/

Tuimavave, L. (2017). *The Pasifika youth court: A discussion of the features and whether they can be transferred*. Victoria University of Wellington.

Ward, T., & Willis, G. M. (2014). The good lives model: An overview. *Sexual Abuse: A Journal of Research and Treatment*, 26(2), 119–131.

Webb, R., Suaalii-Sauni, T., Wright-Bardohl, T., & Tauri, J. (2022). Building understandings of Maori and Samoan experiences of youth justice: Navigating beyond the limits of official statistics. *New Zealand Sociology*, 37(1), 70–92.

4 Colonisation, Racism, and Neoliberalism

Addressing Structural Oppression to Support Māori and Pasifika Youth in the Justice System

Logan Hamley and Yvonne Ualesi

Across contexts, Māori and Pasifika youth continue to be positioned as a criminal or "wicked" problem to address, and the subject of moral panics (Roguski & Tauri, 2013) whether concerns are raised about youth gangs (Tunufa'i, 2017), ram raids (Howie & Block, 2023), or general violence (Cunneen, 2020; Webb et al., 2022). This representation of Indigenous youth reflects their wider positioning within systems of power that continue to criminalise Indigenous peoples. This chapter aims to provide a brief introduction to how structural and social factors play a considerable role in the context of youth justice for Māori and Pasifika peoples.

The chapter first begins with a brief introduction of the authors by way of positionality and an overview of colonialism in the South Pacific, its differential impacts across nations, and its role in shaping the contemporary justice system, like many other systems. It then discusses how racism is shaped by the colonial histories of the South Pacific, looking at how Indigenous peoples are racialised within New Zealand, and how this affects different experiences of the justice system. Attention is given to the increasing impact of neoliberalism on Māoriand Pasifika peoples though we suspect that there will be relevance to First Nations community in Australia. This section then discusses how poverty and precarity are shaped by colonialism and racism, as well as how neoliberalism has further increased the criminalisation of Indigenous peoples. We discuss the significance of the Va and conclude with a case study highlighting its importance among Māori and Pacific youth.

Positionality

Logan Hamley hails from the iwi (nations) of Ngāti Rangi-Whanganui and Te Atihaunui-a-Pāpārangi, part of the broader Te Ranga Tupua of the North Island of New Zealand. He grew up in North Waikato before moving to Tāmaki Makaurau (Auckland) to study psychology. He now calls Morningside home, where he lives with his partner. He is a senior researcher with Whakauae Research Services, a kaupapa Māori health research centre that is owned by Ngāti Hauiti. His PhD research explored identity development for young Māori men growing up in the city, exploring how to resist colonial and racial discourses that impact young Māori men.

DOI: 10.4324/9781003298410-7

Yvonne Ualesi is Aotearoa New Zealand born to parents of Samoan, Tokelauan and Fijian descent. She hails from the villages of Mulivai Safata, Pu'apu'a, Saipipi, Savalalo, Fakaofo and Bureta. She is a proud Southsider who grew up in Ōtara, Tāmaki Makaurau, and currently resides in Māngere East with her husband and four children. She is a Senior Lecturer at Auckland University of Technology in the School of Education and her PhD examined culturally responsive, sustaining and safe youth mentoring for racialised and minoritised Māori and Pasifika rangatahi in alternative education who were targeted as part of a youth mentoring programme in a Eurocentric tertiary context.

Colonialism in the South Pacific

While the focus of this section is on the relevance of colonialism in understanding the context for youth justice, it is important to recognise the long histories of Indigenous peoples across the South Pacific prior to colonisation. These deep histories of belonging, movement, and most importantly relationality continue to inform the lives of Indigenous youth in the South Pacific today (Cliffe, 2013; Geia et al., 2013; Tunufa'i, 2017). The ancestors of many Pacific peoples sailed across the Pacific Ocean over 3000 years ago, beginning in Papua New Guinea, the Solomon Islands and Vanuatu, and eventually reaching Eastern Polynesia, including New Zealand, around 1000 years ago (Walker, 1990).

For thousands of years, Indigenous communities formed a tapestry of vibrant collectives who often engaged with one another and who developed complex polities to manage tension, conflict and instances of (in)justice (Cunneen & Tauri, 2017; Jackson, 1987). These systems of justice and balance included an array of different localised practices, but nevertheless ensured their wellbeing across the South Pacific. Specifically, youth have an elevated position within society as future keepers and practitioners of knowledge and leaders (Hamley & Le Grice, 2021; Ullrich, 2019). It is from this foundation that many Indigenous peoples draw their strength, energy, and passion in resisting coloniality and colonialism.

Beginning from the 16th century, many Indigenous communities experienced the brutal impacts of colonialism, as different European and Asian empires and the United States sought to dominate and exploit the region across the Pacific Ocean (Banivanua-Mar, 2019; Salmond, 2018; Tecun et al., 2022). Colonialism, according to Canadian First Nation scholar Glen Coulthard, is the structure of dispossession, enabling the theft of land and the extinction of Indigenous peoples' political authority over land and community (Coulthard, 2014). Expanding on this notion of colonialism, Veracini (2011) makes the distinction between two different forms of colonialism: extractive or exploitative colonialism, where colonial forces are interested in the extraction of a raw material (or use of a territory for production of a raw material); and settler colonialism, where an Indigenous population is forcibly removed from a territory, so the land is available for settlers. Both forms of colonialism were seen in the Pacific, for example, the seizure of Fijian vanua (land) by the British for sugar plantations, or the widespread settlement of Europeans in places like New Zealand, Australia, and New Caledonia. As such, through colonial invasion, Indigenous sovereignty has been displaced or curtailed across the Pacific (McGuire, 2023).

Seizure of Indigenous land is crucial to the process and structure of colonialism. Part of this process thus requires fracturing the relationships that Indigenous peoples and the land have to one another (Tuck & McKenzie, 2015). Many Indigenous peoples were thus dislocated from their nations and economic and collective foundations, leading them to rely on Western and capitalist economic policies that, from the outset, have disadvantaged Indigenous peoples relative to settlers (Orange, 2004). Indigenous separation from land thus not only opened up the land for settlers but also displaced Indigenous peoples from their networks of connection, destabilising intergenerational communities of kin (Gilchrist, 2017). Collectives like whānau (extended family or kin) have become increasingly fractured through forced migration and increasingly coerced assimilation towards the colonial nation-state. Equally important are state interventions on Indigenous families, such as the large-scale abuse in state care that occurred in New Zealand to Māori and Pasifika children, young people, and adults (Abuse in Care Royal Commission of Inquiry, 2020). Understanding colonialism, and the ongoing social, political, cultural, and spiritual consequences, is therefore foundational to addressing the wider social inequities in the South Pacific.

Contemporary Impacts of Colonisation

Colonial acts of violence have had such long-term impacts on Indigenous communities that contemporary literature has focused on their relationship to intergenerational trauma (Cavino, 2016; Pihama et al., 2014; Wirihana & Smith, 2014). Evans-Campbell (2008) defines this trauma as

> a collective complex trauma inflicted on a group of people who share a specific group identity or affiliation [. . .] it is the legacy of numerous traumatic events a community experiences over generations and encompasses the psychological and social responses to such events.
>
> (p. 320)

Davoine and Gaudillière (2004) argue that such trauma can become "frozen" within communities, continuing to impact people across generations even if they are removed from the initial impacts of colonial violence. Menzies (2019), for example, notes that the loss suffered by the Indigenous communities across the globe continues to shape communities today through issues such as attachment relationships, mental health, addiction, community violence, and early mortality. For practitioners then, it is important to recognise how colonial violence might be pathologised as an individual or familial dysfunction but is instead linked to wider structural issues. From this perspective, rather than a purely individualised approach, healing will often require community engagement and draw on traditional modes of healing in combination with Western interventions (Marsh et al., 2018).

Colonialism is also not simply a historical event but is also embedded within all systems of power in South Pacific colonies (Smith, 1999). The legal systems, prisons, schools, and health systems have all been imposed on Indigenous peoples by colonial forces (Bennett & Liu, 2018; Hamley & Le Grice, 2021). Indigenous systems that support healing and justice were positioned as inferior and actively suppressed by colonial powers (Mikaere, 2011). Indigenous peoples within the South Pacific thus experienced both epistemological and ontological violence through the denial of their own ways of being and knowing on their own sovereign territories (King, 2019; Teo, 2010). It is for these reasons that Cunneen and Porter (2017) use the term "immiseration" (p. 668) to describe the detrimental impact colonisation had across the social, educational, health, and economic quality of life for Indigenous peoples as we had to navigate systems that were not designed for us.

Various studies have highlighted how the justice system continues to perpetuate colonial violence against Indigenous peoples. Within the New Zealand context, Moana Jackson's (1987) report, *He Whaipānga Hou*, is a seminal report of how the New Zealand Justice System is founded in colonialism. It demonstrates how Māori justice practices had been marginalised through the forced imposition of British law onto Māori. Successive acts of legislation sought to eliminate Māori epistemologies and practices within education, health, and the law. These changes saw the decline of te reo Māori (the Māori language), the forced suppression of tōhunga (Māori healers), a decline in health for Māori, cultural disenfranchisement and disconnection and the loss of 96% of Māori land through decades of settler efforts to undermine Māori tino rangatiratanga (self-determination) (Glover et al., 2004).

Today, more than half the prison population in New Zealand is Māori, and within certain demographics, Māori are more than ten times as likely to be jailed as other ethnicities (McIntosh & Workman, 2017). Further, Māori youth make up 58% of police apprehensions and 61% of Youth Court appearances (Quince, 2017). This proportion is even higher in some Youth Courts, where Māori were 100% of Youth appearances in four Youth Courts, and 70% in a further 20 (Taumaunu, 2015). Te Kooti Rangatahi, a tikanga Māori (Māori customs, protocols) extension of the Youth Court, has been presented as an alternative which has been successful at reducing rates of reoffending. However, the justice system continues to ignore its duties and obligations owed between the Crown and Māori as partners to te Tiriti o Waitangi (the Treaty of Waitangi), a relationship that has been largely overlooked to date in criminal justice (Quince, 2017). Crucially, it ignores Māori right to self-determination.

Thus, there is an imperative for the Crown to engage with Māori to generate kaupapa Māori and tikanga-informed approaches to justice. However, Māori continue to be excluded from meaningful decision-making about our lives (Mihaere, 2015; Quince, 2017; Webb, 2017). The Government's response to addressing Māori overrepresentation within the Justice system currently focuses on adapting imported programmes from overseas to meet the needs of the New Zealand context (Tauri & Webb, 2012). This approach tends to view Māori approaches as only relevant to focus on addressing cultural disconnection, and by proxy, only suitable as an add-on to a Western solution plan. Mihaere (2015) discussed the issues when Māori cultural identity inputs become subsumed within Western-based programmes. In many situations, because the Western framework is the normative one, Māori tikanga and concepts become diluted in order to claim that Treaty obligations have been met (Tauri & Webb, 2012).

As such, different strategies of colonialism have been employed across the Pacific, but the core of these different expressions of colonialism is the belief that Europeans were more equipped and worthy of control of the Pacific region and its rich resources (Tauri, 2014). Further, colonialism is not simply a historical event, but an ongoing set of practices that are maintained within national systems, including the justice system, and many of the norms found within the system (Cunneen & Tauri, 2017; Gone, 2019; Teo & Afşin, 2020). The settler-colonial goals of assimilation, elimination, and control continue to exist through different forms. In particular, criminal justice systems function as an apparatus for state control.

Race, Racism, and Racialisation

While colonisation is foundational to understanding how Indigenous peoples are impacted by the justice system, there are additional structural factors to consider. Researchers have highlighted the centrality of race, racism, and racialisation to understanding how particular groups of people enter the justice system. Racism is often understood at the individual level, considering how someone may express racist attitudes, belief, or behaviours (Salter & Haugen, 2017; Watego, 2021). However, critical race scholars consider racism as entrenched within society; racism is not an issue of a minority of racist individuals but instead a part of the wider social norms. From this perspective, we are interested in how racism is reproduced and maintained, its origins, and how it might be undone (Delgado et al., 2017; Salter & Haugen, 2017).

As such, it is important to understand how race and racialisation function to enable racism within society. Race is typically understood as a social construct that assumes innate difference based on phenotype, ancestry, and or culture (Paradies, 2020). Racialisation is the process by which race becomes naturalised, typically referred to groups that are negatively impacted by racism (including Black communities, Indigenous peoples, and other people of colour). Racialisation marks some bodies as superior and others as inferior. Finally, racism is defined as the "organized systems within societies that cause avoidable and unfair inequalities in power, resources, capacities and opportunities across racial or ethnic groups" (Paradies et al., 2015, p. 2). Together, race, racialisation, and racism have functioned to entrench power inequities between different groups based (often) on phenotypic differences. Race, racialisation and racism produce hierarchies that position "whiteness" as the top of the race hierarchy, with those closer to whiteness afforded more power and advantage relative to those at the bottom of the hierarchy (Moreton-Robinson, 2015). As such, the racialisation of Indigenous peoples was a crucial tool of the colonial project to justify British theft of the land based on *terra nullius* (so-called "nobody's land", Moreton-Robinson, 2015; Watson, 2014).

Research continues to remind us of the ways in which racism operates within justice systems (like all systems of power). Data from the Department of Corrections in New Zealand in 2007 highlighted that Māori were four to five times more likely to be apprehended, prosecuted, and convicted than non-Māori (Department of Corrections, 2007). For Māori youth, offending rates, appearances in Youth Court, and remands in custody remain higher than those of other young people (Ministry of Justice, 2023). Similarly, Pacific peoples are also disproportionately represented across all stages of the criminal justice process (Department of Corrections, 2007). Pacific youth are the third largest group of youth offenders, and figures show they have the largest percentage of violent apprehensions compared to their Māori and European peers (Ioane et al., 2016).

As such, across the entire process of engaging with the justice system, from police contact, through to charging and conviction, there are clear inequities that impact Indigenous peoples in the South Pacific that are linked to institutional racism. Any initiatives then that seek to support Indigenous youth in the South Pacific must also have a clear anti-racist stance, seeking to dismantle the racism that is embedded within the justice system (Johnson & Bristol, 2024). This needs to occur across all levels of the system, from policy through to community engagement.

Neoliberalism, Class, and the Carceral State

Research has long identified that poverty is also strongly related to entrance into the justice system (Wacquant, 2009). However, it is important to locate the roots of poverty in wider social contexts. For Indigenous peoples, economic impoverishment has occurred since the colonial period, with the theft of land and forced removal of many communities creating additional hardships for communities. However, neoliberalism has only served to further worsen these conditions. Neoliberalism refers to a particular political and economic model that emerged in the 1970s that includes the following key features: privatisation of services and opening up of markets; limiting of public spending on social services; and deregulation and emphasis on individual responsibility (Barnett & Bagshaw, 2020; Sugarman & Thrift, 2020).

Following the embrace of neoliberalism by the New Zealand state, income inequality has skyrocketed, with a rising number of people increasingly living in poverty (Groot et al., 2017). For example, most Pacific youth offenders live in areas of high socio-economic deprivation, with over a third living in the most deprived areas of Aotearoa New Zealand (Ioane et al., 2016). As such, neoliberalism and the immense class disparities it has created, have radically and negatively impacted the lives of Indigenous peoples, in ways that both directly and indirectly affect their likelihood of entering the justice system.

Wacquant (2009) uses the term, hyper-incarceration to demonstrate how neoliberalism, racism and colonialism intersect to create the conditions for a select group being targeted for mass incarceration by the state. In particular, Wacquant's work in hyper-incarceration in the United States focuses on how impoverished African American men are targeted by the justice system. In contrast, "the rest of society – including, most remarkably, middle and upper-class African Americans" are left "practically untouched" (Wacquant, 2010, p. 78). Within the New Zealand context, Indigenous and allied scholars have used the term hyper-incarceration to describe the current criminalisation of Indigenous peoples that is normalised (Cunneen & Tauri, 2019; Curcic, 2019; McIntosh & Workman, 2017).

Hyper-incarceration also describes the relationship between prisons and disadvantaged areas, with the spaces often sharing norms and expectations that reinforce offending behaviour and the normalcy of prison in these communities (Cunneen, 2015). High imprisonment rates thus erode the stability, cohesion, and vitality of whole communities, leading to intergenerational cycles of imprisonment and precarity (McIntosh & Curcic, 2020). Equally, hyper-incarceration of Indigenous peoples in prisons means Indigenous communities bear the brunt of these realities. For example, one area of increasing interest for Indigenous peoples in the justice context is the school-to-prison pipeline (SPP). The term refers to the collective institutional forces that target some groups of young people for expulsion from school and entry into the justice system (McIntosh & Curcic, 2020). A term originally used in the United States context to refer to the "zero tolerance" policies that disproportionately led to the expulsion of African American young people, the term nonetheless is relevant for the South Pacific context. For example, Māori disproportionately experience student stand-downs relative to other ethnic groups, and Māori and Pasifika youth are expelled at higher rates from schools than other young people (Ministry of Education, 2022).

However, this "pipeline" to prison can begin even earlier. One-third of all children in state care in New Zealand from 1950 to 1999 have been in prison at some point, and 70% of inmates have a state care history (Abuse in Care Royal Commission of Inquiry, 2020). As such, both school and state care systems are significant systems of the settler colonial apparatus (Ināia Tonu Nei, 2019). McIntosh (2020) thus adapted the model of the pipeline to refer to the soft pipeline (exclusion from education to prison) and hard pipeline (state care to prison) to reflect the broader state impacts on the hyper-incarceration of Indigenous youth. As such, Indigenous hyper-incarceration is not simply an issue of reducing the number of Indigenous peoples in prison but addressing wider social/community harms produced and reproduced by colonisation, racism, and neoliberal policy (Curcic, 2019). Additionally, given 80% of students in residential care are Māori and 16% Pacific, the Education Review Office report recommends implementation of solutions are underpinned by Te Tiriti o Waitangi and be culturally responsive (Education Review Office, 2021).

Transforming Youth Justice and Practice

Increasingly, there is work being done today to address how neoliberalism, racism and colonialism shape the lives of young people in the South Pacific. The justice system is not a neutral space that invariably leads to justice, but instead must be directed towards addressing inequity and injustice. There have been some steps taken to include a meaningful measure of Indigenous autonomy through alternative systems of justice, like Te Kooti Rangitahi and the Pasifika Courts (Cunneen & Tauri, 2019). However, there are still ways to go when it comes to embedding a decolonial approach to justice for Indigenous peoples into the South Pacific context (Cunneen & Tauri, 2019; McIntosh, 2018; Tauri & Webb, 2012). Further, prevention and early intervention represent key leverage points for addressing the structural factors that enable the hyper-incarceration of Indigenous young people within the South Pacific.

In terms of practice within the justice system, many Indigenous peoples within the system focus on family and community-oriented work, drawing on Indigenous ways of knowing and being to the greatest possible extent (Ināia Tonu Nei, 2019; Ioane, 2023). Further, work should be trauma-informed, both at a person-centred level, but also a wider family and intergenerational lens (Wirihana & Smith, 2014). A cross-sectoral approach is required, focusing on holistic wellbeing and engaging with health, education, and social services. Research also calls attention to this work being done alongside those with lived experience of incarceration who can provide the expertise about escaping the justice system (McIntosh & Curcic, 2020). Finally, Indigenous peoples have called for greater attention to decarceration, with the shifting of resourcing and control towards communities most impacted by incarceration to create pathways of divergence out of the justice system, and to enable the flourishing of communities.

In addressing the structural forms of oppression that shape who enters the justice system, we can transform society to better support Māori and Pasifika peoples to thrive. Turning our attention to a Pasifika framework, we discuss the concept of Va and the systemic and societal factors on youth offending that have been exacerbated by ongoing colonialism, racism, neoliberalism and criminalisation.

Va Relationality, Our Shared Ancestral, and Historical Whakapapa/ Gafa (Genealogical) Connection of Pacific and Māori Youth

Va as a concept is the view of living and relating to others. The concept of va (space) is an example, as Wendt (1999) asserted in his expression of the meaning of the "space between", a space that is far from empty but rather relates and holds separate entities together. The notion of cherishing, nurturing and caring for va relationships supports group unity and takes precedence over individualism:

> Tuagalu (2008) pointed out that whilst the context of Wendt's (1999) article was about Samoan tatau (traditional tattoo) he is, in essence, describing a specifically Samoan world view. Moreover, the va gives context and is meaningful and subject to change as relationships and contexts change over time. Thus, in a communal culture, nurturing an individual is activated within the terms of the collective group. In his examination of texts relevant to va, Tuagalu (2008) also asserted there were at least 37 different types of va. The relational space between people are governed by protocols that people show one another, for example va fealofani between brother and sister.

The va is seen as a helpful organising principle for Pacific cultures (Suaalii-Sauni, 2017), and is seen to govern "all inter-personal, inter-group, and sacred/secular relations and is intimately connected to a Pasifika sense of self or identity" (Suaalii-Sauni, 2017, p. 163). The utility of va relational space through a va relational approach supports the unique relationship between Māori and Pasifika youth (Ualesi, 2021). Given the mixed heritage of our youth, we see va relationality as an opportunity to build on the strengths of longstanding ancestral, historical and genealogical connections.

As mentioned earlier, in the Aotearoa New Zealand context, both Māori and Pasifika youth are overrepresented in youth justice. Intervention programmes that are family-based and consider Pasifika values, cultures and worldviews are strengthened when underpinned by va relational approaches (Ualesi, 2021, 2024). A va relational approach from a diasporic Samoan specific lens in the context of Aotearoa takes into consideration the historical ongoing tuakana-teina (elder-younger sibling) relationship of Māori with Pacific/Pasifika peoples, that is, peoples of Moana-Nui-a-Kiwa (the Pacific Ocean). We see elements of such va relationships between Māori and Pacific/Pasifika peoples in the case study that follows.

The Dawn Raids: A Case Study in Racism, Neoliberalism, and Criminalisation

Pasifika communities, like other racialised communities in New Zealand, have often borne the brunt of racist policing (Anae, 2020). In 1974 and 1976, following the economic downturn in the country, Pasifika peoples became scapegoats for the nation's mass unemployment. In response to this, the Auckland police task force was created with the explicit purpose of "addressing" Polynesian violence. Police would engage in street checks, as well as raiding churches, homes, and Pasifika community spaces, detaining anyone who was unable to produce a passport as evidence of their "right" to be in New Zealand. This police act was legal because of the New Zealand Immigration Act 1968 amendment, with this power being used to racially profile Pasifika peoples, despite constituting fewer than 20% of all overstayers (the majority of whom were from nations that are racialised as white such as Australia, the United Kingdom, and the United States) (Ministry of Pacific Peoples, 2021).

The Dawn Raids showed how racism was actively encouraged through parliamentary acts and within policing (Anae, 2012) and how racism is often embedded within institutions and can be positioned as legitimate or accepted. Equally, there continues to be a longstanding impact on Pasifika communities from the Dawn Raids, as well as the neoliberal reform that occurred in the 1980s and 1990s that disestablished many of the industries in which Pasifika peoples worked (Groot et al., 2017). Despite the negative experiences of Pasifika peoples during the Dawn Raids, there were clear va relationships through collaborations with the Māori activist group Ngā Tamatoa that shared the vision for a society that was fair and just. Key activists in the Polynesian Panthers insisted on the "supportive role in some of the seminal Māori struggles over land dispassion in the 1970s – the great Land March . . . hikoi of 1975. . . and occupation of Takaparawhā or Bastion Point in 1977–78." (Anae, 2020, p. 74). Associate Professor Melanie Anae (2020) illuminates the commitment alongside Māori in their fight for self-determination and sovereignty by asserting that the relationship of Pacific peoples was "one of unity through diversity and not uniformity . . . informed by . . . activism against racism" (p. 73).

The Dawn Raids affected between 5,000 and 12,000 Pasifika people between 1974 and 1976 and led to an intergenerational mistrust of government systems, as recognised in the New Zealand government apology in 2021 (Ministry of Pacific Peoples, 2021). Today, Pasifika peoples are more likely to come from lower socio-economic communities than other young people (Ioane et al., 2016; Ravulo, 2016). Additionally, Pasifika peoples are less likely to access health and social services tied to both precarity and limited trust in services (Kapeli et al., 2020). These inequities flow into engagements with the justice system, where Pasifika youth are more likely to experience precarity and have limited trust in the system (Ioane, 2023).

This is particularly concerning given the offending profile for Pasifika youth in New Zealand, who engage in more violent offending than other youth (Ioane et al., 2013, 2016). Ioane (2023), in qualitative research with 24 Pasifika youth who had engaged in offending behaviour, highlights how the Va had been breached by the system, and that there was a mismatch between their worldviews and the Western Justice System (Anae, 2010; Ioane, 2023). While there are promising gains being made with the creation of the Pacific Courts and greater Pasifika capacity within the system to support Pasifika youth, there continue to be major gaps in system transformation to support Pasifika youth and their families to flourish (Ioane, 2023; Ioane et al., 2013).

To work holistically with Pasifika youth and their families, Ioane and Tudor (2023) advocate for a family-centred, rather than person-centred approach, weaving through spirituality as a central element of Pasifika cultures. Further, there is a need for intervention programmes that are family-based, and tailored to Pasifika values, cultures and worldviews, and can support people through alcohol and substance use, emotional and behavioural problems, often within peer and gender-based collectives (Ioane, 2023). Importantly, centring the va, and developing a Pasifika framework for service delivery at the system-level is a crucial pathway towards addressing the inequities Pasifika youth face within the justice system.

Conclusions

In this chapter, we have explored the need for a broader lens in addressing youth justice in the South Pacific. The criminal justice system functions as an apparatus for state control, and our young people have a continued pipeline to prison as racialised bodies. Our discussion shows that both Māori and Pasifika youth continue to be impacted by the ongoing effects of colonialism rampant in our structures and systems. This includes an understanding of the intersections of colonialism, racism, and poverty. We also discussed the need for a familial and va relational approach in youth justice in the South Pacific. Through our shared ancestral and historical relationships and ongoing work, we have shared what this means for us as Māori and Pacific, respectively, in our work and the implications for those working to make structural and systemic shifts in youth justice at all levels.

References

Abuse in Care Royal Commission of Inquiry. (2020). *Tāwharautia: Pūrongo o te Wā: Interim Report*. Abuse in Care Royal Commission of Inquiry. https://www.abuseincare.org.nz/our-progress/reports/interim-report-volume-one/

Anae, M. (2010). Research for better Pacific schooling in New Zealand: Teu le va – A Samoan perspective. *MAI Review*, 1(1), 1–24.

Anae, M. (2012). All power to the people: Overstayers, dawn raids and the polynesian panthers. In S. Mallon, K. U. Māhina-Tuai, & D. I. Salesa (Eds.), *Tangata o le moana: New Zealand and the people of the Pacific* (pp. 221–240). Te Papa Press.

Anae, M. (2020). *The platform: The radical legacy of the Polynesian Panthers*. Bridget Williams Books Ltd.

Banivanua-Mar, T. (2019). *Decolonisation and the Pacific indigenous globalisation and the ends of empire*. Cambridge University Press.

Barnett, P., & Bagshaw, P. (2020). Neoliberalism: What it is, how it affects health and what to do about it. *The New Zealand Medical Journal*, 133(1512), 76–84.

Bennett, S. T., & Liu, J. H. (2018). Historical trajectories for reclaiming an indigenous identity in mental health interventions for Aotearoa/New Zealand – Māori values, biculturalism, and multiculturalism. *International Journal of Intercultural Relations*, 62, 93–102. https://doi.org/10.1016/j.ijintrel.2017.05.005

Cavino, H. M. (2016). Intergenerational sexual violence and Whanau in Aotearoa/New Zealand – Pedagogies of contextualisation and transformation. *Sexual Abuse in Australia and New Zealand*, 7(1), 4–17.

Cliffe, T. (2013). *Transitory Māori identities: Shape-shifting like Māui. Pūrākau of Māori secondary school students experiencing "complex needs"* (Master of Education). University of Auckland. https://pdfs.semanticscholar.org/dbb9/5d5fac4a841089d5073e04e1b7a76909a096.pdf

Coulthard, G. S. (2014). *Red skin, white masks: Rejecting the colonial politics of recognition*. University of Minnesota Press.

Cunneen, C. (2015). Surveillance, stigma, removal: Indigenous child welfare and juvenile justice in the age of neoliberalism. *Australian Indigenous Law Review*, 19(1), 32–45.

Cunneen, C. (2020). Youth justice and racialization: Comparative reflections. *Theoretical Criminology*, 24(3), 521–539. https://doi.org/10.1177/1362480619889039

Cunneen, C., & Porter, A. (2017). Indigenous peoples and criminal justice in Australia. In A. Deckert & R. Sarre (Eds.), *The Palgrave handbook of Australian and New Zealand criminology, crime and justice* (pp. 667–682). Springer.

Cunneen, C., & Tauri, J. (2017). *Indigenous criminology/Chris Cunneen and Juan Tauri*. Policy Press.

Cunneen, C., & Tauri, J. M. (2019). Indigenous peoples, criminology, and criminal justice. *Annual Review of Criminology*, 2(1), 359–381. https://doi.org/10.1146/annurev-criminol-011518-024630

Curcic, M. (2019). *The making of Māori hyper-incarceration: Narratives of imprisonment and the violence continuum* (PhD). University of Auckland. https://researchspace.auckland.ac.nz/bitstream/handle/2292/48907/whole.pdf?sequence=2&isAllowed=y

Davoine, F., & Gaudillière, J.-M. (2004). *History beyond trauma: Whereof one cannot speak, thereof one cannot stay silent*. Other Press.

Delgado, R., Stefancic, J., & Harris, A. (2017). *Critical race theory: An introduction*. New York University Press.

Department of Corrections. (2007). *Overrepresentation of Māori in the criminal justice system. An exploratory report*. Department of Corrections.

Education Review Office. (2021). *Learning in residential care: They knew I wanted to learn*. Education Review Office.

Evans-Campbell, T. (2008). Historical trauma in American Indian/Native Alaska communities: A multilevel framework for exploring impacts on individuals, families, and communities. *Journal of Interpersonal Violence*, 23(3), 316–338. https://doi.org/10.1177/0886260507312290

Geia, L. K., Hayes, B., & Usher, K. (2013). Yarning/aboriginal storytelling: Towards an understanding of an indigenous perspective and its implications for research practice. *Contemporary Nurse*, 46(1), 13–17. https://doi.org/10.5172/conu.2013.46.1.13

Gilchrist, T. (2017). *Āwhinatia tāu Whānau: Kua Wehea ai, Kua Ngaro ai. Māori experiences of reconnecting and rebuilding relationships with kin based systems of Whānau, Hapū and Iwi* (Doctor of Clinical Psychology). University of Auckland. https://researchspace.auckland.ac.nz/bitstream/handle/2292/33566/whole.pdf?sequence=2

Glover, M., Dudgeon, P., & Huygens, I. (2004). Colonisation and racism. In G. Nelson & I. Prilleltensky (Eds.), *Commmunity psychology: In pursuit of liberation and well-being* (pp. 330–347). Palgrave Macmillan.

Gone, J. P. (2019). "The thing happened as he wished": Recovering an american indian cultural psychology. *American Journal of Community Psychology*, 64(1–2), 172–184. https://doi.org/10.1002/ajcp.12353

Groot, S., van Ommen, C., Masters-Awatere, B., & Tassell-Matamua, N. A. (Eds.). (2017). *Precarity: Uncertain, insecure and unequal lives in Aotearoa NewZealand*. http://public.ebookcentral.proquest.com/choice/publicfullrecord.aspx?p=5061916

Hamley, L., & Le Grice, J. (2021). He kākano ahau – Identity, Indigeneity and wellbeing for young Māori (indigenous) men in Aotearoa/New Zealand. *Feminism & Psychology*, 31(1), 62–80. https://doi.org/10.1177/0959353520973568

Howie, C., & Block, G. (2023, July 14). Retail crime: Almost 400 ram raids in six months, judge tells young offender the public have had enough. *NZ Herald*. https://www.nzherald.co.nz/nz/retail-crime-almost-400-ram-raids-in-six-months-judge-tells-young-offender-the-public-have-had-enough/L7X4UDED5FB5PD74DEK7NJ5BZU/

Ināia Tonu Nei. (2019). *Inaia Tonu Nei: Hui Māori Report*. Ināia Tonu Nei. https://static1.squarespace.com/static/60d12cb5a665b46504ad8b32/t/60fe31b1735d6f7990bf3f5a/1627271661386/d8s653-Inaia-Tonu-Nei-Hui-Maori-English-version.pdf

Ioane, J. (2023). *You've just got to think about your family and what type of person you want to be. Listening to young Pasifika people in the youth justice system and their families. Research and recommendations*. Health Research Council of NZ and Massey University School of Psychology. https://mro.massey.ac.nz/server/api/core/bitstreams/77615d2f-0192-46dc-8fdf-bc047469aeb5/content

Ioane, J., Lambie, I., & Percival, T. (2013). A review of the literature on Pacific Island youth offending in New Zealand. *Aggression and Violent Behavior*, 18(4), 426–433. https://doi.org/10.1016/j.avb.2013.05.002

Ioane, J., Lambie, I., & Percival, T. (2016). A comparison of Pacific, Māori, and European violent youth offenders in New Zealand. *International Journal of Offender Therapy and Comparative Criminology*, 60(6), 657–674. https://doi.org/10.1177/0306624X14560725

Ioane, J., & Tudor, K. (2023). Family-centered therapy: Implications of Pacific spirituality for person-centered theory and practice. *Person-Centered & Experiential Psychotherapies*, 22(1), 58–76. https://doi.org/10.1080/14779757.2022.2100812

Jackson, M. (1987). *Māori and the criminal justice system: A new perspective, he Whaipānga Hou*. NZ Department of Justice. https://www.ncjrs.gov/pdffiles1/Digitization/108675NCJRS.pdf

Johnson, M. E., & Bristol, S. C. (2024). Anti-racism and racial justice in the criminal justice system. In E. Verona & B. Fox (Eds.), *The handbook of evidence-based criminal justice practices* (pp. 386–394). Routledge.

Kapeli, S. A., Manuela, S., & Sibley, C. G. (2020). Understanding pasifika mental health in New Zealand: A review of the literature. *MAI Journal: A New Zealand Journal of Indigenous Scholarship*, 9(3). https://doi.org/10.20507/MAIJournal.2020.9.3.7

King, P. (2019). The woven self: An auto-ethnography of cultural disruption and connectedness. *International Perspectives in Psychology*, 8(3), 107–123. https://doi.org/10.1037/ipp0000112

Marsh, T. N., Marsh, D. C., Ozawagosh, J., & Ozawagosh, F. (2018). The sweat lodge ceremony: A healing intervention for intergenerational trauma and substance use. *International Indigenous Policy Journal*, 9(2). https://doi.org/10.18584/iipj.2018.9.2.2

McGuire, M. M. (2023). Exposing the complexities of the colonial project. In C. Cunneen, A. Deckert, A. Porter, J. Tauri, & R. Webb, *The Routledge international handbook on decolonizing justice* (1st ed., pp. 11–21). Routledge. https://doi.org/10.4324/9781003176619-3

McIntosh, T. (2018). Indigenous rights, poetry and decarceration. In E. Stanley (Ed.), *Human rights and incarceration* (pp. 285–301). Springer International Publishing. https://doi.org/10.1007/978-3-319-95399-1_12

McIntosh, T. (2020, May 20). *Imagining a world without prisons*. https://www.auckland.ac.nz/en/alumni/whats-happening/alumni-video-and-audio/raising-the-bar--home-edition-2020/tracey-mcintosh---imagining-a-world-without-prisons.html

McIntosh, T., & Curcic, M. (2020). Prison as destiny? Descent or dissent? In L. George, A. N. Norris, A. Deckert, & J. Tauri (Eds.), *Neo-colonial injustice and the mass imprisonment of Indigenous women* (pp. 223–238). Springer International Publishing. https://doi.org/10.1007/978-3-030-44567-6_11

McIntosh, T., & Workman, K. (2017). Māori and prison. In A. Deckert & R. Sarre (Eds.), *The Palgrave handbook of Australian and New Zealand criminology, crime and justice* (pp. 725–735). Palgrave Macmillan. https://doi.org/10.1007/978-3-319-55747-2

Menzies, K. (2019). Understanding the Australian aboriginal experience of collective, historical and intergenerational trauma. *International Social Work*, 62(6), 1522–1534. https://doi.org/10.1177/0020872819870585

Mihaere, R. (2015). *A Kaupapa Māori Analysis of the Use of Māori Cultural Identity in the Prison System* (Doctor of Philosophy). Victoria University of Wellington. http://researcharchive.vuw.ac.nz/bitstream/handle/10063/4185/thesis.pdf?sequence=2

Mikaere, A. (2011). *Colonising myths – Māori realities he rukuruku whakaaro*. Huia Publishers. http://www.myilibrary.com?id=857199

Ministry of Education. (2022). *Briefing note: Release of 2021 student engagement data*. Ministry of Education. https://assets.education.govt.nz/public/Documents/our-work/information-releases/Advice-Seen-by-our-Ministers/November-2022/9.-BN-1297963-Release-of-2021-Student-Engagement-Data.pdf

Ministry of Justice. (2023). *Youth justice indicators summary report*. Ministry of Justice. https://www.justice.govt.nz/justice-sector-policy/research-data/justice-statistics/youth-justice-indicators/

Ministry of Pacific Peoples. (2021). *Dawn raids apology*. Ministry of Pacific Peoples.

Moreton-Robinson, A. (2015). *The white possessive: Property, power, and indigenous sovereignty*. University of Minnesota Press.

Orange, C. (2004). *An illustrated history of the Treaty of Waitangi*. Bridget Williams Books.

Paradies, Y. (2020). Racism. In B. Carson, T. Dunbar, R. D. Chenhall, & R. Bailie (Eds.), *Social determinants of indigenous health* (1st ed., pp. 65–86). Routledge. https://doi.org/10.4324/9781003117247

Paradies, Y., Ben, J., Denson, N., Elias, A., Priest, N., Pieterse, A., Gupta, A., Kelaher, M., & Gee, G. (2015). Racism as a determinant of health: A systematic review and meta-analysis. *PLoS ONE*, 10(9), e0138511. https://doi.org/10.1371/journal.pone.0138511

Pihama, L., Reynolds, P., Smith, C., Reid, J., Smith, L. T., & Nana, R. T. (2014). Positioning historical trauma theory within Aotearoa new Zealand. *AlterNative: An International Journal of Indigenous Peoples*, 10(3), 248–262. https://doi.org/10.1177/117718011401000304

Quince, K. (2017). Rangatahi courts. In A. Deckert & R. Sarre (Eds.), *The Palgrave handbook of Australian and New Zealand criminology, crime and justice* (pp. 711–723). Palgrave Macmillan. https://doi.org/10.1007/978-3-319-55747-2

Ravulo, J. (2016). Pacific youth offending within an Australian context. *Youth Justice*, 16(1), 34–48. https://doi.org/10.1177/1473225415584983

Roguski, M., & Tauri, J. (2013). The politics of gang research in New Zealand. In K. Richards & J. Tauri (Eds.), *Crime, justice and social democracy: Proceedings of the 2nd international conference* (Vol. 2, pp. 26–44). Queensland University of Technology.

Salmond, A. (2018). *Two worlds: First meetings between Māori and Europeans, 1642–1772*. Penguin New Zealand.

Salter, P. S., & Haugen, A. D. (2017). Critical race studies in psychology. In B. Gough (Ed.), *The Palgrave handbook of critical social psychology* (pp. 123–145). Palgrave Macmillan UK. https://doi.org/10.1057/978-1-137-51018-1_7

Smith, L. T. (1999). *Decolonizing methodologies: Research and indigenous peoples*. Zed Books; University of Otago Press; Distributed in the USA exclusively by St. Martin's Press.

Suaalii-Sauni, T. (2017). The Va and Kaupapa Māori. In T. K. Hoskins & A. Jones (Eds.), *Critical conversations in Kaupapa Māori* (pp. 132–144). Huia (NZ) Ltd.

Sugarman, J., & Thrift, E. (2020). Neoliberalism and the psychology of time. *Journal of Humanistic Psychology*, 60(6), 807–828. https://doi.org/10.1177/0022167817716686

Taumaunu, H. (2015). Latest statistics: Māori overrepresentation in youth court. *Rangatahi Courts Newsletter*, 6, 11.

Tauri, J. (2014). Criminal justice as a colonial project in contemporary settler colonialism. *African Journal of Criminology and Justice Studies*, 8(1), 20–37.

Tauri, J. M., & Webb, R. (2012). A critical appraisal of responses to Māori offending. *The International Indigenous Policy Journal*, 3(4), 1–16. https://doi.org/10.18584/iipj.2012.3.4.5

Tecun, A., Lopesi, L., & Sankar, A. (Eds.). (2022). *Towards a grammar of race in Aotearoa New Zealand*. Bridget Williams Books.

Teo, T. (2010). What is epistemological violence in the empirical social sciences?: What is epistemological violence in the empirical social sciences? *Social and Personality Psychology Compass*, 4(5), 295–303. https://doi.org/10.1111/j.1751-9004.2010.00265.x

Teo, T., & Afşin, B. (2020). The impossible conditions of the possibility of an alter-global psychology. In L. Sundararajan, K.-K. Hwang, & K.-H. Yeh (Eds.), *Global psychology from indigenous perspectives* (pp. 159–174). Springer International Publishing. https://doi.org/10.1007/978-3-030-35125-0_10

Tuagalu, I. (2008). Heuristics of the Vā. *AlterNative: An International Journal of Indigenous Peoples*, 4(1), 107–126. https://doi.org/10.1177/117718010800400110

Tuck, E., & McKenzie, M. (2015). *Place in research: Theory, methodology, and methods*. Routledge.

Tunufa'i, L. (2017). Samoan youth crime. In A. Deckert & R. Sarre (Eds.), *The Palgrave handbook of Australian and New Zealand criminology, crime and justice* (pp. 175–189). Springer International Publishing. https://doi.org/10.1007/978-3-319-55747-2_12

Ualesi, Y. (2021). *Culturally responsive, sustaining and safe youth mentoring practice in Aotearoa New Zealand-a va relational approach*. University of Auckland. https://researchspace.auckland.ac.nz/items/d35f3fa3-9fb0-4fe4-8612-c0a1a9225ef2

Ualesi, Y. (2024). Lessons from a Va relational approach – Embedding indigenous constructs for classroom practice. *New Zealand Journal of Educational Studies*. https://doi.org/10.1007/s40841-024-00316-8

Ullrich, J. S. (2019). For the love of our children: An indigenous connectedness framework. *AlterNative: An International Journal of Indigenous Peoples*, 15(2), 121–130. https://doi.org/10.1177/1177180119828114

Veracini, L. (2011). *Settler colonialism: A theoretical overview*. Palgrave Macmillan. http://site.ebrary.com/id/10445635

Wacquant, L. (2010). Class, race & hyperincarceration in revanchist America. *Daedalus*, 139(3), 74–90. JSTOR.

Wacquant, L. J. D. (2009). *Punishing the poor: The neoliberal government of social insecurity*. Duke University Press.

Walker, R. (1990). *Ka whawhai tonu matou =: Struggle without end*. Penguin Books.

Watego, C. (2021). *Another day in the colony*. University of Queensland Press. https://go.openathens.net/redirector/umoncton.ca?url=https%3A%2F%2Febookcentral.proquest.com%2Flib%2Fumoncton-ebooks%2Fdetail.action%3FdocID%3D6786847

Watson, I. (2014). Re-centring first nations knowledge and places in a Terra Nullius space. *AlterNative: An International Journal of Indigenous Peoples*, 10(5), 508–520. https://doi.org/10.1177/117718011401000506

Webb, R. (2017). Māori experiences of colonisation and Māori criminology. In R. Sarre & A. Deckert (Eds.), *The Palgrave handbook of Australian and New Zealand criminology, crime and justice* (pp. 683–696). Palgrave Macmillan. https://doi.org/10.1007/978-3-319-55747-2

Webb, R., Suaalii-Sauni, T., Wright-Bardohl, T., & Tauri, J. (2022). Building understandings of Maori and Samoan experiences of youth justice: Navigating beyond the limits of official statistics. *New Zealand Sociology*, 37(1), 70–92.

Wendt, A. (1999). Tatauing the post-colonial body. In V. Hereniko & R. Wilson (Eds.), *Inside out: Literature, cultural politics, and identity in the New Pacific* (pp. 399–412). Rowman & Littlefield.

Wirihana, R., & Smith, C. (2014). Historical trauma, healing and well-being in Maori communities. *MAI Journal: New Zealand Journal of Indigenous Scholarship*, 3(3), 197–210.

Section Two

A Case Study

Pasifika Interventions

5 Pasifika Interventions for Talavou (Youth)

Rochelle Nafatali, Vaoiva Natapu-Ponton, and Julia Ioane

'O fanau a manu e fafaga i fugala'au, ae 'o fanau a tagata e fafaga i 'upu – the offspring of birds are fed with flower nectar, but the children of men are nurtured with words.

This Samoan proverb acknowledges the importance of young people being raised in environments which are nurturing and loving. However, for a small group of Pasifika youth, this is not a reality. Difficult childhood environments can contribute to adverse adolescent or adult outcomes. This chapter proposes to outline Pasifika youth in general, followed by a discussion of Pasifika youth involved or at risk of involvement in the justice system in Aotearoa New Zealand (Aotearoa New Zealand) and Australia. We provide a brief overview of Youth Justice in Aotearoa New Zealand and Australia with a Pasifika focus where appropriate, a discussion on Pasifika youth offending, offer a cultural understanding of offending behaviour, and identify interventions for Pasifika youth offending; highlighting family, community, and cultural interventions. We conclude with a case study from clinical experience.

Within Aotearoa New Zealand, Pasifika youth are ethnically and linguistically diverse. Half of all Pasifika youth identify with a primary Pasifika ethnicity, while half identify with two or more Pasifika ethnicities (Ministry of Social Development, 2023). For example, Samoan (55%) and Tongan (26%) were the largest Pasifika youth ethnic groups, and almost a third (31%) identified as both Māori and Pasifika. Accordingly, a new challenge for those working within youth justice is the prioritisation and appropriate response to the growing number of Pasifika youth with dual or more ethnic identities. This is currently a gap in policy and practice. Overall, Pasifika youth remain the most youthful and one of the fastest-growing population groups in Aotearoa New Zealand (StatsNZ, 2024).

Pasifika youth statistics in Australia are more difficult to ascertain, given the large multi-ethnic populations there. However, further exploration indicated that between 1.3% (337,000) and 1.6% (415,033) of the total Australian population has Pasifika heritage, and this group was both younger (more people 0–29 years), and growing more than twice as fast as the general Australian population (Gerace et al., 2023; Liu & Howes, 2023). Taken together, it is clear that the Pasifika population, including youth, continues to grow across both Australia and Aotearoa New Zealand.

DOI: 10.4324/9781003298410-9

Identity Among Pasifika Youth

Pasifika youth highlight conflict and tension within their identities in Aotearoa New Zealand and Australia (Mila-Schaaf, 2013; White et al., 1999). These tensions arise from being raised in a diasporic community where the collective framework of self is often in contradiction with individualistic and Western societal ways of being. Relationships can also change with extended family members as youth connect with Aotearoa New Zealand/Australian culture, and inadvertently disconnect from parental and cultural support networks.

Strained identities can be exacerbated further when young people become engaged in a justice system where (within a cultural context) parents can also be held responsible for their child's offending behaviour. In Aotearoa New Zealand, Pasifika youth are seen to be in an "identity crisis" and need support to strengthen their identity given the complexities of the environments they live in (Alefaio-Tugia et al., 2023). A recent study in south-east Queensland found that many Pasifika youth faced insecurities and felt a lack of belonging due to their diasporic background and often living in underserved and marginalised communities in Australia (Radclyffe et al., 2024). This was likely worsened by racialised stereotyping and derogatory labelling of Australian Pasifika youth, which impacted negatively on their sense of self-worth. Symptoms of this include the overrepresentation of Pasifika youth in the justice system and high suicide rates (Radclyffe et al., 2024).

Whilst family and culture were rated as important amongst Pasifika youth, they also reported confusion in trying to balance the tensions and differences between their Pasifika and non-Pasifika cultures (Liddell et al., 2017). Further, Pasifika youths' understanding of identity appeared contradictory. They reported pride in their Pasifika heritage and family, yet their understanding of Pasifika identity was distorted, as they referenced alcohol abuse and violence as part of Pasifika identity (Ioane, 2023). As a result, in Australia there are continued efforts to promote a community and government approach which is culturally inclusive, alongside an increased awareness of issues faced by Pasifika youth (Liddell et al., 2017). Similarly, in Aotearoa New Zealand, a targeted response is being promoted to eliminate the cultural, social, and systemic barriers which impact positive Pasifika youth outcomes (Ravulo, 2016; Ioane et al., 2016).

Much has been written about Pasifika youth in Aotearoa New Zealand (Veukiso-Ulugia et al., 2024) and Australia (Durham et al., 2023). However, it is our view that to truly understand how our Pasifika youth are doing, one must look at the most vulnerable Pasifika youth; those engaged in offending behaviour. While the impact of Pasifika youth offending on the Pasifika and wider community is significant, knowledge remains limited and requires further understanding and exploration.

Youth Offending

Experts have advised that halting the "natural" trajectory of vulnerable youth toward serious adult offending requires early interventions which are intensive, community-based, and which bring together policy and practice across child health and development, social services, education, and youth and adult justice (Department of Corrections, 2001, p. 26; Gluckman, 2018). Intervening with youth at risk of, or already on a pathway of, offending behaviour, is imperative to stem the tide of young people flowing through the prison pipeline. Previous research has shown that following imprisonment, released young people were very likely to reoffend quickly, and multiple times, and further offending was likely to be serious (Nadesu, 2009). Recent evidence shows that this remains true (Polglase & Lambie, 2024). Therefore, keeping youth out of prison altogether should lead to better outcomes for all (Ministry of Justice, 2022).

In surveying the literature on youth offending, an immediate issue in definition is the lack of age clarity for this group. Legally, in Aotearoa New Zealand, the age of adulthood is 18 years, and the age of maturity is 17 years. Young people are therefore considered legally capable adults, while developmentally, the prefrontal cortex has not matured (Steinberg et al., 2018). Full brain maturation is generally believed to conclude around the mid- to late-twenties, although some researchers believe it to be later due to the digital age (Crone & Konijn, 2018). Perhaps due to this fact, together with the "maturity gap" observed in adolescents who offend, adults aged 18–24 years old are also often included in youth crime statistics and targeted in youth interventions. Ara Poutama Aotearoa | Department of Corrections has typically defined youth to be between the ages of 17 and 20 years old (Ara Poutama, n.d.b). Often, youth offending data focuses on youth aged 14–17 years, as adults who offend (from 18 years) go to men's or women's prisons, while youth are often directed to other interventions.

Given the focus on Pasifika youth offending in this chapter, the definition of "youth" from a Pasifika perspective is important. The age of Pasifika youth within a cultural context is not limited to chronological age. The transition from youth to adulthood among Pasifika cultures is influenced by cultural rites of passage and status that can be privileged over age (Suaalii & Mavoa, 2003).

Youth Justice (Aotearoa New Zealand and Australia)

The Aotearoa New Zealand youth justice system has been called innovative in its emphasis on both a developmental and family systems approach to youth offending, reframing early criminal behaviour as normal adolescent risk-taking behaviour, and seeking solutions within the young person's wider family system (Suaalii-Sauni, 2006). Accordingly, young people under 18 years who offend are usually given diversionary options, with the intention of keeping them out of Aotearoa New Zealand's 19 adult prisons. The Youth Court deals with young people who seriously criminally offend and who cannot be dealt with by community Police (Youth Court of New Zealand, n.d.). The Youth Court can order Family Group Conferences, which develop plans for remediation and preventing the young person from further offending. If plans are incomplete, a range of options are available to the Youth Court, with transfer to the District Court being the last resort. If young people are incarcerated, they may be given an order for Supervision with Residence at one of five Youth Justice residences. If within this time they turn 18 years old, they may be transferred to the general adult prison population. The Rangatahi Court, for Māori youth, and the Pasifika Youth Court, for young people of Pasifika heritage, mirror the Youth Court's basic provisions and are held in culturally appropriate spaces, operating according to Māori or Pasifika cultural protocols.

Pasifika Youth Court incorporates Pasifika languages and protocols with the presence of Pasifika elders and professionals dressed in Pasifika attire. Experiences of Pasifika youth (Samoan) were explored and youth attending Pasifika Youth Court reported favouring the cultural processes, including positive interactions with the Judge they stated were similar to recrimination from their families (Urale-Baker, 2016). This was further substantiated in a more recent study of Pasifika youth offending (Ioane, 2023) where Pasifika Youth Court was seen by youth as a positive experience which was responsive to their cultural and family needs. Furthermore, the direct oversight of Pasifika Judges contributed to a young person and their family's motivation to authentically engage with programmes and interventions.

Australia does not have a Pasifika Youth Court, but established its Children's Koori Court in 2005 (Borowski, 2010). The Children's Koori Court seeks to enable greater participation by the Koori community through involving Aboriginal Elders and fostering Indigenous participation. This is discussed further in another chapter in this book.

Given the overrepresentation of Pasifika youth in juvenile justice, this chapter focuses on the current interventions available in Aotearoa New Zealand and Australia for Pasifika youth offending behaviour. These interventions are available for Pasifika young people who have broken the law to reduce the likelihood of further offences and prevent them from becoming embroiled in the "prison pipeline" (Ministry of Justice, 2024).

Cultural Understanding of Offending Behaviour

The cultural concepts of *Vā* and *Soli le vā* help us to appreciate a Pasifika cultural understanding of offending behaviour. *Vā,* is a multi-layered trans-Pasifika concept referencing the interconnected relationships and relational spaces between Pasifika people, the Christian God, all living and inanimate things, and environments (Matapo & McFall-McCaffery, 2022; Mo'a, 2015). These connections are considered *tapu* or sacred and are healthiest when in harmony with each other (Anae, 2016).

Within the Samoan context, we draw on three dimensions of the V*ā* – namely *Teu le Vā, Tausi le Vā,* and *Soli le Vā* (Ioane, 2023; Pereira, 2011). All three dimensions occur in reciprocity within the Vā and it is therefore important to recognise and acknowledge that whilst relationships and relational spaces can be established, nurtured and maintained, they can also be disrespected, breached, or violated. *Teu le vā* and *tausi le* v*ā* are often used synonymously with one another (Pereira, 2011), although here, we separate these dimensions. *Teu le vā* is essentially building and establishing a relationship and connection with people and/or the environment

(Anae, 2016). This is the general foundation for many Samoan (and Pasifika communities), given that one's identity is relational; based on their relationship with others, community, and environment (Tamasese et al., 2005). *Tausi le vā* is the nurturing of established relationships and relational spaces drawing on Samoan values including (although not limited to) Respect, Reciprocity, Humility, and Love. Included in this concept is the maintenance of the *vā tapuia*, or harmonious interconnected relationships between people, which are of utmost importance to Pasifika people (Mo'a, 2015; Matapo & McFall-McCaffery, 2022). The concepts of vā influence how Pasifika people live and conduct themselves, and therefore Pasifika people recognise each other through their adherence to vā values (Anae, 2016).

In the *vā tapuia*, when a Pasifika individual succeeds, the wider family and Pasifika community are uplifted. Conversely, *Soli le Vā* occurs when there is disharmony, tension, or conflict in the relationship. This is generally seen when a Pasifika individual engages in negative behaviour which reflects unfavourably on the wider family and Pasifika community (Anae, 2016). For example, Samoan youth born in Aotearoa generally controlled the way they expressed their anger so as *not* to harm relational values (Mulipola et al., 2024). Offending behaviour within a Pasifika perspective, then, not only represents a transgression of the prevailing Western laws but also a breach and a trampling of the sacred relational spaces between Pasifika family and community members (Pita, 2018; Ioane, 2023). Such violations lead to distancing as the individual at fault has neglected to *teu le vā* or maintain relational harmony. Distance can be both psychological and/or physical, with separation from parents or the community being a result of a severe offence (Pita, 2018.

Serious criminal offending (e.g. violent and sexual offending, murder) represents the most severe breaches of the *vā* (Ioane et al., 2021). As with young people engaged in offending behaviour, the *vā* has been violated, and this violation is experienced by all parties, given the collective identity of Pasifika people. To illustrate, within offending behaviour, *soli o le vā* has occurred between: a) the Pasifika youth and their victim(s); b) the Pasifika youth and the family of their victim(s); c) the family of the Pasifika youth and the victim(s); and, d) the family of the Pasifika youth and the victim'(s') family (Ioane, 2023).

Pasifika Youth Offending

In Aotearoa New Zealand, the overall youth offending rate (14–17 years old) increased by 9% from 2023 to 2024, while the Pasifika youth offending rate increased by 12%. This was the highest increase in overall offending rates among youth from 2023 to 2024 in Aotearoa New Zealand (Ministry of Justice, 2024). Pasifika young people represent the third-largest ethnic group to offend after Māori and NZ European youth in Aotearoa New Zealand (Paongo, 2024).

In 2015, Pasifika youth under 20 years in Aotearoa New Zealand prisons were 5.2% of the offending population (Department of Corrections, 2015). Recently, youth under 25 years old represented approximately 10% of the Aotearoa New Zealand prison population, with 1.2% of those under 20 years old (Ministry of Justice, 2022). Additionally, Pasifika people represented 11.2% of the total Aotearoa New Zealand prison population (Boshier & New Zealand Office of the Ombudsman, 2023). As ethnicity information in the justice system is limited, Pasifika data underestimates reality (Ministry of Justice, 2024). For example, in Aotearoa New Zealand, previous ethnicity prioritisation meant that where a young person self-identified as both Tongan *and* Māori, the recorded ethnicity was Māori (Ministry of Health, 2017). Anecdotally, the same process also exists for Pasifika communities in Justice.

Pasifika youth in Australia are also overrepresented within the Juvenile Justice system despite people of Pasifika backgrounds making up 2.1% and 1.9% of the national youth population aged 10–14 years and 15–19 years, respectively (Australian Bureau of Statistics, 2011 as cited in Ravulo, 2016). More recent data shows that almost 40% of the Pasifika population in Australia is under 19 years (Oxley, 2021). According to past data on Pasifika youth on community-based orders, the majority were Māori,[1] followed by Samoan, Tongan, and Fijian youth (NSW Department of Attorney General & Justice, 2012, as cited in Ravulo, 2016). In New South Wales, Pasifika are the second most overrepresented group in youth justice statistics (Department of Human Services, 2010) and have the highest proportion of violent youth offending (Ravulo, 2016).

In Victoria, Pasifika youth are overrepresented in youth offending, with 8.5% in youth detention centres compared with comprising 0.1% of the youth population, and are the second most overrepresented group in the juvenile justice system (Liddell et al., 2017). Pasifika youth are typically older than non-Pasifika youth in the Australian juvenile justice system and are more likely to engage in serious violent offences compared with other ethnic groups (Department of Human Services, 2010). Previous research has reported that a tangible loss of culture within Pasifika youth in Australia may be a factor in their overrepresentation (Mission Australia, 2009).

Research in Aotearoa New Zealand, too, has shown that Pasifika youth tended to offend later but were more likely to have a violent offence as their first offence, and for violent offences to be serious (Ioane et al., 2016; Polglase & Lambie, 2024). Factors found to increase the likelihood of Aotearoa Pasifika young people offending included multiple social (e.g. peer pressure), environmental (e.g. societal disconnection, exposure to violence), and socio-economic (e.g. inadequate education, financial strain) factors (Paongo, 2024). Substance use was more likely in Pasifika young people with poor parental and peer connections, and having parents and friends who engaged in substance use themselves (Tamapeau & Kingstone, 2020). A recent study hearing directly from Pasifika youth in the justice system highlighted a desire for money (initially for basic needs, before materialistic goods), credibility, and status among peers as key drivers for criminal offending (Ioane, 2023). However, when these youth were asked what would prevent them from entering the Justice system, all of the young people talked about staying in education and for the system to help them stay in school. This is despite the young people in the study all being disengaged from education.

Retaining Pasifika Students in Education

Keeping young people in school minimises the probability of offending and reoffending. Helping Pasifika learners stay in school involves a combination of culturally responsive support, community engagement, and educational strategies tailored to their needs and strengths (Ioane, 2023; Ponton, 2017). One way of encouraging Pasifika student retention is through Culturally Responsive Teaching. When students see themselves reflected, not only in the staff hired within their educational environment but also represented in the classroom activities and learning tasks they complete, their desire to participate increases. The expression, "You cannot be who you cannot see" speaks to the impact of role-modelling regarding students seeing people who look like them written in to exciting, positive novels or films, and having teachers and educators of Pasifika heritage. Acknowledgement and the valuing of Pasifika identity within educational contexts is imperative. Furthermore, seeking Pasifika student perspectives across the curriculum is critical when considering strategies to reduce learning disengagement. This is a strategy which forms a bond, reflecting a process of *Teu le vā* (Anae, 2016). Through this process, a relationship of genuine care is established between teachers and learners through exchanging knowledge and experience and valuing the perspectives of Pasifika students. Further, there is a need for pedagogical methods and curricula used by educators to be effective and engaging. The following strategies work to engage Pasifika learners by creating mindful, safe learning environments.

Staff Professional Development to Engage Pasifika Learners Critical to retaining Pasifika students is ongoing training for staff in cultural competency, recognition of unconscious biases, and understanding the socio-economic realities faced by many Pasifika youth. Further, encouraging staff to engage in reflective practice, and to co-design solutions with Pasifika students, their families and carers, has been shown to be effective. Research shows that many students struggle to navigate living between traditional Pasifika values and beliefs, and Western educational practices and ideologies (Samu, 2006). To make a difference in the education that Pasifika students are receiving, it has been suggested that training educators to best support the learning styles, metacognitive strategies, and educational outcomes for learners, will be most effective (Ponton, 2017).

Academic and Wellbeing Support For educational institutions to best support Pasifika learners, utilisation of Pasifika methodologies is imperative and requires first learning about who Pasifika people and communities are. The current curriculum does not provide adequate opportunities for engaging diverse learners. Significant evidence continues to encourage schools to maximise student learning and minimise barriers so that all students are successful learners (Barrett, 2014). Further suggestions for creating safe, inclusive learning environments include:

- Targeted learning support: Offering tutoring, study groups, and tailored learning plans.
- Pastoral care: Providing culturally responsive support workers who understand the pressures and experiences of Pasifika youth.
- Flexible pathways: Recognising different learning styles and providing vocational, academic, and blended learning options.
- Celebrate cultural identity: Creating Pasifika groups, cultural days, or language weeks to foster belonging.

Pasifika Youth Interventions

While strong evidence suggests that investing in prevention and early intervention actions, such as educational stability are critical to reducing the pipeline to prison (Polglase & Lambie, 2024), the remainder of this chapter focuses on what interventions are available once Pasifika youth enter the justice system. Previous research has shown that interventions aimed at reducing recidivism amongst Pasifika youth should involve family-based interventions (Advisory Group on Conduct Problems, 2009) and community supports, rather than individual support and interventions (Ioane, 2023).

Family-Based Interventions

Given the collective identity of Pasifika communities, a collective community approach to Pasifika youth offending is needed. Young people are vulnerable to the overall health of their families. In this way, offending behaviour could be seen as a barometer for the environments young people find themselves in. By extension, this means that when families and communities are well, young people will be well. Restoring family relations can counter young peoples' search for "family" within gangs when they experience familial disconnection (Gluckman, 2018). Evidence reviewed by Aotearoa New Zealand youth offending experts showed that those most likely to be involved in the youth justice system were those with the most significant child trauma and maltreatment histories (Polglase & Lambie, 2024). Recent Aotearoa New Zealand research further confirms the rationale for a family-based approach for Pasifika youth (Ioane, 2023; Ioane, 2017). Specifically, Pasifika youth in the justice system stopped their offending behaviour when there was: (a) a change in motivation and mindset to offend; (b) positive changes within their family, particularly with their parents; and (c) access to appropriate programmes and education (Ioane, 2023). An Australian study with Pasifika youth in the justice system reported that avoiding of alcohol and drugs, staying home, and listening to parents was successful in reducing recidivism (Blake et al., 2015). Accordingly, family-based interventions can be effective for our Pasifika youth involved in the justice system.

From a prevention perspective, parenting programmes such as Incredible Years have been identified by Pasifika parents as beneficial to their learning to parent their children (Maiava, 2014). However, more research is needed to explore this within a justice setting, particularly when there is interparental violence and parental criminality (Ioane et al., 2016; Ioane, 2023). Furthermore, it is not uncommon for Pasifika parents to disengage from children who have offended. In Australia, for example, Pasifika parents will not attend Court as a form of punishment for their child's misbehaviour reflecting on the family; therefore, an older sibling will often attend instead (Ravulo, 2016). Recent research has also shown that a unique prevention approach to youth gangs for Pasifika youth includes the development and delivery of family-centred activities via mentoring (Alefaio-Tugia et al., 2023).

One innovative and unique programme currently offered in a Pasifika faith-based community organisation (Village Connect in Hosanna Church – Logan, Brisbane), aims to reduce reoffending by providing culturally safe, holistic support to young people with experience of the youth justice system and their families. Partnering with Children Youth Justice and Multicultural Affairs (CYJMA) through the Community Partnership Innovation Grant 2022–2023, the *KOKO Village (Keep Our Kids Out)* project works with young people aged 10 to 17 years. This project aims to intervene early to support young people with their health, education, safety, and wellbeing (KOKO Village: Changing Futures, 2022). Educational programmes meet the needs of young people by addressing risky behaviours to keep them out of the court system. Through a 12-week programme with the assistance of industry experts and KOKO Community Connectors, cultural activities are incorporated in topics including film, music, sports, entrepreneurship, and performing arts to engage children and youth. Young people are offered the opportunity to learn positive habits and a safe place to live, with appropriate supervision and support available to reconnect with families as well as communities, rather than incarceration.

Interventions for Pasifika Youth in the Justice System

Cultural interventions for youth in the justice system are seen to be useful (Liddell et al., 2017; Urale-Baker, 2016) although a recent study has shown that they can be "tricky" amongst our Pasifika youth when identification with their ethnic culture is seen as antisocial (Ioane, 2023). A cultural intervention seen to have early signs of success with Pasifika youth in the justice system in New South Wales introduced Pasifika youth to Pasifika cultural artefacts during a museum visit. The youth were proud of their Pasifika heritage and cultural identities, and following the visit, approximately 36% of the participants reported no further offending behaviour. Whilst it is difficult to state clearly the cause of the youths' desistance from criminal behaviour, the authors acknowledged a rehabilitative cultural intervention may be positive for Pasifika youth in the justice system (Blake et al., 2015). The effectiveness of cultural interventions is still being evaluated (Gluckman, 2018). However, there is increasing evidence highlighting positive outcomes from connection with culture and language through the strengthening of identity and overall wellbeing (Mila-Schaaf, 2013).

Within our own Pasifika clinical experience, the role of relationships is seen as fundamental to a young person's journey. Pasifika identity is relational as it provides a sense of belonging and acceptance (Tamasese et al., 2005). Further, the messenger is seen as being pivotal amongst Pasifika youth and their families, while the message is secondary to the experiences of Pasifika youth and their families in the justice system. Therefore, interventions with Pasifika youth must be holistic in their approach and incorporate family, social, and economic determinants that impact and inform Pasifika worldviews (Ioane et al., 2021).

Pasifika Cultural Advisors and Lay Advocates

Cultural advisors are a growing occupational role in Aotearoa New Zealand. Alongside Māori cultural advisors, Pasifika cultural advisors provide cultural advice, guidance, and in some circumstances supervision to clinicians and practitioners working with Pasifika youth and their families in the Justice system. Agencies and government departments working with justice-involved youth and families employ cultural advisors as part of their resources. However, the demand can often outweigh the supply. As clinicians and academics, we continue to encourage the involvement of cultural advisors when working with Pasifika families. It is not uncommon for Pasifika families involved in the Justice system to decline the involvement of cultural advisors. However, it is our view that practitioners should still consult with cultural advisors to ensure their cultural responsiveness and integrity.

In Aotearoa New Zealand, lay advocates are statutorily appointed to support a child or young person in Youth Court through the Oranga Tamariki Act 1989, 163 Appointment of lay advocate (New Zealand Legislation). Their role involves making the Court aware of cultural matters relevant to proceedings, and representing the interests of the child's family and cultural belonging. Efforts are made to ensure cultural matching when appointing a lay advocate for a young person (Ministry of Justice, 2023).

Talavou Programme – SAFE (Aotearoa (NZ))

SAFE is a community treatment programme for children, youth, and adults engaged in harmful sexual behaviour towards children. The Talavou Programme is a group therapy programme within SAFE for Pasifika youth engaged in harmful sexual behaviour. It was developed by Pasifika practitioners (including the third author JI) to respond to the growing need for a culturally informed programme for Pasifika youth alongside offence-based treatment, mental health intervention, and working with families. It was developed within a '*by Pasifika, with Pasifika, for Pasifika*' approach. The programme was based on a cognitive behavioural therapy group programme for youth; and was contextualised to suit Pasifika worldviews. An evaluation of this programme has not been carried out, however, preliminary reviews from young people and their families are positive.

Affirming Works (Aotearoa New Zealand)

A faith-based initiative by Affirming Works focused on preventing youth gang recruitment for Pasifika youth in the community. Their approach was grounded in community responsiveness and working collaboratively in the communities that Pasifika young people reside in. Affirming Works prioritises a holistic approach that includes the young person and their family to ensure they all receive the necessary resources to thrive. The success of this initiative has drawn on accessing local knowledge, valuing young people, key staff enablers, and drawing on wraparound support (Alefaio-Tugia et al., 2023).

Tuilaepa Youth Mentoring Services (Aotearoa New Zealand)

Tuilaepa Youth Mentoring Services (TYMS) is a Pasifika-led cultural and relationship-based intervention service that works primarily with Pasifika and Māori at-risk youth, including those in the youth justice system. Services include (though are not limited to) mentoring, transition support services for young people exiting state care, and cultural and sporting programmes. An impact report found positive changes for young people participating in TYMS programmes (Tuilaepa Youth Mentoring Services, n.d.).

Fautasi Pasifika Youth Outreach Programme (Australia)

This community-based early intervention programme is for Pasifika and Māori youth at risk of school exclusion or entering youth justice in Melbourne, Australia. They support young people to maintain educational engagement or support them into their chosen profession. They also provide targeted short-term interventions for Pasifika youth and support them to build their access and connection to Pasifika culture and community (Les Twentyman Foundation, n.d.).

Manawise Care (Australia)

With a diverse offering of services across Australia, including employment opportunities, research, school mentoring, and workplace training, Manawise Care provides "therapeutic out-of-home-care services and programmes using evidence-based approaches". Manawise Care provide a holistic, responsive approach using Pasifika cultural frameworks to implement effective care plans. Their Youth Justice programme aims to reintegrate young people transitioning from detention centres into community surroundings (schools/families/connecting with supportive stakeholders).

Charis Youth and Community Organisation

Charis Youth aims to support Pasifika youth with opportunities to grow as individuals, utilising Pasifika core values and beliefs at the heart of their programmes. The mission is that all young people would "Know who they are, Grow in character, and Sow into others", as they develop through individual and group workshops and training (Charis Youth and Community Programs, n.d.). The organisation also works to build culturally responsive, needs-based support for the reduction of recidivism through RENIU. The aptly named "RENIU" or Renew (RE: to return; NIU (Samoan): fresh coconut) programme is designed to reconnect youth with their culture, family, and community. RENIU is founded on the belief that cultural identity and heritage are key social protective factors that enhance holistic wellbeing. Whilst undertaking this experience on a practical level, young people are empowered as leaders as they work towards achieving agreed goal.

Interventions for Pasifika Youth in Prison (Aotearoa New Zealand)

Pasifika interventions within Ara Poutama Aotearoa | Department of Corrections include the Vaka Fa'aola Pasifika Focus Unit, Saili Matagi Pasifika Violence Prevention Programme, and the Fauina o le Fale Pasifika engagement model which sets out Pasifika values for working with Pasifika men from a cultural, systemic approach. Men under 20 years old and those over 20 years who meet programme eligibility (Alefaio-Tugia, 2015) can be accepted into the Vaka Fa'aola Pasifika Focus Unit, and/or Saili Matagi Pasifika Violence Prevention Programme, while Fauina o le Fale can be used with all Pasifika people who have committed an offence.

Saili Matagi and Vaka Fa'aola Pasifika Focus Unit

Saili Matagi is a 17-week non-violence programme for Pasifika men over 20 years old who are at moderate risk[2] of further violent offending. Saili matagi, meaning 'in search of favourable winds', combines Pasifika cultural values and protocols with offence-focused modules, and family involvement, to decrease risk factors and rehabilitate participants. Programme participants reside in the Vaka Fa'aola Pasifika Focus Unit which assists participants to maintain treatment gains through a therapeutic community approach which models Pasifika values and beliefs. A 2017 evaluation showed impressive completion rates and reduced reconviction and reimprisonment rates over a 12-month period (King & Bourke, 2017).

Case Study Research Participant NW – Holistic Interventions

NW, a 16-year-old male of Pasifika (Tongan/Māori) descent in Australia was disengaged from school and engaged with the local gang. His father was in prison for severe violence towards his mother, although his parents remained in contact. His father was reported to consume high levels of alcohol on a regular basis and both parents were unemployed. NW's two younger siblings were also living at home but under the care of Child Services. NW's older brother was also affiliated with a local gang. The family lived in one of the lower socio-economic areas in the city and had extensive support from social services for basic needs; the younger children were also supported by social and education services.

NW's offending was of a violent nature towards a stranger and it was his first offence. He was reportedly under the influence of alcohol and cannabis at the time of the offence. Throughout our involvement with NW, he regularly attended interviews and participated appropriately. At times, however, he was observed to be under the influence of substances, and as such, some interviews were postponed. His parents also participated well in the interviews, although one incident occurred where the parents argued incessantly (verbally) in front of the interviewer. The family were seen over a period of three to four years.

By the end of the engagement period, NW had secured employment in road construction in another city. He lived in that city with his older brother and would visit his family regularly. When he was interviewed for the final time, he talked about the changes in his parents. They were no longer arguing – they had found ways to communicate without yelling – and this had been a significant influence on NW's motivation to seek employment. NW's older brother had also become a parent and was reportedly no longer engaged with gangs.

Summary

Pasifika youth offending across Aotearoa New Zealand and Australia continues to be overrepresented and, alarmingly, is often violent offending. This chapter has highlighted the complexities that contribute to Pasifika youth offending and the need for a holistic approach which incorporates social, economic, and familial factors. Furthermore, an understanding of the identity issues faced by Pasifika youth and recognising the impact of migration, racism, and discrimination is crucial to working authentically with this cohort and their families.

Interventions that incorporate culture, family, and community alongside clinical and offending needs are most beneficial. Programmes that are developed and led by Pasifika, for Pasifika, are one way to ensure success for our Pasifika youth in Aotearoa New Zealand and Australia. However, this needs to be balanced alongside the intersectionalities that exist when dealing with more than one ethnic identity, alongside other factors such as a young person's sexual orientation and/or disabilities. It is also the view of the authors that an agile response is needed when addressing Pasifika youth offending. It is not necessarily a 'one size, fits all' approach, given the diversity of Pasifika youth in relation to ethnicity, migration stories (e.g. first or second migration), and/or socio-economic status.

We also recognise that for some Pasifika youth and their families, they may not desire cultural interventions or services. It is our view that efforts should still be made by practitioners to engage with cultural services for background guidance and support. We also remind those working in the justice system that all practitioners are primarily trained in Western theories, models, and practices. Therefore, expect that working with Pasifika communities is likely to be in contrast or even contradict one's own practice; and there may not necessarily be any "evidence-based practice" that informs why a different approach is needed. However, our key message is that relationships with Pasifika communities are critical. The identity of Pasifika people is relational (Tamasese et al., 2005). Therefore, prioritising relationally-based clinical skills and practice can go a long way in working effectively with our Pasifika youth and their families in the youth justice system, and in changing youth environments to nurture better outcomes.

Notes

1 Māori youth are included in data on Pasifika youth in Australia.
2 According to Ara Poutama | Department of Corrections' actuarial risk algorithm, which classifies reoffending risk into categories according to the likelihood of reimprisonment within five years of release from a community or custodial sentence (Bakker et al., 1999).

References

Advisory Group on Conduct Problems. (2009). Conduct problems: Best practice report. *Ministry of Social Development.* https://www.msd.govt.nz/documents/about-msd-and-our-work/publications-resources/research/conduct-problems-best-practice/conduct-problems.pdf

Alefaio-Tugia, S., Ioane, J., Satele, P., Satele, J., & Naepi, M. (2023). *Talanoa participatory-impact evaluation: A Pacific youth gang prevention and intervention programme developed by Affirming Works (AW).* Massey University. https://mro.massey.ac.nz/items/fbb658ba-7099-449d-9472-a12266ea5828

Alefaio-Tugia, S. T. (2015). *Galuola: A NIU way for informing psychology from the cultural context of Fa'aSamoa* (Unpublished Doctoral Thesis). Monash University, Melbourne, Australia. https://doi.org/10.4225/03/58abad465cdc1

Anae, M. (2016). Teu Le Va: Samoan relational ethics. *Knowledge Cultures*, 4(3), 117–130. https://link.gale.com/apps/doc/A458164605/AONE?u=vuw&sid=AONE&xid=787194af

Bakker, L., Riley, D., & O'Malley, J. (1999). *Risk of reconviction: Statistical models predicting four types of re-offending.* Department of Corrections.

Barrett, C. A. (2014). *School social work in the State of Victoria, Australia: 65 years of student wellbeing and learning support* (Ph.D. Thesis). University of Melbourne.

Blake, M., Liddell, M., & Singh, S. (2015). Artifacts, identity and youth: A cultural intervention with Pacific Islander young people who offend in Western Sydney, Australia. *Curator The Museum Journal*, 58(2), 313–333.

Borowski, A. (2010). Indigenous participation in sentencing young offenders: Findings from an evaluation of the children's Koori Court of Victoria. *Australian & New Zealand Journal of Criminology, 43*(3), 465–484. https://doi.org/10.1375/acri.43.3.465

Boshier, P., & New Zealand Office of the Ombudsman. (2023). *Kia whaitake = Making a difference: He tūhuratanga nā te kaitiaki mana tangata ki te Ara Poutama Aotearoa: Investigation into Ara Poutama Aotearoa, Department of Corrections.* Tari o te Kaitiaki Mana Tangata/The Office of the Ombudsman. https://ndhadeliver.natlib.govt.nz/delivery/DeliveryManagerServlet?dps_pid=IE87972549

Charis Youth and Community Programs. (n.d.). https://www.charis-youthandcommunity.com/programs

Crone, E. A., & Konijn, E. A. (2018). Media use and brain development during adolescence. *Nature Communications*, 9, 588. https://doi.org/10.1038/s41467-018-03126-x

Department of Corrections. (2001). *About time: Turning people away from a life of crime and reducing re-offending.* Department of Corrections. https://www.corrections.govt.nz/__data/assets/pdf_file/0014/10652/abouttime.pdf

Department of Corrections. (2015). *Topic series young offenders April 2015.* https://corrections.govt.nz/resources/research/topic_series_reports/young_offenders_topic_series_report

Department of Human Services, New South Wales. (2010). *Pacific islander young people on community supervision in the juvenile justice metropolitan region.* Juvenile Justice Statistical Information System (JJSIS).

Durham, J., Tafa, S., Etuale, J., Nosa, V., Fa'avale, A., Malama, E., Yaranamua, M., Taito, T., Ziesman, C., & Fa'avale, N. (2023). Belonging in multiple places: Pasifika young peoples' experiences of living in Logan. *Journal of Youth Studies,* 26(2), 196–212. https://doi.org/10.1080/13676261.2021.1994130

Gerace, G., Itaoui, R., Moors-Mailei, A,. Williams, B., Patu, P., & Ponton, V. (2023). *Pasifika communities in Australia: 2021 census.* Centre for Western Sydney. https://doi.org/10.26183/9qbb-cy24

Gluckman, P. (2018). *It's never too early, never too late: A discussion paper on preventing youth offending in New Zealand.* Office of the Prime Minister's Chief Science Advisor. Wellington, New Zealand. https://www.dpmc.govt.nz/sites/default/files/2021-10/pmcsa-Its-never-too-early-Discussion-paper-on-preventing-youth-offending-in-NZ.pdf

Ioane, J. (2017). Talanoa with Pasifika youth and their families. *New Zealand Journal of Psychology,* 46(3), 38–45.
Ioane, J. (2023). *You've just got to think about your family and what type of person you want to be. Listening to young Pasifika people in the youth justice system and their families.* Research and recommendations. Health Research Council of NZ and Massey University School of Psychology.
Ioane, J., Lambie, I., & Percival, T. (2016). A comparison of Pasifika, Māori, and European violent youth offenders in New Zealand. *International Journal of Offender Therapy and Comparative Criminology*, 60(6), 657–674.
Ioane, J., Tofaeono, R., & Lambie, I. (2021). Pasifika youth with harmful sexual behaviour differ from other young people and need a different response. *New Zealand Journal of Psychology*, 50(3).
King, L., & Bourke, S. (2017). A review of the Saili Matagi Programme for male Pacifica prisoners. *Practice: The New Zealand Corrections Journal,* 5(2).
KOKO Village: Changing Futures. (2022). *Village connect.* https://www.villageconnect.org.au/koko-project
Les Twentyman Foundation. (n.d.). *Fautasi Pasifika Youth outreach.* https://ltfoundation.au/fautasi-pasifika/
Liddell, M., Blake, M., & Singh, S. (2017). Over-represented and misunderstood: Pacific young people and juvenile justice in NSW. *Australian & New Zealand Journal of Criminology,* 50(4), 529–547. https://doi.org/10.1177/0004865816666614
Liu, H., & Howes, S. (2023). *Pacific islanders in Australia/Pacific Islanders in Australia: 2021 census results*. Devpolicy Blog from the Development Policy Centre.
Maiava, M. (2014). *Exploring the acceptability and accessibility of the incredible years parenting programme for Pasifika peoples* (Doctoral Dissertation). ResearchSpace@ Auckland.
Matapo, J., & McFall-McCaffery, J. T. (2022). Towards a Va knowledge ecology: Mobilising Pasifika philosophy to transform Higher Education for Pasifika in Aotearoa New Zealand. *Journal of Higher Education Policy and Management*, 44(2), 122–137. https://doi.org/http://www.tandfonline.com/loi/cjhe20
Mila-Schaaf, K. (2013). Not another New Zealand-born identity crisis. In M. N., Agee, T. McIntosh, P. Culbertson, & C. O. Makasiale (Eds.), *Pasifika identities and well-being: Cross-cultural Perspectives* (pp. 49–64). Otago University Press.
Ministry of Health. (2017). *HISO 10001:2017 ethnicity data protocols.* https://www.tewhatuora.govt.nz/assets/Our-health-system/Digital-health/Health-information-standards/HISO-10001-2017-Ethnicity-Data-Protocols.pdf
Ministry of Justice. (2022). *Justice sector long-term insights briefing: Long-term trends in imprisonment and exploring future responses*. https://www.justice.govt.nz/justice-sector-policy/key-initiatives/key-initiatives-archive/justice-sector-long-term-insights-briefing/
Ministry of Justice. (2023). *Lay advocate and court registry handbook* (4th ed.). Lay-Advocate-Handbook–2023.pdf
Ministry of Justice. (2024). *Youth justice indicators summary report December 2024.* https://www.justice.govt.nz/justice-sector-policy/research-data/justice-statistics/youth-justice-indicators/
Ministry of Social Development. (2023). *What about me? Pacific report*. New Zealand Government. https://www.msd.govt.nz/documents/about-msd-and-our-work/publications-resources/consultations/youth-health-and-wellbeing-survey-results/2021-yhws-pacific-cohort-report-final-june-2023-.pdf
Mission Australia. 2009. *Young people and the criminal justice system: New insights and promising responses.* Mission Australia Research and Social Policy. http://goo.gl/5OKQXm
Mo'a, V. (2015). *Culture as a foundation for care* (Ed. Pasifika Perspectives Limited, pp. 1–6). Aniva Pasifika Health Workforce Fono. https://www.Pasifikaperspectives.co.nz/_files/ugd/840a69_da1886ebb72841068fe683307b035666.pdf

Mulipola, L., Wiles, J., & Fa'alau, F. (2024). Understanding anger with New Zealand-born Samoan youth: A Samoan qualitative exploration. *Australian and New Zealand Journal of Public Health*, 48(4), 100162.

Nadesu, A. (2009). *Reconviction patterns of released prisoners: A 60-months follow-up analysis.* Auckland, NZ: Department of Corrections.

Oxley, L. (2021). *Engaging Pasifika young people at UTS.* University of Technology Sydney Engaging Pasifika young people at UTS | University of Technology Sydney.

Paongo, A. (2024). *An exploration of the factors that contribute to violent offending within the population of young Pacific Islanders in Auckland Aotearoa New Zealand* (Master's Thesis). University of Auckland.

Pereira, F. T. (2011, 10–12 June). *Tausi Le Vā.* Paper presented at the When Culture and Care Connects Conference, Auckland, New Zealand.

Pita, S. M. (2018). *Mata'ifale: Navigating the context of incest in Samoa.* University of Auckland.

Polglase, L., & Lambie, I. (2024). A sharp decline in youth crime: Reviewing trends in New Zealand's youth offending rates between 1998 and 2019. *Current Issues in Criminal Justice, 1*(36), 42–62. https://doi.org/10.1080/10345329.2023.2236730

Ponton, V. (2017). An investigation of Samoan student experiences in two homework study groups in Melbourne. *Sociology Study, 7*(7), 349–363. https://doi.org/10.17265/2159-5526/2017.07.001

Radclyffe, C. J., Aia-Fa'aleava, A., Avia, P., Utiku-Roberts, D., Soo Choon, G., Tafa, S., & Durham, J. (2024). "FOB", 'plastic'and polycultural capital: experiences of social labelling of Pasifika young peoples in South-east Queensland, Australia. *Journal of Youth Studies*, 27(7), 1058–1077.

Ravulo, J. (2016). Pasifika youth offending within an Australian context. *Youth Justice, 16*(1), 34–48.

Samu, T. W. (2006). The 'Pasifika umbrella' and quality teaching: Understanding and responding to the diverse realities within. *Waikato Journal of Education*, 12(1), 35–49. https://doi.org/10.15663/wje.v12i1.297

StatsNZ. (2024). *2023 Census of population and dwellings* [Dataset]. https://datainfoplus.stats.govt.nz/item/nz.govt.stats/7c1335e0-c2c7-4217-ac48-bfc7a68aea48

Steinberg, L., Icenogle, G., Shulman, E., Breiner, K., Chein, J., & Bacchini, D. H. (2018). Around the world, adolescence is a time of heightened sensation seeking and immature self-regulation. *Developmental Science*, 21, e12532.

Suaalii, T. M., & Mavoa, H. (2003). Who says yes? Collective and individual framing of Pasifika children's consent to, and participation in research in New Zealand. *Pasifika Health Dialog*, 10(2), 193–197.

Suaalii-Sauni, T. M. (2006). *Le matuamoepo: Competing 'spirits of governing' and the management of New Zealand-based Samoan youth offender cases* (Doctoral Thesis). University of Auckland, ResearchSpace.

Tamapeau, M., & Kingstone, S. (2020). *Tau Amanaki Onoono Ki Mua: Pasifika peoples' youth substance use analyses from the pooled Youth Insights Survey (2014–2018).* Te Hiringa Mahara Health Promotion Agency.

Tamasese, K., Peteru, C., Waldegrave, C., & Bush, A. (2005). Ole Taeao Afua, the New Morning: A qualitative investigation into Samoan perspectives on mental health and culturally appropriate services. *Australian and New Zealand Journal of Psychiatry*, 39(4), 300–309. https://doi.org/10.1080/j.1440-1614.2005.01572.x

Tuilaepa Youth Mentoring Services. (n.d.). *Home*. http://www.tyms.org.nz

Urale-Baker, N. (2016). *Aua le limatētē ina ne'i ola pala'ai fanau: Samoan youths' views on their experience in the Pasifika Youth Court* (Doctoral Dissertation). ResearchSpace@Auckland.

Veukiso-Ulugia, A., McLean-Orsborn, S., Clark, T. C., Yao, E., Kuresa, B., Drayton, B., & Fleming, T. (2024). *Talavou o le Moana. The health and wellbeing of Pasifika secondary school students in Aotearoa New Zealand. A Youth19 report.* Youth19 Research Group, the University of Auckland and Victoria University of Wellington.

White, R., Perrone, S., Guerra, C., & Lampugnani, R. (1999). *Ethnic youth gangs in Australia: Do they exist? Report no. 3, Pacific Islander young people.* Australian Multicultural Foundation.

Youth Court of New Zealand. (n.d.). *Youth court.* https://www.youthcourt.govt.nz/home-2/

Section Three

Special Populations Amongst Youth Offending

6 Harmful Sexual Behaviour

A First Nations and Pasifika Perspective

Carmen Julie Shelley and Esther Leauanae Earl

"We are all visitors to this time, this place. We are just passing through. Our purpose here is to observe, to learn, to grow, to love . . . and then we return home."

Aboriginal Proverb

"E le falala fua le niu, ae falala ona o le matagi."
(The coconut tree does not sway by itself, but because of the wind.)

Samoan Proverb

Introduction

A culture of silence and shame exists across many indigenous cultures throughout Australia, Aotearoa New Zealand (NZ) and the Pacific Islands when it comes to sex, reproduction, and sexual violence. In contrast, the overrepresentation of indigenous youth in the sexual offending statistics (Molnar et al., 2021; Ministry of Justice, 2025a) emits a piercing sound demanding our attention. Understanding how the wind, as mentioned in the Samoan proverb above, causes the coconut tree to sway is the purpose of this chapter. In other words, we look at adolescent sexual offending through the lenses of two indigenous clinicians, one representing a perspective on the First Nations people of Australia, and the other a view of Pasifika youth in NZ. Specifically, we explore the extent of adolescent sexual offending in these populations, victim characteristics, risk factors, and the relationship between youth and adult sexual offending.

Harmful sexual behaviour (HSB) is a term widely used and accepted to refer to a continuum of developmentally and culturally inappropriate sexual behaviours displayed by young people under 18 years old which may cause harm towards self and/or other children, youth or adults (Hackett, 2014; Hackett et al., 2016). These behaviours may be obsessive, aggressive, or degrading and might include forced, compulsive, or penetrative and non-penetrative sexual acts; violations of privacy and exposure to sexual acts and materials; violent or coercive controlling patterns of behaviour including non-consensual kissing, touching or other unwanted sexual contact toward others; and excessive or public self-stimulation or public exposure. Such behaviours are often towards other individuals over whom the child or young person has power by virtue of age, emotional maturity, gender, physical strength, or intellect and where the victim in the relationship has suffered a betrayal of trust. Research also suggests that

DOI: 10.4324/9781003298410-11

a significant proportion of online sexual offending against children is committed by young people due to advancements in technology and the internet (Cahill et al., 2024).

There has been debate amongst researchers and professionals regarding the appropriate terminology to describe these sexual behaviours (O'Brien, 2010; Shlonsky et al., 2017). Where some sexual acts would be considered abusive within the criminal justice system if not for a young person's age, the terms "sexualised behaviour" or "problem sexual behaviours" have been more aptly applied to young people, thus avoiding the misuse of terminology which can lead to inappropriate labelling of young people. Clear terms allow for meaningful communication between professionals and the accurate assessment of sexual behaviours (Hackett et al., 2016). For the purposes of this chapter, the term HSB will be used.

Empirical research on young people with HSB indicates they are a heterogeneous population with diverse backgrounds, drivers, age of onset, victims, and behaviours exhibited (Hackett et al., 2024). Given that HSB covers a spectrum of behaviour, many of which may not come to the attention of authorities, the true incidence of HSB in this population is unknown. However, estimates in the United States and the United Kingdom suggest that about one-third of HSB is committed by children and youth (Finkelhor, 2009; National Society for the Prevention of Cruelty to Children [NSPCC], 2024), while Australian literature has reported figures of between 30% and 60% (El-Murr, 2017). In contrast, official justice data indicate lower proportions. In Australia, young people aged 10–17 years account for approximately 16% of individuals with a principal sexual offence (Molnar et al., 2021). In NZ, approximately 11%[1] (Ministry of Justice, 2025b) of sexual offences are attributed to young people, with around 5% committed by 10- to 17-year-olds[2] (Ministry of Justice, 2025a).

Adolescents with HSB

Adolescence is an age of rapid growth and development. There are three primary stages of adolescent development, beginning (10–13), middle (14–17), and late (17–21); however, this can differ significantly from one young individual to another, and age does not define maturity. Adolescence is a point in time where a young person's attempts at autonomy begin. This is where the development of their sexual identity begins, risk-taking, navigating boundaries and experimentational behaviours (NSW Kids and Families, 2014).

Sexual behaviour in most children and young people is age-appropriate and a typical expected part of their development. Nevertheless, there are behaviours that are not within the typical range of behaviours that are expected for the child or young person's level of development. The Royal Commission in Australia have found that children with HSB have frequently been victims themselves, with histories of adverse childhood experiences including trauma, prior physical and sexual abuse, exposure to family violence and excessive or harmful pornography. (Royal Commission into Institutional Responses to Child Sexual Abuse, 2017). However, some young people who have not been exposed to these negative childhood experiences also demonstrate HSB, and most young people who have been victims of maltreatment do not exhibit HSB.

The Australian Bureau of Statistics recorded crime data in 2017–2018 that indicated children and young people aged 10–19 years were the alleged offenders in 14% of sexual offences committed in Australia. The NSW Child Protection Helpline received reports concerning over 5,000 children exhibiting concerning and harmful sexual behaviours between 2018 and 2019 (Spangaro et al., 2020).

Aboriginal and Torres Strait Islander Young People and Families

Traditionally, Aboriginal family and extended kinship systems have always been a key component of the functioning of Aboriginal and Torres Strait Islander societies as the social fabric and cultural attachment systems for nurturing healthy, happy children. These systems have been supported by cultural knowledge, governance structures and lore, enabling Aboriginal and Torres Strait Islander peoples to adapt and thrive for at least two thousand generations (Thomas, 1993).

The principles of Grandmothers Law (Langton, 1997) – traditional knowledge, experience, and practices of senior women in a community for supporting mothers before and after their birth (Ramsamy, 2014); and yarning, a respectful and informal conversation where knowledge is often shared through storytelling, are important examples of such cultural practices. The wellbeing and safety of children were fostered within collectivist systems of kinship and community care (Lowell et al., 2018).

Since colonisation, Aboriginal and Torres Strait Islander communities have been impacted by successive waves of violence and trauma (Atkinson, 2002). The impacts of this collective trauma are cumulative and intergenerational, compounded by ongoing personal, lateral, and structural violence and oppression, discrimination, an inadequate access to social, cultural, and economic determinants of health (Clark et al., 2020).

Perinatal and family services are significant sites of past and ongoing trauma; many infants were removed from their parents in hospitals or homes shortly after birth. The ongoing and escalating high rates of Aboriginal and Torres Strait Islander children in out-of-home care signify ongoing structural violence and a failure to address compounding intergenerational trauma (O'Donnell et al., 2019)

The issues of HSB are not limited to Aboriginal and Torres Strait Islander young people, families or communities and are experienced by children and young people worldwide of all social classes and backgrounds. In Aboriginal and Torres Strait Islander communities, HSB is not part of their cultural practices or culture. In some communities, young people with HSB are shunned and isolated by their community as a way of protecting the other children. Aboriginal and Torres Strait Islander people do not usually discuss matters relating to sex or sexual behaviours, practices, identity, preferences, and interests openly. Sex is a taboo topic for many, and they still maintain their own beliefs and practices about sexual health.

For many Aboriginal and Torres Strait Islander peoples, sexual health practices and beliefs are kept separate as men's and women's business. There are topics that are taboo and neither gender would be involved in the practices, have knowledge of, or discuss matters relating to the other gender. Men do not talk about women's business, nor do women talk about men's business. Aboriginal and Torres Strait Islander cultural values and beliefs, including those around sex, have been influenced by colonisation and cultural and religious ideologies. Many Aboriginal and Torres Strait Islander people were subject to government control and rules for many aspects of their lives. This included the way people pursue relationships, needing permission from government officials for marriage (Queensland Health, 2013).

When working with Aboriginal and Torres Strait Islander young people who display HSB, you need to work holistically and think about the cultural considerations not just for the young person who has harmed but also for the person that has been harmed, the families, extended families, communities, schools and other Aboriginal and Torres Strait Islander organisations, out-of-home-care agencies. There are many things we need to consider when working with this population. Cultural consultation with a local Aboriginal consultant is crucial.

In Australia, the Aboriginal and Torres Strait Islander communities are so diverse that we need to consult with someone who knows the local community and has local knowledge. This helps us to understand what the considerations might be for working with the Aboriginal young people and their families who display HSB. The issues, needs and histories of each community will be different in each Aboriginal community.

The consultation process varies in different services, but the importance of this is widely recognised in NSW Health services and at New Street, we have at least 1 Aboriginal position in each service across NSW and in some services, we have male and female designated positions to provide cultural consultation. Our NSW under tens service Safewayz also have an Aboriginal position at each sexual assault service across NSW, and our Violence prevention services have a network of Aboriginal workers who can be consulted about cultural issues.

Adolescent HSB in Australian Aboriginal Communities

The National Agreement on Closing the Gap Priority Reform Areas for Joint National Action has three crucial outcomes, relevant to HSB. Outcome 11: Aboriginal and Torres Strait Islander young people are not overrepresented in the criminal justice system. Outcome 12: Aboriginal and Torres Strait Islander children are not overrepresented in the child protection system. Outcome 13: Aboriginal and Torres Strait Islander families and households are safe (NSW Health, 2022).

There is a limited amount of research or literature that has been completed from an Australian First Nations perspective regarding Aboriginal young people with HSB and of any tailored responses to Aboriginal clients across all Australian areas. Shlonsky highlights the need for a culturally appropriate intervention that addresses the specific needs of Aboriginal and Torres Strait Islander children and their families and communities and that recognises and respects cultural variation in understandings of behaviour without minimising their impact (Shlonsky et al., 2017).

Identifying the prevalence of child HSB within Aboriginal and Torres Strait Islander communities, determining the prevalence of children and young people engaging in HSB is difficult (Bromfield et al., 2017). This is partly due to the varying definitions of HSB and associated data collection issues, but also due to the secrecy within which HSB occurs, regardless of who is causing it. Knowledge, understanding, and support in the Aboriginal and Torres Strait Islander communities will help to break this cycle. Herbert and Bromfield (2018) observed a similar figure of 31% (named offenders 10–19 years within a forensic environment) in a local WA sample during their review of the Multiagency Investigation and Support Team.

Factors that may contribute to children and young people who have been involved in HSB. There is no single pathway that contributes to children and young people developing HSB. Children and young people of all genders, ages, life experiences, ethnicities and abilities can display PHSB (NSW Health, 2022). However, among Aboriginal and Torres Strait Islander young people, the over-representation of Aboriginal and Torres Strait Islander children and young people in the out-of-home care and the criminal justice systems, the ongoing oppression, structural racism, and intergenerational and transgenerational trauma have added to the risk factors.

According to the Australian Institute of Health and Welfare Productivity Commission, of the 45,000 Australian children living in OOHC, Aboriginal and Torres Strait Islander children comprise over one-third of the total population or 11 times the rate for non-Indigenous children, that is, about 18,000 children. Of every 1000 Indigenous children, 54.2 are in OOHC compared to only 5.1 per 1000 non-Indigenous children (Australian Institute of Health and Welfare, 2020; Productivity Commission, 2020). With high levels of social disadvantage, histories of mistrust associated with past government practices due to colonisation mean that there has historically been difficulty in delivering therapeutic services that effectively engage Aboriginal clients (O'Brien, 2010). It is also statistically more likely for Aboriginal children and young people to experience or engage in concerning or HSB due to their vulnerability.

Contributing factors include: a biased view of social perspective of gender norms and expectations, trauma due to experiences of sexual violence. experiences of violence, abuse and or neglect, domestic and family violence, male privilege and entitlement and exposure to pornography (Yamurrah & Secretariat of National Aboriginal and Islander Child Care [SNAICC], 2023). Due to the shame associated with sexuality, Aboriginal and Torres Strait Islander young people may place themselves at great risk when exploring their sexuality, including being in a state of intoxication to make them feel okay about it and accepting advances by strangers. Risk behaviours may also include multiple partners, trading and the use of drugs and other substances (Queensland Health, 2013).

Children and Young People with Disabilities

Children and young people with intellectual disabilities are more likely to suffer impulse control issues; are less likely to be redirected by adults when displaying HSB and less likely to receive sex education and more likely to present with concerning or HSB compared to other children. They are also at a greater risk of being exploited and experiencing abuse and neglect, placing them at increased risk of trauma and sexualisation (Evertsz & Miller, 2012).

In Aboriginal communities, there are high rates of prenatal exposure to alcohol including other biological and psychosocial risk factors that increase behavioural and neurodevelopmental issues amongst children (Fitzpatrick et al., 2015). However, prior to colonisation, there was limited alcohol production amongst Aboriginal and Torres Strait Islander communities. The use of alcohol for medical and ceremonial purposes and the consumption of alcohol by Aboriginal and Torres Strait Islander people were governed by strict cultural lore.

The impact of colonisation introduced recreational alcohol use to Aboriginal and Torres Strait Islander people, and alcohol began to be used as a payment for labour. FASD has emerged as an issue for Aboriginal and Torres Strait Islander people from a combination of factors, some of which are related to historical violence, dispossession, and intergenerational trauma (2021). Most Aboriginal and Torres Strait Islander women do not consume alcohol during their pregnancy. However, high alcohol consumption has been reported in some communities in remote areas.

When children with intellectual disabilities do show HSB, they will need a response from a treatment programme that considers their intellectual abilities including difficulties in social understanding of behaviour. They may also be more vulnerable than other children due to additional complexities such as communication difficulties (Evertsz & Miller, 2012).

The Extent of the Problem

Of the 1,129 private sessions attendees that spoke to the Royal Commission into Institutional Responses to Child Sexual Abuse about being sexually abused by another child, 473 (41.9%) told them they were abused by another child or children only, with the remainder telling them about abuse by both adults and other children. Some of these survivors also informed the Royal Commission that, as children, they then sexually abused other children (Royal Commission into Institutional Responses to Child Sexual Abuse, 2017).

The Commission found Australia is one of the few developed countries where a nationally representative prevalence study on child maltreatment and child sexual abuse has not been conducted. Therefore, there is no uniform data collection on children with HSB. Increasing methods of defining and counting occurrences of child sexual abuse have led to different conclusions, and most official figures underestimate the occurrence. It is imperative that data is collected so we have a better idea of the ongoing needs and impact of HSB on Aboriginal and Torres Strait Islander young people to provide more culturally safe and responsive services.

According to the Crime data in Australia, there is an indication of the potential impact of sexual abuse by children. In the period from July 2015 to June 2016, 21% of those who were against whom the police initiated legal action for a sexual offence were aged between 10 and 17 years. And reported that the Australian Bureau of Statistics reports that this amounted to 1,672 children (Royal Commission into Institutional Responses to Child Sexual Abuse, 2017).

There is less information about the extent of children's harmful sexual behaviours that do not meet the criminal threshold or are not reported to police. The research explored contemporary incidents of child sexual abuse using various administrative datasets, such as police data, education department data and child protection data and looked specifically at child sexual abuse in institutional contexts in Australia from 2008 to 2013. The research demonstrated that, where information was available regarding the subject of a report, children were the subject of most reports to police between 2008 and 2013 regarding child sexual abuse in institutional settings, and this was the case across most Australian areas (Royal Commission into Institutional Responses to Child Sexual Abuse, 2017).

The reports of child sexual abuse in institutional contexts between 2008 and 2013, children made up 67% of those reported to police in Victoria; 76% in New South Wales; and 93% in Queensland (Royal Commission into Institutional Responses to Child Sexual Abuse, 2017). It is important to note that there was a considerable amount of missing data in relation to the characteristics of the reports, and that recording practices varied across areas.

The Royal Commission initiated a research peace regarding the extent of child sexual abuse in Australia and was concerned with the way cases of child sexual abuse were reported to police and finalised. Research concluded that children were the subject of 20% of child sexual abuse reports to police between 2010 and 2014, and that the details of the report were disclosed. It is important to observe that the details of the subject were not disclosed in 41% of reports (Royal Commission into Institutional Responses to Child Sexual Abuse, 2017). The 1,642 reports involving children in institutional settings accounted for 8% of all reported occurrences of child sexual abuse by a child. It is important to note that the number of reports involving child sexual abuse by a child in institutional settings was an underestimate.

Based on the private sessions held by the Royal Commission into Institutional Responses to Child Sexual Abuse, the victims of child sexual abuse by other children (15%) of survivors are Aboriginal. That suggests an estimated 9,000 Aboriginal survivors, and is likely to be an underestimation (67%), were female, while children who sexually abuse other children were mostly male (87%). Due to numerous variations in recording practices across districts and the significant amount of missing data, cautious interpretation of these findings is necessary (Royal Commission into Institutional Responses to Child Sexual Abuse, 2017).

The Relationship Between Youth with HSB and Adult Sex Offending

Studies into recidivism indicated that most children's HSB will cease in childhood, with average sexual recidivism rates for children ranging from 3% to 14%. And offending in children tends to peak at about 17 years old with sexual offending, and then dramatically reduces. "The likelihood of it continuing is low". In Australia, studies of children with HSB who have attended therapeutic treatment show low rates of the behaviours recurring post-intervention (Royal Commission into Institutional Responses to Child Sexual Abuse, 2017).

It is difficult to accurately calculate recidivism rates in a methodological manner. Recidivism studies focus on children who have committed criminal sexual offences, and as a result, these studies do not capture the rates at which children with problematic sexual behaviours and less severe harmful sexual behaviours continue to exhibit these behaviours (Royal Commission into Institutional Responses to Child Sexual Abuse, 2017).

In a 2010 meta-analysis of male adolescent sexual offenders, there are two primary risk factors that may indicate whether harmful sexual behaviours in childhood are likely to continue past adolescence. These are: antisocial traits, such as a criminal history, and sexual deviance, including atypical sexual desires (Royal Commission into Institutional Responses to Child Sexual Abuse, 2017). However, based on current research and knowledge about recidivism, it is not possible to predict which children with HSB will continue the behaviours. Available data from recidivism studies contradicts the common assumption that children who commit sexual offences will become adult sex offenders (Royal Commission into Institutional Responses to Child Sexual Abuse, 2017).

Risk Factors

Research has demonstrated that HSB is frequently impacted by several risk and protective factors that occur at the individual child, family, peer, school, neighbourhood, and community levels. There is no single explanation for sexual behaviours, or a one-size-fits-all approach for addressing them. There are a variety of characteristics and circumstances that enhance the children and young people's vulnerability. Adverse Childhood Experiences have been viewed at a higher rate among children and young people with HSB (Felitti et al., 1998).

Experience of child sexual abuse and other forms of child abuse: physical abuse, emotional abuse, neglect, and family violence (with 80% of some samples of children with HSB also having experienced family violence) (Fox, 2017 as cited in Malvaso et al., 2020). The instability of the caregiver, absence, and/or difficulties with parent–child attachment relationships. Children with a learning disability (Hackett et al., 2013; Seto & Lalumiere, 2010). Children with impulsivity, social difficulties, and difficulty with following rules (O'Brien, 2010). Male children (some samples note 97% of children displaying HSB are males) (Friedrich et al., 2001; Hackett et al., 2013). Children living in out-of-home care and exposure to pornography and/or adult sexual activity (Malvaso et al., 2020; Wright et al., 2016).

The Role of External Influences on Offending

In Australia, the House of Representatives Standing Committee on Social Policy and Legal Affairs (2020) reported that children were to first access online pornography between the ages of 10 and 13 years. Young people's exposure to pornography influences with the online world are rising exponentially, with numerous mobile internet-connected devices being commonplace. This exposure is observed in children and young people who are "logging on" to various social media platforms, interactive gaming forums and online learning. However, with this increased exposure to the internet, children and young people are more likely to be exposed to unfiltered and often developing inappropriate content from various sources. Despite the limitations, this means children and young people can more easily access and be exposed to pornographic material online, either intentionally or not.

Pornography is a term that is typically used to describe sexually explicit material that is intended to provoke the viewer. Pornography can be varied and encompasses a variety of content that would be considered both common and extreme, including images, videos, text, and cartoons or anime illustrating sexual themes, practices, and scenarios. The internet is primarily used to access pornography, although printed material, DVDs, and other image storage devices are also used to exchange, view, and store pornographic material.

Quadara noted that 44% of children aged 9–16 years had been exposed to sexual images (with males being more likely), either via intentional searching or through accidental exposure while on the internet. Suggesting that the impact of exposure to and the use of online pornographic content on children and young people can be profound. It can impact their knowledge and attitudes towards sex and relationships, including sexual violence, and influence their sexual behaviours and practices (Quadara et al., 2017).

Although it is widely accepted that young children are being exposed to pornography, the consequences are potentially harmful. Therefore, it requires both a general and targeted approach to prevent and eliminate harmful impacts. This is particularly evident when a child moves from accidental exposure to more repeated, purposeful searching for the material and as the material content becomes more explicit, violent or deviates from acceptable sexual practices of mutuality and consent.

Pasifika Youth in NZ with HSB

Seated in a circle on vintage wooden school chairs, our eyes closed, and heads bowed, we silently waited for the opening prayer. Fourteen-year-old Sione[3] stood to offer the invocation, asking for God's Spirit to be with us, to protect our families and loved ones, and to "help us choose the right". With a united "amen", we all stood to sing our weekly anthem, an original composition by group members of several years before, handed down as a legacy. To the idle observer, we might have been mistaken for a church youth group, but the words of the song told a different story:

> [4] *Every day is a new day*
> *Opportunities for us to change*
> *We are brothers from the South Pacific*
> *Polynesians*

Amanaki Pasifika[5]
One heart, one soul
Making good choices is our goal
That's how we roll in Talavou
Every week we all come together
Three to half-past four
Feeling safe, supporting each other
HSB no More

As one of two NZ-born female clinicians of Samoan descent, co-facilitating a weekly therapy group named "Talavou" (meaning "youth" in Samoan) for Pasifika adolescent males who had engaged in HSB, both embodied and challenged many of the dichotomies within Pasifika culture regarding our attitudes, values and beliefs about sex, morality, and mental health. Here we were, two Pasifika psychologists regularly engaging in talanoa[6] (talk or discussion) about sexual offending with youth who had typically never met a therapist before, never been encouraged to talk about their emotions in a meaningful way, and never talked about sex with anyone, least of all females. It was not a complete surprise to me, therefore, that in discussions about physical intimacy, words such as "masturbation", "condoms", "penetrative sex", and "vagina" elicited embarrassed laughter from the same youth whose HSB included initiating sex acts with younger or similar-aged male and female peers and/or siblings, indecent exposure of genitals to women unknown to them in public, and stealing female family members' underwear to masturbate with.

The Talavou group, formed in recognition of the need for a more culturally responsive programme for Pasifika youth, sought to foster an understanding of HSB within the context of Pasifika identities, languages, and worldviews – separate from the mainstream youth group which viewed HSB through a purely Western lens. Talavou group members represented a larger number of Pasifika young people referred to community-based specialist treatment facilities for HSB, a heterogeneous group comprising youth of various Pasifika ethnicities, mostly NZ-born with English as their preferred, if not their first or only language. Their HSB was similarly diverse, ranging in frequency, duration and severity, from one-off incidents towards a single victim lasting 30 minutes to multiple incidents towards multiple victims over a timespan of years. Whilst they experienced shared vulnerabilities which had led to their HSB, a key commonality was a connection to family and faith, which, despite variations of what this looked like in their individual lives, was a cornerstone of their Pasifika identity and sense of belonging.

Pasifika Peoples in NZ

The history of settlement by Pasifika peoples in NZ dates from the early half of the 20th century, when the number of "Pacific Polynesians" grew from less than 1,000 (Friesen, 2018) and accelerated post-World War II to comprise NZ's current Pacific population of 8.9% (Statistics New Zealand, 2024a). Whilst this population is dynamic and diverse in terms of language, culture, migration histories and settlement patterns (Ministry of Business, Innovation and Employment, 2024), the general label of "Pasifika" will be used throughout this chapter to describe people living in NZ who migrated from or identify through ancestry with Pacific Island nations including Samoa, Tonga, Fiji, Tokelau, Tuvalu, Niue, the Cook Islands and Kiribati. Today, more than 60% of NZ's Pasifika population was born in NZ, with over two-thirds of Pasifika young people in Years 9–13 living in Auckland (Malatest International, 2023). Four key values commonly held by Pasifika peoples are family, collectivism, reciprocity and respect (Ministry for Pacific Peoples, 2017). Understanding the role these values play across Pasifika cultures and generations provides valuable insight into the context for HSB amongst Pasifika youth in NZ.

Pasifika Views on Sex and Sexual Violence

I write this chapter from my position as a NZ-born Samoan woman from South Auckland, whose identity as a teenager in the 1990s was rooted strongly in religion, and where Christian values of obedience, service, and duty to God aligned with Pasifika values of familial duty and service to others. Both systems upheld clear behavioural rules, roles and etiquette, both implicit and explicit, across various settings. One such unspoken rule was that sex was not openly spoken about. Yet, the skeletons of incest, extramarital affairs, and single, unwed mothers that hung in my ancestral family closet told me that sexual silence did not equate to sexual abstinence or the absence of sexual harm. "Ka'i lua kaukalaiki kele!" ("You two are talking too much about naughty things!") was the scolding my mother and her friend, Alofa, received from an aunt when, as two 13-year-old girls in 1960s Samoa, they were overheard talking about how Alofa's father would make her massage his thighs after sending other family members away from the house on errands. When Alofa fell pregnant to him the following year, she was sent away to have the baby in secret. Her father, a man of high standing in the village, received no censure, protected as he was by status and the silence surrounding sex.

Research shows that within Pasifika communities, conversations about sex, which are traditionally considered tapu (sacred or forbidden), often meet with discomfort and shame and are therefore rarely discussed in either public or private settings (Young et al., 2024). This is due to the strong influence of cultural and Christian values which have historically discouraged open conversation about sexuality and reproduction for fear of encouraging young people to engage in sex and other behaviours deemed unacceptable (Katavake-McGrath, 2021). With the majority of Pacific Aotearoa (68%) identifying with a Christian religion (Statistics New Zealand, 2019), conventional gender roles that highlight family responsibility and duty often position males as the protectors of female safety, including sexual purity and family honour (Tupuola, 1996) as reflected in the Samoan proverb, "O le tuafafine o le ioimata o lana tuagane" (A sister is the pupil of her brother's eye). For this reason, in some Pasifika households, boys and girls might be raised separately, and post-pubertal males being in the same room as female relatives alone may be considered a breach of tapu (Scroope, 2018).

The operation of these roles and relationships, within a Pasifika worldview, is governed by a theoretical construct known as vā or "the space between", which describes a spiritual, physical or emotional space established to build meaningful connections with others and the environment (Ministry for Pacific Peoples, 2024). To nurture the vā that exists between parents and children, husbands and wives, brothers and sisters, older and younger siblings, or friends and extended family members is to respect and maintain the sacred space, harmony and balance within these relationships (Le Va, 2020). Furthermore, research indicates that the strong respect inherent in the brother–sister relationship (which also applies to opposite gender relatives and foster children) is a protective factor for Pasifika peoples (Percival et al., 2010). Therefore, any offence towards another person, especially one of a sexual nature, represents a significant breach of the vā (Ioane et al., 2021). This impacts not only the wellbeing of the individuals affected but that of the wider family and community (Young et al., 2024).

In a NZ research project exploring Pasifika views on sexual violence, participants described the use of social sanctions for sexual perpetrators in their native homelands, which included physical punishment, banishment, family or public shaming, and curses by village leaders (Percival et al., 2010). However, although the public shame of exposed sexual offending was intended to act as a deterrent for further violence, where a family member had been sexually harmed, the stigma, shame and reputation of the victim's family or of the perpetrator were often prioritised over safety and support for the victim. This reflects the value of relationships in collectivist cultures, wherein "individualism within the family can work against the common good and is often frowned upon" (Ministry of Social Development, 2012, p. 24).

Extent of the Problem for Pasifika Youth with HSB

In NZ between 2014 and 2023, Pasifika children[7] and young people with a Youth Court proven outcome or who were convicted and sentenced in the District or High Court for sexual assault and related offence(s) accounted for 14% of the total number[8] of children and young people committing such offences (Statistics New Zealand, 2024b). All were male, with 90% aged between 14 and 16 years and 10% aged 17 years.[9] Although numbers were lower when compared with NZ-European (Pākehā) (51%) and Māori (35%) adolescents, Pasifika are overrepresented.

Victim Characteristics

There is limited data on the victim-offender relationship of NZ youth with HSB. However, a report by Oranga Tamariki – Ministry for Children indicates that between 2020 and 2021, out of 580 victims of children or young people aged 10–13 years old requiring a Family Group Conference (FGC),[10] 3% experienced a sexual assault[11] (Spier & Casswell-Laird, 2023). Of these victims, the majority were female (70%), children (70%), and whānau (family) members such as siblings or cousins (52%). This, compared with the minority of victims who were adults (17%), adolescents (11%), and either knew (e.g. attended the same school) (29%) or had no prior relationship (17%) with the child or young person. While the report identified that 11% of the total number of child or youth offenders were of mixed Māori/Pasifika descent and 6% of Pasifika descent, no inferences can be made specific to the ethnicity of those who committed sexual offences.

Research exploring the characteristics of victims targeted by youth with HSB has yielded mixed results including amongst the general population (Leonard & Hackett, 2019) and indigenous populations (Ioane et al., 2021). However, most young people choose to target victims known to them (Leonard & Hackett, 2019) and HSB towards strangers is relatively rare (Finkelhor, 2009). Contrary to such findings, a recent NZ study found that Pasifika youth were more likely to engage in HSB towards same-age peers or older victims who were not known to them (Ioane et al., 2021). While HSB directed towards peers may reflect normative adolescent sexual interests enacted in inappropriate, deviant and abusive ways (Leonard & Hackett, 2019), HSB towards strangers may be associated with high levels of assaultive, predatory behaviour or physical violence (Finkelhor, 2009) and higher rates of recidivism (Carpentier & Proulx, 2011). Finkelhor et al. (2009) found a relationship between age and gender of youth with HSB and their victims, suggesting that when males are targeted, they tend to be younger, sexually immature boys; and when females are targeted, they tend to be older, sexually developed girls. Given the findings that Pasifika youth tend to target peers/adults, Ioane et al. (2021) suggested this might be a reflection of sexual experimentation and immaturity rather than evidence of sexual deviance. While further research on victim characteristics of Pasifika youth with HSB is warranted, it is clear that the great variability across subgroups of youth with HSB is based on a range of factors including victim characteristics, age at HSB onset, personality differences, and ethnicity – thus requiring substantially different intervention responses (Leonard & Hackett, 2019).

Risk Factors for Pasifika Youth with HSB

Pasifika youth with HSB have been found to display a more extensive history of non-sexual offending behaviour prior to their sexual offending, and higher levels of emotional and behavioural problems when compared with Pākehā youth (Ioane et al., 2021). This contrasts with findings from a meta-analytic review showing that youth sex offenders tend to present with less extensive criminal histories, fewer antisocial peers, and fewer substance use problems than youth non-sex offenders (Seto et al., 2010). In addition, internalising behaviours are seen more typically in youth whose HSB is towards children rather than peers or adults (Chaffin et al., 2002). Another significant risk factor is childhood adversity including highly problematic family backgrounds, attachment difficulties, and social and economic disadvantages (Leonard & Hackett, 2019). These are significant challenges for Pasifika communities, where risk factors such as overcrowding, low educational achievement (Allard et al., 2016), acculturation, social deprivation and racial discrimination contribute to higher rates of family violence (Malatest International,

2021) and mental illness such as anxiety and depression (Tucker-Masters & Tiatia-Seath, 2017) when compared with other ethnic groups. Factors specific to NZ-born Pasifika youth include growing up in conflicting value-based systems and settings that challenge their ability to strengthen and maintain cultural identity in the face of racism and discrimination (Malatest International, 2021).

A study exploring the sexual development histories of 277 adolescent males (including 5% Pasifika) with HSB found that sexual-related factors commonly present in their pasts included engagement in normative non-harmful sexual behaviours, experiences of child sexual abuse, and exposure to pornography (Patterson et al., 2022). Although no direct relationships were identified between the latter two factors and subsequent engagement in HSB, Pasifika overrepresentation in "out-of-home" care placements (Royal Commission of Inquiry into Historical Abuse in State Care and in the Care of Faith-based Institutions, 2024), as well as a high rate of pornography use (72%) amongst Pasifika youth (Office of Film and Literature Classification [OFLC], 2018), suggest that these are factors to be considered.

Pornography, in particular, has received much attention due to an increase in consumption over the last two decades (Irizarry et al., 2023). Despite a lack of research establishing a definitive relationship between pornography use and sexual offending, there exists an assumption that there is a causal role that may increase recidivism risk (Holt et al., 2024). Since viewing pornography is not in itself atypical in adolescence, the greater concern is the role that it may play in shaping unhealthy views, attitudes, and beliefs about sex, sexuality and relationships, especially in the absence of open, honest and non-judgemental conversations about such topics with trusted adults. The AIM3 Assessment Model, which is the key tool used by all specialist agencies in NZ to assess youth aged 12–18 with HSB, includes the use of pornography as a factor for scoring analysis. Clinicians are asked to consider the nature of the content being viewed (e.g. depictions of violence, self-generated, illegal, adult vs child) and its impact on the young person's sexual development and functioning (Leonard & Hackett, 2019).

While little research has been undertaken to assess the cross-cultural efficacy of the AIM3, which was originally developed in the United Kingdom, framework developers have encouraged specialist agencies to create their own cultural guidelines specific to the populations they work with. Currently, Safe Network, one such specialist agency based in Auckland, has provided a resource for clinicians working with Māori. One of the recommendations when assessing a young person's sexual behaviour is to be clear about the context in which this occurs, noting that in Te Ao Māori[12] (and similar to Pasifika cultures), a kiss on the cheek, hongi[13] or hug when people meet is acceptable, especially during pōwhiri,[14] whakatau,[15] or tangihanga.[16] The clinical relevance of such a consideration is that normative behaviours in Polynesian cultures may be considered inappropriate in Western cultures, subsequently increasing risk scores on western-based assessment tools.

Although Pasifika youth have been found to demonstrate more restrictive attitudes towards pornography use compared to NZ European peers, they are more likely to access it for information (OFLC, 2018). Interestingly, the most popular search term on Pornhub in 2022 for the Auckland region, which is home to the largest Pasifika community in NZ, was "Tongan" (Pornhub Insights, 2022).

Although no definitive conclusions can be drawn from this, studies on adolescent pornography use suggest that viewers may prefer to search for content featuring actors of the same race (Rothman et al., 2015). Adolescent use of pornography as a learning tool highlights findings from a study with Pasifika high school students where a lack of sexual and reproductive health (SRH) information at school, parental expectations of sexual abstinence before marriage, and limited communication about sex at home were identified as contributing factors to young people engaging in sexual behaviours outside the home to avoid detection or reprimand, and sharing sexually compromising images with others (Cammock et al., 2025).

Relationship between Youth with HSB and Adult Sex Offending

Youth sex offending literature has evolved in the past three decades from viewing young people who engage in HSB as "adult sex offenders in the making" to a current view of HSB as being part of a general pattern of antisocial behaviour, with no clear causal links to adult sex offending (Daly et al., 2013; Lussier et al., 2024). However, like Pasifika youth with HSB, Pasifika adult sex offenders are overrepresented for this offence type (Tuiburelevu et al., 2023), committing around 14% of sexual offences in NZ between 2023 and 2024[17] Ministry of Justice (2025a). In a qualitative study exploring the values and practices relating to sexual assault among migrant Pasifika communities in NZ, Rankine et al. (2017) found that the communal values and practices of participants did not fit the individualistic assumptions of the predominant Western models of domestic violence. For example, whilst some male participants, including many older men, highlighted the sacredness of women and the respect required in the brother–sister relationship, some younger Pasifika men described being excused for sexually violent behavior toward women they were not married to. While this may speak to generational and post-migratory differences, it also highlights a common misconception that females are more at risk of sexual violence from strangers than from people they know (Pacific Women Lead, 2023). In reality, lifetime prevalence rates for sexual violence toward women and girls across the Pacific Islands are between 10% and 60% by partners compared with 6% to 50% by non-partners (United Nations Population Fund, 2019). Other false but commonly held beliefs in the Pacific Islands, including that "gender equality is a Western concept that has no place in Pacific culture", "violence is a private issue", or "sexual violence against women is caused by women's personal behaviour" (Pacific Women Lead, 2023) have undoubtedly shaped and perpetuated such views amongst Pasifika youth in NZ, including those who have engaged in HSB.

We might ask, how is it that such harmful beliefs can co-exist alongside traditional Pasifika values of faith, respect, and the preservation of sacred relationships? That the father who prays for God's protection on his family in the morning might be the same man who molests his niece at night; or that the male youth who refuses to talk to a female therapist about his HSB, believing it disrespectful to talk to a woman about sex, could be the same youth who masturbated next to a woman on a public train an hour before his session.

The answer lies in yet another dichotomy in which protective cultural values, when misused, become harmful, often resulting in the outward *appearance* of the vā being prioritised over *actions* that authentically maintain the sacredness of the vā. This focus on appearances reflects a common characteristic of communal cultures, with collective pride and shame being two sides of the same coin. Therefore, although an act of HSB towards an individual might be recognised as a breach of the vā with one person, the fear of potential public exposure, collective family shame, and a subsequent breach of the vā with the wider community is often considered a worse fate, thus keeping silence.

Conclusion

For First Nations and Pasifika peoples across Australia and NZ, the culture of silence and shame regarding sex and sexuality stands as a significant contributor to adolescent HSB and as a barrier to effective intervention. We can trace this to the historical and ongoing impacts of European colonisation, shared by both populations, which led not only to the dispossession of land, resources and communities, but of culture, language, values and beliefs – including those about gender, violence and sex. This chapter has addressed some of the consequences of this dispossession, including large inequities in health, wealth, education and social justice, leading to higher rates of poverty, racial discrimination, childhood trauma, and mental illness (Malatest International, 2021; Yamurrah & SNAICC, 2023) – all risk factors for adolescent criminal offending.

Furthermore, the imposition of European cultures, languages, and customs during colonial rule led to the erosion of traditional indigenous practices and the perpetuation of cultural norms that continue today to support rigid gender roles, male dominance over women, and violence as an acceptable practice and private family issue (Cripps et al., 2019; Pacific Women Lead, 2023). In the same way, colonial-era narratives on sex as a taboo or tapu subject have led to a continued stifling of open discussions about sexual intimacies – a "colonial moral hangover" (Sullivan, 2018, p. 406) passed down through previous generations to our youth of today. Coupled with the influence of harmful online pornography, so easily accessed in the privacy of a bedroom and so often used by young people to learn about sex in the absence of healthy sexual education, it is easy to see how pornography consumption has increased over time while the age of first exposure has gotten younger (Quadara et al., 2017; OFLC, 2018). The overrepresentation of HSB by First Nations and Pasifika adolescents must be understood within the context of these factors.

Given that indigenous youth are at higher risk of dropping out of HSB treatment programmes (Ioane et al., 2021) or reoffending despite them (Allard et al., 2016), how do we utilise our understanding of their respective histories and cultures to reduce recidivism risk? Although answers to this question are beyond the scope of this chapter, we proffer some key recommendations from existing research. For First Nations youth, Allard et al. (2016) suggest that effective treatment programmes include field-based services to ensure more equitable access to support, especially for remote communities; collaborative partnerships between indigenous community members and professionals; and individualised multisystemic assessment and treatment approaches. These components, which incorporate First Nations' worldviews and customs, can help to increase cultural safety for programme participants (Funston, 2013), thus improving engagement and responsivity.

For Pasifika youth, recommendations include community-wide sexual violence prevention programmes (Percival et al., 2010) and holistic approaches involving family members that recognise HSB as part of a wider pattern of offending in homes where violence exists (Ioane et al., 2021). Other recommendations include interventions that promote transparency and openness between parents and schools about what is being taught (Cammock et al., 2025), provide family-based psychoeducation on sex and sexuality, and focus on developing appropriate communication with peers and parents/caregivers (Ioane et al., 2021).

The Samoan saying, "Sili le oti i lo le ma" (Death is better than shame) (MacPherson & MacPherson, 1987) highlights the tremendous barrier that exists in talking about and addressing HSB in First Nations and Pasifika communities. However, if "shame derives its power from being unspeakable" (Brown, 2015, p. 58), let us speak, talanoa, yarn in the oral traditions of our ancestors, until the shame is silenced and the richness of our cultures bears sway to bring about change.

Notes

1 Between 2020 and 2024, an average of 11.2% of people with finalised charges for sexual offences were aged 19 years or under when the offence occurred (an average of 170.2 people).

2 Between 2020 and 2024, an average of 5% of children and young people with finalised charges in any court had sexual assault and related offences as their most serious offence (an average of 78.6 people).

3 All names have been changed.

4 Lyrics shared with permission.

5 Amanaki is a Tongan word meaning "hope".

6 Talanoa is more than just talking; it is about communicating openly and respectfully to share ideas and stories (Le Va, 2020).

7 The NZ court system defines "children" as those aged 10–13 years and "young people" as those aged 14–16 years, and 17-year-olds from 1 July 2019 onwards.

8 Between 2014 and 2023, Pasifika accounted for 30/213 sexual assaults, NZ-European 108/213, and Māori 75/213.

9 Between 2014 and 2023, 27/30 Pasifika were aged 14–16 years old, and 3/30 were aged 17 years old.

10 A Youth Justice FGC is held when children and youth break the law, and provides an opportunity for change without getting a criminal record.

11 In 2020/2021, 17/580 victims of children aged 10–13 years old at the time of offence experienced sexual assault.

12 The Māori worldview encompasses a holistic understanding of the interconnectedness between humans and the environment.

13 A traditional Māori greeting where two people press their noses together, symbolising the actions of the gods giving the breath of life to humans.

14 A traditional ceremony welcoming people onto a marae, the courtyard of the meeting-house where formal greetings and discussions take place.

15 A less formal customary welcome than a pōwhiri that can be undertaken at any location.

16 A traditional funeral rite practiced by Māori.

17 In 2023/2024, 83/609 people convicted of sexual offences were Pasifika.

References

Aboriginal and Torres Strait islander adolescent sexual health guideline. Published by the State of Queensland (Queensland Health). (2013, May) This document is licensed under a Creative Commons Attribution 3.0 Australia licence. To view a copy of this licence, visit creativecommons.org/licenses/by/3.0/au © State of Queensland (Queensland Health).

Allard, T., Rayment-McHugh, S., Adams, D., Smallbone, S., & McKillop, N. (2016). Responding to youth sexual offending: A field-based practice model that "closes the gap" on sexual recidivism among indigenous and non-indigenous males. *The Journal of Sexual Aggression*, 22(1), 82–94.

Atkinson, J. (2002). *Trauma trails, recreating song lines: The transgenerational effects of trauma in indigenous Australia*. North Melbourne, VIC: Spinifex Press.

Australian Institute of Health and Welfare. (2020). *Australia's health 2020: In brief*. https://www.aihw.gov.au/reports/australias-health/australias-health-2020-in-brief

Bromfield, L., Hirte, C., Octoman, O., & Katz, I. (2017). *Child sexual abuse in Australian institutional contexts 2008–13: Findings from administrative data*. Royal Commission into Institutional Responses to Child Sexual Abuse.

Brown, B. (2015). *Daring greatly: How the courage to be vulnerable transforms the way we live, love, parent, and lead*. Avery.

Brown, L. (2016). *10 Profound quotes from aboriginal elders that will change your perspective*. https://ideapod.com/10-aboriginal-australian-quotes-will-change-perspective-life/

Cahill, M., Napier, S., Thomsen, D., McCaig, M., & Wolbers, H. (2024). *Recorded sexual offences among juveniles in Australia* (Statistical Bulletin 43). Australian Institute of Criminology. https://www.aic.gov.au/sites/default/files/2024-04/sb43_recorded_sexual_offences_among_juveniles_in_australia.pdf

Cammock, R., Pousini, T., Andrews, M., Vaka, S., & Tautolo, E.S. (2025). Pacific high school students' experiences of sexual and reproductive health education in Aotearoa New Zealand. *Sex Education: Sexuality, Society and Learning*, 25(1), 111–125. https://doi.org/10.1080/14681811.2023.2279561

Carpentier, J., & Proulx, J. (2011). Correlates of recidivism among adolescents who have sexually offended. *Sexual Abuse*, 23(4), 434–455. https://doi.org/10.1177/1079063211409950

Chaffin, M., Letourneau, E., & Silovsky, J. F. (2002). Adults, adolescents, and children who sexually abuse children: A developmental perspective. In J. E. B. Myers, L. Berliner, J. Briere, C. T. Hendrix, C. Jenny, & T. A. Reid (Eds.), *The APSAC handbook on child maltreatment* (2nd ed., pp. 205–232). Sage Publications, Inc.

Clark, Y., Gee, G., Ralph, N., Atkinson, C., Brown, S., Glover, K., McLachlan, H., Gartland, D., Hirvonen, T., Andrews, S., & Chamberlain, C. (2020). The healing the past by nurturing the future: Cultural and emotional safety framework. *Journal of Indigenous Wellbeing*, 5(1), 38–57.

Cripps, K., Diemer, K., Honey, N., Mickle, J., Morgan, J., Parkes, A., Politoff, V., Powell, A., Stubbs, J., Ward, A., & Webster, K. (2019). *Attitudes towards violence against women and gender equality among Aboriginal people and Torres Strait Islanders: Findings from the 2017 National Community Attitudes towards Violence against Women Survey (NCAS)* (ANROWS Insights, Issue 03/2019). Sydney: ANROWS. https://www.anrows.org.au/publication/attitudes-towards-violence-against-women-and-gender-equality-among-aboriginal-people-and-torres-strait-islanders-findings-from-the-2017-national-community-attitudes-towards-violence-against-women-surv/read/#_Toc75343285

Daly, K., Bouhours, B., Broadhurst, R., & Loh, N. (2013). Youth sex offending, recidivism and restorative justice: Comparing court and conference cases. *Australian & New Zealand Journal of Criminology*, 46(2), 241–267.

Felitti, V. J., Anda, R. F., Nordenberg, D., Williamson, D. F., Spitz, A. M., Edwards, V., & Marks, J. S. (1998). Relationship of childhood abuse and household dysfunction to many of the leading causes of death in adults: The Adverse Childhood Experiences (ACE) Study. *American Journal of Preventive Medicine*, 14(4), 245–258.

Finkelhor, D. (2009). The prevention of childhood sexual abuse. *The Future of Children*, 19(2). https://muse.jhu.edu/article/361498

Fitzpatrick, J. P., Latimer, J., Ferreira, M. L., Carter, M., Oscar, J., Martiniuk, A. L.,. . .& Elliott, E. J. (2015). Prevalence and patterns of alcohol use in pregnancy in remote Western Australian communities: The Lililwan Project. *Drug and Alcohol Review*, 34(3), 329–339.

Friesen, W. (2018). Beyond the RSE: Systems of Pacific labour migration to New Zealand. *New Zealand Population Review*, 44, 111–129.

Funston, L. (2013). Aboriginal and Torres Strait Islander worldviews and cultural safety transforming sexual assault service provision for children and young people. *International Journal of Environmental Research and Public Health,* 10(9), 3818–3833. https://doi.org/10.3390/ijerph10093818

Hackett, S. (2014). *Children and young people with harmful sexual behaviours: Research review*. London: Research in Practice. https://www.researchinpractice.org.uk/children/publications/2014/june/children-and-young-people-with-harmful-sexual-behaviours-research-review-2014/

Hackett, S., Darling, A. J., Balfe, M., Masson, H., & Phillips, J. (2024). Life course outcomes and developmental pathways for children and young people with harmful sexual behaviour. *The Journal of Sexual Aggression*, 30(2), 145–165. https://www.tandfonline.com/doi/full/10.1080/13552600.2022.2124323

Hackett, S., Holmes, D., & Branigan, P. (2016). *Harmful sexual behaviour framework: An evidence-informed operational framework for children and young people displaying harmful sexual behaviours*. UK: NSPCC.

Hackett, S., Masson, H., Balfe, M., & Phillips, J. (2013). Individual, family, and abuse characteristics of 700 British child and adolescent sexual abusers. *Child Abuse Review*, 22, 232–245. https://onlinelibrary.wiley.com/doi/10.1002/car.2246

Herbert, J. L., & Bromfield, L. (2018). *National comparison of cross-agency practice in investigating and responding to severe child abuse* (Child Family Community Australia Paper No. 47). Australian Institute of Family Studies. https://aifs.gov.au/resources/policy-and-practice-papers/national-comparison-cross-agency-practice-investigating-and

Holt, K., Kissinger, J., Spickler, C., & Roush, V. (2024). Pornography use and sexual offending: An examination of perceptions of role and risk. *International Journal of Offender Therapy and Comparative Criminology*, 68(6–7), 613–637. https://doi.org/10.1177/0306624X211049183

House of Representatives Standing Committee on Social Policy and Legal Affairs. (2020). *Protecting the age of innocence. Report of the inquiry into age verification for online wagering and online pornography*. Commonwealth of Australia.

Ioane, J., Tofaeono, R., & Lambie, I. (2021). Pasifika youth with harmful sexual behaviour differ from other young people and need a different response. *New Zealand Journal of Psychology (Online)*, 50(3), 17–28. https://ezproxy.auckland.ac.nz/login?url=https://www.proquest.com/scholarly-journals/pasifika-youth-with-harmful-sexual-behaviour/docview/2669610822/se-2

Irizarry, R., Gallaher, H., Samuel, S., Soares, J., & Villela, J. (2023). How the rise of Meiksans, J, Bromfield, L. Ey, L. (2017). *A continuum of responses for harmful sexual behaviours. Commissioner for children and young people western Australia.* University of South Australia. Australian Centre for Child Protection.

Katavake-McGrath, F. (2021). *Our way to home: An exploratory study of Pasifika gay men in New Zealand, their lived experience and their navigation of sexual orientation related legislative change* (PhD diss.). Auckland University of Technology. https://www.manalagi.org/_files/ugd/b7eedf_b56d70106c7d4da1a5748ffef6f730f8.pdf

Langton, M. L. (1997). Grandmothers' law, company business and succession in changing Aboriginal land tenure systems. In G. Yunupingu (Ed.), *Our land is our life: Land rights—past, present and future* (pp. 84–117). University of Queensland Press.

Leonard & Hackett (2019). *AIM3 Assessment Model*. The AIM Project.

Le Va (2020). *Respectful relationships: Pasifika people living our values*. https://www.leva.co.nz/wp-content/uploads/2020/04/Respectful-Relationships-CatchYourself-Factsheet-.pdf

Lowell, A., Maypilama, E. L., Fasoli, L., Gundjarranbuy, R., Godwin-Thompson, J., Guyula, A., Yunupiŋu, M., Armstrong, E., Garrutju, J., & McEldowney, R. (2018). The "invisible homeless": Challenges faced by families bringing up their children in a remote Australian Aboriginal community. *BMC Public Health, 18*, Article 1382. https://doi.org/10.1186/s12889-018-6306-7

Macpherson, C., & Macpherson, L. (1987). Towards an explanation of recent trends in suicide in Western Samoa. *Man,* 22(2), 305–330. https://doi.org/10.2307/2802867

Malatest International (2021). *Nga take o nga wheako o te kaikiri ki nga manene o Aotearoa: Drivers of migrant New Zealanders' experiences of racism.* https://communityresearch.org.nz/wp-content/uploads/formidable/8/Malatest_migrant-research-report-20210324_FINAL.pdf

Malatest International (2023). *Whataboutme.nz – the national youth and wellbeing survey 2021.* https://www.msd.govt.nz/documents/about-msd-and-our-work/publications-resources/consultations/youth-health-and-wellbeing-survey-results/2021-yhws-pacific-cohort-report-final-june-2023-.pdf

Malvaso, C., Proeve, M., Delfabbro, P., & Cale, J. (2019). Characteristics of children with problem sexual behaviour and adolescent perpetrators of sexual abuse: A systematic review. *Journal of Sexual Aggression,* 26(1), 1–26. https://doi.org/10.1080/13552600.2019.1651914

Malvaso, C. G., Proeve, M., Delfabbro, P., & Cale, J. (2020). Characteristics of children with problem sexual behaviour and adolescent perpetrators of sexual abuse: a systematic review. *Journal of Sexual Aggression*, 26(1), 36–61. https://doi.org/10.1080/13552600.2019.1651914

Ministry for Pacific Peoples (2017). *Yavu: Foundations of Pacific engagement.* https://www.mpp.govt.nz/assets/Resources/Yavu-Booklet.pdf

Ministry for Pacific Peoples (2024). *Pacific study finds vā can lift mood.* https://www.mpp.govt.nz/news-and-events/news-from-2/pacific-study-finds-va-can-lift-mood/#:~:text=V%C4%81%20is%20an%20important%20concept,with%20others%20and%20the%20environment

Ministry of Business, Innovation and Employment. (2024, December 21). *Pacific migrants' trends and settlement outcomes report.* https://www.mbie.govt.nz/immigration-and-tourism/immigration/migration-research-and-evaluation/pacific-migrants-trends-report

Ministry of Justice. (2025a). *Number and percentage of children and young people with finalised charges in any court, by offence type, 2015 - 2024* [Dataset]. https://view.officeapps.live.com/op/view.aspx?src=https%3A%2F%2Fwww.justice.govt.nz%2Fassets%2FDocuments%2FPublications%2F9mvMML_Children-and-young-people-with-charges-finalised-in-any-court_dec2024_v1.0.xlsx&wdOrigin=BROWSELINK

Ministry of Justice. (2025b). *Number and percentage of people with finalised charges for sexual offences, by victim type and age group of person charged, 2015 – 2024* [Dataset]. https://view.officeapps.live.com/op/view.aspx?src=https%3A%2F%2Fwww.justice.govt.nz%2Fassets%2FDocuments%2FPublications%2F12OrdNa_Sexual-offences_dec2024_v1.0.xlsx&wdOrigin=BROWSELINK

Ministry of Social Development. (2012). *Nga Vaka o Kāiga Tapu: A Pacific conceptual framework to address family violence in New Zealand.* Wellington: Author.

Molnar, T., McKillop, N., Allard, T., Rynne, J., & Adams, D. (2021). Patterns of rearrest for Aboriginal and/or Torres Strait Islander and non-Indigenous youth who have sexually harmed. *The Journal of Sexual Aggression,* 27(2), 167–184. https://doi.org/10.1080/13552600.2020.1850894

National Society for the Prevention of Cruelty to Children. (2024). *Statistics briefing: Harmful sexual behaviour.* https://learning.nspcc.org.uk/media/dlnp4m3d/statistics-briefing-harmful-sexual-behaviour-hsb.pdf

NSW Health. (2022). *Children First: Our shared framework for preventing and responding to problematic and harmful sexual behaviours by children and young people.* https://www.health.nsw.gov.au/parvan/hsb/Documents/children-first.pdf

NSW Kids and Families. (2014). Understanding and responding to harmful sexual behaviours in children and young people: A practice guide. NSW Ministry of Health.

O'Brien, W. (2010). *Australia's response to sexualised or sexually abusive behaviours in children and young people.* Canberra: Australian Crime Commission. dro.deakin.edu.au/eserv/DU:30065114/obrien-australias–2010.pdf

O'Donnell, M., Burrow, S., Usher, R., Wood, L., Fisher, C., & Gayde, R. (2019). Infant removals: The need to address the over-representation of Aboriginal infants and community concerns of another "stolen generation." *Child Abuse & Neglect,* 90, 88–100. https://doi.org/10.1016/j.chiabu.2019.01.017

Office of Film and Literature Classification. (2018). *NZ Youth and Porn: Research findings of a survey on how and why young New Zealanders view online pornography.* Wellington, NZ: Office of Film and Literature Classification.

Pacific Women Lead. (2023). *Thematic brief: Myths about gender equality in the Pacific.* https://pacificdata.org/data/dataset/cb248af3-23ac-4da6-8eeb-5d1a3ce780dc/resource/38b3e82c-ca53-4725-8d62-bf7a25f0e77a/download/spc-pwl_thematicbrief_myths.pdf

Patterson, T., Hobbs, L., Lorimer, M., & Rapsey, C. (2022). Sexual developmental histories of adolescents who engaged in harmful sexual behaviour. *The Journal of Forensic Psychiatry & Psychology,* 33(6), 810–827. https://doi.org/10.1080/14789949.2022.2122856

Percival, T., Robati-Mani, R., Powell, E., Kingi, P., Peteru, M. C., Hope, L.-T., Finau, E., Selu, E., Rankine, J., & Percival, T. (2010). *Pacific pathways to the prevention of sexual violence: Overview report.* Pacific Health, School of Population Health, University of Auckland.

Pornhub Insights. (2022). *New Zealand Insights.* https://www.pornhub.com/insights/new-zealand-insights-2022

Productivity Commission. (2020). *Mental health: Productivity Commission inquiry report (No. 95).* Canberra: Australian Government. Released publicly 16 November 2020. Retrieved from https://www.pc.gov.au/inquiries/completed/mental-health/report

Quadara, A., El-Murr, A., Latham, J., & Australian Institute of Family Studies, Issuing Body. (2017). *The effects of pornography on children and young people: An evidence scan: Research report.* Melbourne, VIC: Australian Institute of Family Studies, Government publication.

Ramsamy, N. (2014). Indigenous birthing in remote locations: Grandmothers' law and government medicine. In O. Best & B. Fredericks (Eds.), *Yatdjuligin: Aboriginal and Torres Strait Islander nursing and midwifery care* (pp. 102–119). Cambridge University Press.

Rankine, J., Percival, T., Finau, E., Hope, L.-T., Kingi, P., Peteru, M. C., Powell, E., Robati-Mani, R., & Selu, E. (2017). Pacific peoples, violence, and the power and control wheel. *Journal of Interpersonal Violence,* 32(18), 2777–2803. https://doi.org/10.1177/0886260515596148

Rothman, E. F., Kaczmarsky, C., Burke, N., Jansen, E., & Baughman, A. (2015). "Without Porn . . . I Wouldn't Know Half the Things I Know Now": A qualitative study of pornography use among a sample of urban, low-income, Black and Hispanic youth. *The Journal of Sex Research,* 52(7), 736–746. https://doi.org/10.1080/00224499.2014.960908

Royal Commission into Institutional Responses to Child Sexual Abuse. (2017). *Final report.* https://www.childabuseroyalcommission.gov.au/final-report

Royal Commission of Inquiry into Historical Abuse in State Care and in the Care of Faith-based Institutions, (2024), *Whanaketia.* Crown Copyright New Zealand 2024 ISBN 978-0-473-71010-1 (online) ISBN 978-0-473-71009-5

Scroope, C. (2018). *Tongan culture.* https://culturalatlas.sbs.com.au/tongan-culture/tongan-culture-family#:~:text=Tonga%20is%20traditionally%20a%20matriarchal,ehi%27ehi)%20his%20sister

Seto, M. C., Lalumière, M. L., & Hinshaw, S. P. (2010). What is so special about male adolescent sexual offending? A review and test of explanations through meta-analysis. *Psychological Bulletin,* 136(4), 526–575. https://doi.org/10.1037/a0019700 Shlonsky, A., Albers, B., Tolliday, D., Wilson, S. J., Norvell, J., & Kissinger, L. (2017). *Rapid evidence assessment: Current best evidence in the therapeutic treatment of children with problem or harmful sexual behaviours, and children who have sexually offended*. Sydney: Royal Commission into Institutional Responses to Child Sexual Abuse.

Spangaro, J., Quadara, A., Katz, I., & Bromfield, L. (2020). *Children and young people with harmful sexual behaviours: A scoping review of policy and practice responses in Australia*. Australian Centre for Child Protection.

Spier, P., & Casswell-Laird, O. (2023). *Victims of offending by children who had a family group conference in 2020/21*. Wellington: Oranga Tamariki—Ministry for Children. https://www.orangatamariki.govt.nz/assets/Uploads/About-us/Research/Latest-research/Victims-of-offending-by-children-with-FGCs/Victims-of-offending-by-children-who-had-an-FGC-in-F2021.pdf

Statistics New Zealand (2019). *2018 Religious affiliations for Pacific people in New Zealand*. https://figure.nz/chart/MLOTJzWBmvHsUl0W

Statistics New Zealand (2024a). *2023 Census national and regional data* [Dataset]. https://www.stats.govt.nz/infographics/2023-census-national-and-regional-data/

Statistics New Zealand (2024b). *Children and young people given an order in court – most serious offence calendar year* [Dataset]. https://explore.data.stats.govt.nz/vis?pg=0&fs[0]=Society%2C0%7CCrime%20and%20justice%23CAT_CRIME_AND_JUSTICE%23&fc=Society&bp=true&snb=20&df[ds]=ds-nsiws-disseminate&df[id]=JUS_CAL_005&df[ag]=STATSNZ&df[vs]=1.0&dq=.00.T.T.T&ly[rw]=YEAR_JUS_CAL_005&ly[cl]=SENTENCE_JUS_CAL_005&to[TIME]=false

Sullivan, C. T. (2018). Indigenous Australian women's colonial sexual intimacies: Positioning indigenous women's agency. *Culture, Health & Sexuality*, 20(4), 397–410. https://doi.org/10.1080/13691058.2017.1349930

Thomas, C. (1993). *Sexual assault: Issues for aboriginal women*. Aboriginal Women's Policy Coordinator Office of Aboriginal Affairs New South Wales.

Tucker-Masters, L., & Tiatia-Seath, J. (2017). Reviewing the literature on anxiety and depression in Pacific youth: A fresh perspective. *New Zealand Medical Student Journal*, 25, 24–28.

Tuiburelevu, L., Lotoa, E., Ieremia, I., Wagner-Hiliau, H., & Coxon-Brayne, G. (2023). *Pacific Peoples and the Criminal Justice System in Aotearoa New Zealand*. Michael & Suzanne Borrin Foundation; University of Auckland.

Tupuola, A.-M. (1996). Learning sexuality: Young Samoan women. *Women's Studies Journal*, 12(2), 59–75.

United Nations Population Fund (2019). *Women who experience intimate partner violence 2000-2019: UNFPA Asia and the Pacific Region*. https://asiapacific.unfpa.org/sites/default/files/resource-pdf/2019_knowvawdata_regional_vaw_map_-_v2_updated_31_july_2020.pdf

Yamurrah & SNAICC. (2023). *The believe inquire respond to disclosures (BIRD) research report*. SNAICC.

Young, C. D., Taumoepeau, M. M., Hohmann-Marriott, B. E., Girling, J. E., & Bird, R. J. (2024). Sexual and reproductive health knowledges: A study with Pacific young people enrolled in an Aotearoa New Zealand tertiary institution. *Culture, Health & Sexuality*, 26(2), 265–283. https://doi.org/10.1080/13691058.2023.2201356

7 Understanding Firesetting in Australia

How Can Current Arson Theory and Treatment Programs Be Better Informed to Provide Culturally Relevant Responses for First Nations Young People?

Therese Ellis-Smith and Glenda Harward-Nalder

Overrepresentation of Indigenous Australians in Custody

According to available national data in 2021 Indigenous peoples in Australia comprise 3.8% of the total population, one-third of whom are aged under 15 years of age (Australian Bureau of Statistics, 2021). Indigenous young people make up just 6% of all Australian young people aged between 10 and 17 years (AIHW, 2023), yet as of 30 June 2022, 61% of those remanded or sentenced to juvenile detention nationally were Indigenous (AIHW, 2023). First Nations adults are also significantly overrepresented, comprising 32% of the Australian adult prisoner population (ABS, 2023).

Overrepresentation of Indigenous people is observed across a range of offence types (Wundersitz, 2010), and research has found that offending by Aboriginal and/or Torres Strait Islander women when compared to their non-Indigenous counterparts is increasing (MacGillivray & Baldry, 2015). The use of alcohol and other substances in the commission of offences by Indigenous people is also reported to be rising (Intergovernmental Committee on Drugs, 2014; Putt et al., 2005), and the proportion of Indigenous offenders with a mental illness is similarly identified as having increased over recent years (Shepherd et al., 2017). These alarming national patterns have pointed to the need for urgent attention for many years, yet mainstream theory and treatment programs continue to dominate. The identification of offence-specific and offender-specific factors is crucial to the development of culturally specific systemic responses and interventions to reduce offending.

Overrepresentation Amongst Juvenile Offending in General

It is estimated that in 2021–2022, Aboriginal and/or Torres Strait Islander young people were 17 times more likely to be under community-based supervision than their non-Indigenous peers, and about 24 times as likely to be in detention (AIHW, 2023). These disproportionate statistics are not new, as it was reported almost 20 years ago that, in 2005, Indigenous juveniles were 23 times as likely as non-Indigenous juveniles to be detained (Year Book Australia, 2008).

DOI: 10.4324/9781003298410-12

New South Wales has the largest number of Indigenous Australians who continue to be overrepresented in the juvenile criminal justice system. The following New South Wales statistics highlight the discrepancies between Indigenous and non-Indigenous juvenile offenders (Bureau of Crime Statistics and Research, 2023):

- In 2022, 54% of all police court actions against young people proceeded against Aboriginal offenders, an increase of 34% over five years.
- Sixty-six per cent of young people refused bail at their first court appearance in 2022 were Aboriginal, and 79% of custodial sentences handed down in juvenile courts were to Aboriginal offenders.
- The number of Aboriginal young people remanded in detention increased by 37% in the two years between June 2021 and June 2023, with males increasing by 42%, while the female rates were stable.

These alarming statistics have prompted considerable research over recent years aimed at identifying causal and contributing factors in order to identify systemic responses, and the criminal justice literature has identified important differences between Indigenous and non-Indigenous offenders, in terms of offence and offender features. For example, in Queensland, Indigenous male offenders have been found to commence offending at an earlier age than non-Indigenous male offenders, and chronic (repeated) offending amongst Indigenous juveniles is higher than that of non-Indigenous juveniles (Crime and Misconduct Commission, 2009). This pattern has also been observed in a South Australian study (Marshall, 2008) which showed that 17% of Indigenous juvenile offenders had been classified as chronic offenders, compared to 2% of non-Indigenous juvenile offenders ($N = 3344$). Community factors such as lower incomes and chronic unemployment, impoverished housing and community facilities, increased use of substances, reduced access to education and boredom are often cited as contributing factors (McCausland & Vivian, 2010).

In Australia the impact of displacement and loss of culture is viewed as having contributed to rising crime rates (Anthony, 2013; Finnane & Richards, 2010; Weatherburn, 2014), as respected Aboriginal leader Charles Perkins noted "we know we cannot live in the past but the past lives with us" (Wanganeen, 2014, p. 267), and is widely considered to be directly responsible for substantially higher rates of mortality, including suicide (Silburn et al., 2014), poorer health outcomes, higher rates of mental illness (Australian Indigenous HealthInfoNet, 2017; Parker & Milroy, 2014) lower educational achievement (Danaher, 2011), and higher crime rates within Indigenous communities. The destructive impact of colonisation began with warfare between the first settlers and First Australians in 1788. Recent research (Ryan et al., 2022) estimates that more than 10,000 Aboriginal and Torres Strait Islander lives were lost in more than 400 massacres. Euphemisms such as "dispersals" and "clearances" were common in reports of the day. Similarly, terms used in subsequent colonial policies: "displacement", "protection", and "assimilation", resulting in the loss of land, language and culture, and the forced separation of First Nations family groups in Australia (Evans et al., 1988; Griffiths et al., 2016;

Holland, 2015; Prior, 2007; Vickery et al., 2007) must be understood as instruments of control over every aspect of First Nations lives in attempts to understand the precipitating factors for criminal behaviour in general, and firesetting in particular.

Colonisation also brought missionaries to First Nations communities, intent upon converting them to various religious beliefs. Sadly, even in recent times, there are examples of religious-based groups and evangelists moving into Kimberley communities in Western Australia, promoting Aboriginal culture as a type of devil worship (Parke, 2019). As one Elder noted "wherever the religious intervened in Aboriginal communities, on-going trauma has resulted" (personal communication, 2025) and another "Christian missionaries have a long history of trying to assimilate Aboriginal people in the Kimberley, and discouraging them from practicing their traditional religious beliefs" As Karajarri man Mr Gordon Marshall, from the Kimberley noted "These people, they're vulnerable, and they [the church] come along and catch them and say, 'I can help you, I think they just prey on vulnerable people'" (Parke, 2019). Australian First Nations communities have been flooded with outside views, rules and oversights, and subjected to paternalistic and disempowering influences which have not met their cultural and traditional needs. Many have called for the communities themselves to resist these influences and forge their own solutions to community problems, which reflect Indigenous viewpoints and cultural knowledge.

Hovane et al. (2014) argue that effective interventions with Indigenous offenders must adopt a holistic or ecological approach which is cognizant of this history and the cultural schemas that are derived from it. An example of this approach would be to recognise that Indigenous people may not value self-disclosure, or an expression of emotion about their offending, which is often expected in non-Indigenous therapeutic settings as a prerequisite to change. This difference in expressive proficiency might appear as though an Indigenous person lacks empathy or denies responsibility for his or her offending.

This difference in expressive proficiency is also reflected in results obtained by Day et al. (2008), who found greater experiences of loss, higher levels of tension-reduction behaviours and dissociation among Indigenous men when compared to non-Indigenous men in their study of South Australian prisoners. The study also found Indigenous prisoners were more likely to have difficulty identifying and describing their feelings, raising implications for the delivery of offender programs. Furthermore, non-Indigenous treatment providers may lack understanding of the complex avoidant relationships between members of Indigenous communities, where customary avoidance is regarded as a gesture of respect such as avoidance of eye contact, or communication between a man and his mother in law (Aboriginal Corporation, 2019), and thereby fail to understand subtle relationship stressors impacting on their clients (Gee et al., 2014) affecting participation in a group setting.

A lack of cultural awareness or understanding of the potential for communication barriers can give rise to non-Indigenous therapists ignoring the subtleties in Indigenous disclosures and thereby neglecting to give sufficient attention to relevant underlying emotions impacting on behaviour.

Responsivity issues such as poor literacy or problems with expressive English, a reluctance to share experiences of trauma due to feelings of shame, loss or grief in Caucasian company, and differences in the identification and treatment of mental illnesses are some of the difficulties identified for Indigenous persons who are engaged in treatment (Dingwell & Cairney, 2010; Dingwell et al., 2014; Macklin & Gilbert, 2011; Mals et al., 2008). As Professor Harry Blagg (2008) notes the pursuit of a single theory of crime in Indigenous communities is both simplistic and reflective of a European empiricism when "we pull with us into the Aboriginal domain a baggage train of theories and perspectives on crime drawn from western research" (p. 4). As mainstream theories appear to lack cultural relevance, we turn to First Nations concepts and ways of interpreting the world, commencing with "social and emotional well-being", to explore an understanding of juvenile crime in general, and firesetting in particular.

Social and Emotional Wellbeing

Social and Emotional Wellbeing (SEWB) is a holistic understanding of life and wellbeing held by Aboriginal and/or Torres Strait Islander peoples. The framework has been developed to guide intervention strategies and treatment modalities for Indigenous peoples (Gee et al., 2014). Described as a "multidimensional concept of health that includes mental health, but which encompasses domains of health and wellbeing such as connections to land or 'country', culture, spirituality, ancestry, family and community" (p. 55), Gee et al. (2014) argue this framework represents the complex relationships between domains of Indigenous life. SEWB was defined by the Social Health Reference Group established by the Australian government in 2004 as "The social and emotional wellbeing concept recognises the importance of connection to land, culture, spirituality, ancestry, family and community, and how these affect the individual" (Social Health Reference Group, 2004, p. 9; Zubrick et al., 2014, p. 76). As shown in Figure 7.1, the domains of SEWB include connection to culture, country, body, mind and emotions, family and kinship, spirituality and ancestors, and connection to community.

By connecting the impact of colonisation and displacement within First Nations communities to intergenerational trauma and a broad reduction in social and emotional well-being, we begin to establish a sense of the underlying factors that need to be addressed to reduce crime rates. Reflecting on the above, this next section will discuss firesetting behaviours and also focus on providing some suggestions for how arson treatment programs can incorporate SEWB, specifically, how these programs can avoid the pitfalls of cultural irrelevance and the "one-size-fits-all" mentality.

Extent of the Problem – Indigenous Juvenile Arson Offending

Indigenous offenders are overrepresented amongst those who set illegal fires (Muller, 2008; Muller & Stebbins, 2008). Early research conducted in 2008 by the Australian Institute of Criminology reviewed all arson cases between 2001 and 2006 in

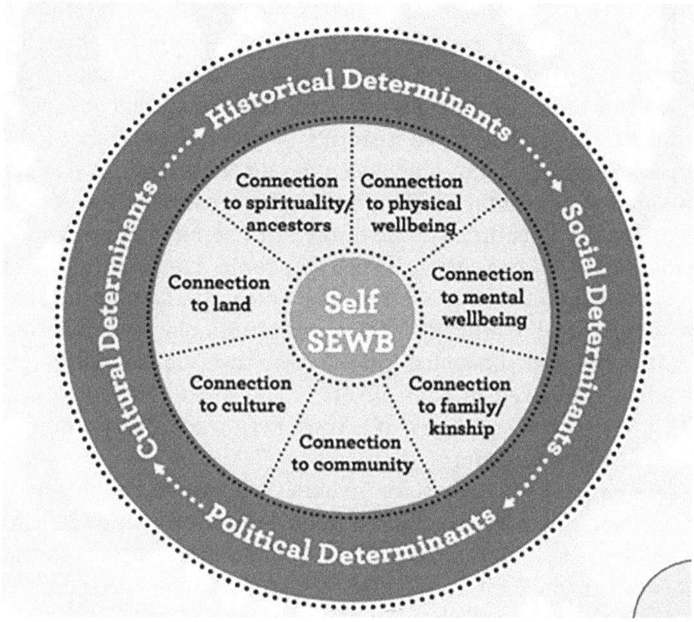

Figure 7.1 The Aboriginal and Torres Strait Islander peoples' Social and Emotional Wellbeing (SEWB) framework (Gee et al., 2014).

Note: This version of the framework design was adapted from: ETS-SEWB-Possible-Protective-Factors-Activity-and-Plan.pdf.

New South Wales. This report identified a total of 1,232 arson and bushfire arson defendants and of these, 22% were aged under 18 years at the time of the index offence. It was also reported that 37% of all juvenile firesetters and 20% of adult firesetters were identified as Aboriginal and/or Torres Strait Islander.

Of all juvenile arson offences between 2001 and 2006 in New South Wales (n = 247), 75% were committed by those aged between 15 and 17 years and 91% were committed by male offenders. More recent research from New South Wales identified a steady increase in the number of fires attributed to juveniles, with 26% of all arson offences in 2015–2016 and 42% in the 2016–2017 period (Perks, 2019).

The Queensland Corrective Services, Department of Justice and Attorney General (2015) identified 34.7% of all arrests for arson in 2015–2016 were juveniles aged between 10 and 17 years, and this rate increased to 48% in the 2016–2017 period (Perks, 2019). These proportions are also reflected in New Zealand statistics, with young people aged between 10 and 19 years responsible for 62% of all fire-related offences between 2014 and 2016 (Perks, 2019). Given the significant proportions of arson offending amongst Australian First Nations youth, it is imperative that criminal justice agencies provide targeted treatment programs in the community and in detention, based on culture-relevant theoretical underpinnings, to reduce these rates in the future.

Perks et al. (2019) conducted a meta-analysis of 34 international studies which were conducted over 30 years, investigating differences in reported behavioural, environmental and psychological factors between adolescents who set fires and those who do not. The authors found that juvenile arsonists had "significantly more extensive histories of problematic behaviours, experienced adverse familial events, elevated rates of emotional dysregulation, and greater prevalence of mental health disorders compared to youth not involved in firesetting" (p. 1). Specifically, one of the most significant environmental risk factors associated with firesetting in young people was a history of abuse and disruptions to the parent–child relationships. Other risk factors such as Attention Deficit-Hyperactivity Disorder (ADHD) and emotional dysregulation, depression and self-harm, and substance misuse were also elevated amongst juvenile firesetters when compared to control sets of non-firesetting juveniles. A fascination with fire and a past history of setting fires were also found to be highly predictive of further firesetting.

While these general risk factors for juveniles who set illegal fires have not been considered in studies of Indigenous young people involved in offending in Australia, it is likely that these risk factors are present amongst this group, given the research on general crime characteristics of adolescent offenders (Jacobs et al., 2020). Firesetting by First Nations youth has not been considered in the research literature despite the significant statistics cited previously. In addition, First Nations young people who set fires for illegal purposes are also neglected in the most recent theory developed to understand firesetting, which focuses on adults. The multi-trajectory theory of adult firesetting, or M-TAFF (Gannon et al., 2012), identifies five trajectories developed to explain firesetting, which are summarised as:

Antisocial cognition trajectory. The antisocial trajectory refers to firesetting behaviour that is predominantly related to antisocial cognitions, scripts and values.

Grievance trajectory. The second trajectory, the grievance trajectory, relates to firesetters whose predominant risk factors are aggression, anger and hostility.

Fire interest trajectory. The fire interest trajectory describes firesetters who demonstrate elevated levels of fire interest.

Emotionally expressive trajectory. The emotionally expressive trajectory describes firesetters who have poor communication and social skills, low self-regulation, and problem-solving deficits.

Multifaceted trajectory. The final trajectory is the multifaceted trajectory which refers to firesetters who hold elevated fire interest and offence supportive attitudes.

While useful in identifying different types of explanations for firesetting, this theory only applies to adults who set illegal fires, leaving quite a gap in the theoretical space dedicated to juvenile firesetters, and specifically those from First Nations communities. The five trajectories highlight alternative pathways to firesetting and identify specific targets for intervention, but the theory lacks reference to an Indigenous standpoint or perspective (Moreton-Robinson, 2004; Nakata, 2007; Tuhiwai

Smith, 2012), and it is silent on how culture and community factors impact the identification of pathways to firesetting.

Given that the M-TTAF, and the trajectories identified within the theory, are based on the cultural context in which they were developed, it is not surprising that they do not fully account for different cultures. The trajectories neglect spirituality and social and emotional wellbeing (SEWB) as distinct elements, and as these elements are fundamental to Indigenous life in Australia, there is an argument to be made for an alternative trajectory for this group. The M-TTAF is also silent on how the pathways to firesetting differ across individualistic and collectivist cultures, an important distinction given that the trajectories appear to be based on an individualistic approach. Those offending within an individualist cultural context, such as Western societies, are more likely to be motivated by what makes them feel good, and to meet their individual needs, as opposed to those offending within a collectivist culture, such as Indigenous societies, who are often motivated by emotions such as sympathy, shame and communion reflected in their environment (Seidler, 2010).

First Nations people have long been differentiated from non-Indigenous people for having an external locus of control (Kingsley et al., 2013). Their reference is their family, their community and their country, and when their family or community is sad or traumatised, then they are likely to reflect this. The M-TTAF does not account for specific cultural influences such as community grieving, socio-economic disadvantage, or higher rates of mental and physical illness amongst Indigenous peoples (Jorm et al., 2012; Parker & Milroy, 2014; Schwartz, 2010; Vos et al., 2009). Features such as community sadness and heightened stress, and the consequential opportunistic acting out behaviours using readily available implements; or heightened levels of frustration and diminished tolerance to stress due to repeated experiences of loss, are not accounted for in the theory. For this reason, the multifaceted trajectory is more likely to be considered for Indigenous firesetters, as a catch-all, which may not target these individualised treatment needs.

Based on the qualitative research conducted in the Northern Territory and South Australia (Ellis-Smith, 2020) an alternative trajectory such as grief and loss saturation would reflect these cultural differences and consider a broader range of etiological factors contributing to firesetting, as opposed to in situ motivations. An offending trajectory for First Nations firesetters might emphasise the impact of their community trauma and family environment, within an historical context. In communities where grief, trauma, and loss are commonplace, resistance to stress or to frustration is likely to be diminished, and while it appears that offending serves a superficial purpose, such as crime concealment, it is likely that this is a simplistic reflection of deeper emotional distress accumulated over generations.

Introduction to Firesetting – Motivation and Offence Factors

One of the useful dichotomies for understanding why a person sets an illegal fire is the "expressive versus instrumental" motivation (Canter & Fritzon, 1998). An expressive motivation for arson includes elements of self-pity, sexual excitement, delusional thinking, or the expression of elevated emotion such as anger, rage, jealousy, or revenge. On the other hand, many fires are set for instrumental purposes to achieve a specific outcome, such as to profit from the fire by claiming insurance or to eliminate or conceal evidence of another crime, such as fingerprints.

In a review of 305 sentencing court transcripts across Australia between 1990 and 2015, several key differences between adult Indigenous and non-Indigenous firesetters were identified (Ellis-Smith, 2020). It was found that Indigenous firesetters were:

- less likely to have a history of diagnosed mental illness attributable to a lower incidence of reporting or the identification of mental illness by clinical services,
- were more likely than non-Indigenous firesetters to set fires for "expressive" purposes, as opposed to "instrumental" purposes,
- were less likely to use accelerants in their firesetting,
- were less likely to have planned their firesetting than the non-Indigenous group, and
- were more likely to have engaged in legitimate firesetting such as setting fires to clear vegetation/land clearing for ecological purposes in the past when compared to non-Indigenous participants.

It was hypothesised that Indigenous firesetters might be more likely to act spontaneously in the heat of a dispute, and therefore were less prepared, having not planned the offence by collecting accelerants or other sources of ignition. It was also suggested that fire might serve to ameliorate negative internal states associated with poor SEWB for the Indigenous offenders and provide for self-soothing or comfort; more so than for the non-Indigenous group, whose use of fire was associated with more explicit or instrumental motivations.

In a qualitative study of the factors contributing to firesetting amongst Indigenous people, 14 First Nations people convicted of illegal firesetting were interviewed across South Australia and the Northern Territory (Ellis-Smith et al., 2019). Grief was a notable theme as one 35-year-old Aboriginal man who was interviewed spoke about his firesetting and his grief and isolation from community "sometimes we do bad things when we lose family." A further participant, a 26-year-old Indigenous man, expressed similar emotions:

> My mum's sister, she grew me up, she raised me – she passed and that sorted of started everything off for me . . . it seemed like anyone I get close to they were passing, and I just didn't know how to deal with it, and me dealing with it was me going out and doing crime and smoking drugs . . . I sent this email to my partner saying if I'm going back to jail it will be for something serious – it won't be for minor things – the way I'm feeling, all my anger and that. I haven't expressed nothing to no-one, I haven't sat down and explained my feelings or how to deal with any of it. In here I'm doing some grief counselling.

Fire was also commonly used by the Indigenous firesetters interviewed in response to relatively minor issues and may signal the use of fire as a function of the "slow burn" of intergenerational trauma, disadvantage and racism experienced in Indigenous communities for many years (Mellor, 2004). Examples of minor frustrations resulting in firesetting in the Indigenous group included being irritated by another's lack of concern or being frustrated following a domestic argument. While these examples are based on adult reflections of their firesetting, the relationship between motivation for illegal firesetting and disturbed social and emotional wellbeing for Indigenous arsonists, both adults and juveniles, warrants further consideration and a prominent place in treatment planning. Given the importance of Social and Emotional Wellbeing for Indigenous people, understanding this relationship would offer treatment pathways that focused on the community and family factors faced by Indigenous youth.

In the study described above, several community members/Elders offered valuable recommendations for interventions or programs involving First Nations people who set illegal fires, particularly those offenders who may have disconnected from their culture. By reconnecting and learning about the positive uses of fire, Elders from several communities suggested that those who have offended with fire in the past should learn to value and revere fire. The view that the potential for deliberate arson might be reduced through interventions or firesetter treatment that assists Indigenous firesetters to establish stronger connections with their culture is significant. Elders can provide local First Nations insights as they have the knowledge and experience to assist in the development of local responses that are culturally aware and therefore more likely to be impactful.

How Can Culture Be Considered in Treatment for Indigenous Juveniles Who Set Fires?

In 2011, Lambie & Randall identified that early interventions for young people who set fires were largely restricted to (1) fire service-operated educational sessions focused on fire safety and awareness, and (2) individual mental health-based psychosocial counselling. In 2025, in Australia, the treatment options for young firesetters continue to be limited to fire services in most jurisdictions, facilitating educational sessions for young people who have been identified as at risk of setting illegal fires, and individual clinicians offering counselling and family assistance. Despite there being a number of treatment programs, including residential treatment facilities for adolescent firesetters, such as the Brandon School and Residential Treatment Centre in Boston, USA, there are no arson/fire-specific group interventions available for young people in Australia. Youth justice agencies across Australia lack a research-informed, coordinated and consistent response to adolescent firesetting (Perks, 2019), and as such, fail to contribute systematically to a reduction in juvenile arson. Not only are there no culturally derived programs for First Nations juvenile firesetters in areas where these offences are prevalent, but there are no generic firesetter treatment programs imbedded in either the primary school educational systems or justice agencies, anywhere across Australia.

As noted by Bruner et al. (2016), "Aboriginal youth development has been mortgaged by multigenerational gaps in the transmission of Indigenous culture, language and identity" and in response, Hovane et al. (2014) argue that effective interventions with Indigenous offenders must adopt a holistic or ecological approach which reflects their cultural schemas and is derived from within their culture. An example of this approach would be to recognise that Indigenous people may not value self-disclosure, or an expression of emotion about their offending, which is often expected in non-Indigenous therapeutic settings as a prerequisite to change. Given the lack of specific research on Indigenous youth firesetting, it can only be hypothesised that these factors also impact adolescents and may contribute to their resistance to discussing their firesetting with others, or considering their feelings and motivations, and insecurities.

Recent evidence of the positive impact cultural engagement can have on reducing antisocial behaviours in Indigenous offenders was found by Shepherd et al. (2018). Incorporating cultural engagement as a protective factor has been shown to reduce violence risk or offending propensity and contribute to desistence. Cultural engagement in custody was also significantly associated with non-recidivism, and these authors argue for enhanced recognition of the therapeutic value of custodial cultural activities. More recently, Doery et al. (2023) found strong evidence for a positive association between cultural engagement and well-being when reviewing 25 studies focused on this relationship in adolescents. Juvenile justice agencies in Australia, where the focus tends to be on education rather than on rehabilitation, could learn from progress made in the adult space, where cultural engagement is more than a simple "add on" activity.

Studies arguing for distinct culture-driven platforms for offender programs, as opposed to the mainstream or generic programmatic foundations, highlight the disadvantages faced by Indigenous people who are required to complete generic programs in order to obtain release/parole. Interventions for First Nations youth firesetters would, therefore, need to be founded on the assessment and understanding of holistic SEWB, and cognizant of the cultural, historical, societal and political factors that may have impeded SEWB. It is suggested that disturbed SEWB is contributing to the formation of negative thoughts and feelings, and addressing this disturbance is likely to be a significant desistance strategy (Ellis-Smith, 2017). If this is true, then effective interventions for First Nations firesetters would be more focused on improving and maintaining the overall social and emotional well-being of the individual and their families and communities, rather than the current positivist and culture-light approach to intervention that tends to focus only on the individual or the specific function served by the behaviour.

Critics of conventional approaches to psychological interventions argue that programs designed to reduce illegal behaviour in Indigenous communities ought not focus solely on the risk-need-responsivity principles, or cognitive behavioural therapy (CBT) models addressing the thoughts, feelings and behaviours associated with the target behaviour (Andrews et al., 1990; Andrews & Bonta, 2010; Cunneen, 2011; Day, 2003). As Dudgeon and Kelly (2014) point out, CBT can only ever be part of the toolkit for interventions with Indigenous peoples, as it lacks cultural responsivity and "miserable thoughts may be entirely realistic for those caught in the poverty trap" (Bennett-Levy et al., 2010). Instead, psychological treatment programs must incorporate content relevant to Indigenous people (meaning, values and beliefs) within a multi-contextual environment, that includes reference to family, social, cultural and ecological responsibilities and obligations (Kilcullen et al., 2016; Kim et al., 2006) to maximise the therapeutic alliance and reduce program drop-out rates (DeSorcy et al., 2016).

Acceptance commitment therapy (ACT) is considered by Kilcullen et al. (2017) to be a more appropriate therapeutic framework when psychologists are working with Indigenous peoples, as this therapeutic approach emphasises acceptance of past and current circumstances, and the development of mindfulness strategies to enhance social and emotional wellbeing. ACT also provides opportunities to incorporate culturally relevant strategies, such as *punya*, and *dadirri*. *Punya* refers to a multidisciplinary and interdisciplinary approach to health and wellbeing from the Indigenous Ngaringman language and encompasses both person and country. It refers to being "strong, happy, knowledgeable, socially responsible, beautiful, clean and safe" (Atkinson, 2002, p. 44). *Dadirri* comes from the Ngangikurungkurr people of the Northern Territory, and means "inner, deep listening and quiet, still awareness" (West et al., 2012, p. 1584). Elders and community members interviewed also called for interventions that reunited Indigenous people with their culture, by incorporating cultural concepts.

The adoption of an Indigenous approach to psychological offender behaviour programs legitimises cultural knowledge so that new culturally grounded perspectives, concepts, theories and interventions can develop to maximise engagement and behavioural change (Marchetti, 2017; Hodgetts et al., 2010). By shifting the emphasis in treatment from a non-Indigenous therapist-centred or manual-driven approach, to a client-centred approach, treatment responses will evolve. Redirecting psychological responses to those areas identified by the individual offender will likely reduce the focus on problematic behaviours and individual deficits, and emphasise a strength-based approach, enhanced agency and self-control, and connection to family and community, all of which are consistent with the aims of treatment in contemporary rehabilitation literature (Kilcullen & Day, 2018; Trotter et al., 2015; Willis et al., 2012).

It is hoped that interventions that join together Indigenous schemas or views of the world, with relevant content, are likely to be more effective, and sustain behavioural change in Indigenous offenders. For firesetter treatment programs, this may mean that the schemas identified by Gannon et al. (2012) would not apply equally to Indigenous and non-Indigenous arsonists. Instead, programs developed to incorporate beliefs valued by Indigenous peoples, such as the importance of family and kinship structures, relationship obligations, reputation preservation, respect and reciprocity, and the centrality of Elders and children (Hovane et al., 2014), are likely to better address needs and reduce risk by maximising protective factors (Ferrante, 2012).

Despite calls for new therapeutic approaches to address Indigenous crime over recent years (Atkinson & Jones, 2005; Calma, 2008; Homel et al.,1999; Macklin & Gilbert, 2011; Mals et al., 2008), the evidence base supporting the efficacy of interventions purposively designed for culturally diverse groups is only just emerging

(Dolan et al., 2015; Murrup-Stewart et al., 2018). Using self-report questionnaires and psychometric scales, including one specifically designed to assess emotional empowerment in Indigenous people (the Growth and Empowerment Measure), Berry et al. (2012) found evidence that cultural components incorporated into a New South Wales substance abuse program enhanced participants' sense of wellbeing and self-efficacy.

Leske et al. (2016) also found support for culture-based interventions in their multi-national review of interventions for Indigenous adults with mental health and substance abuse problems. These authors evaluated outcomes for participants engaged in 16 interventions across Australia, New Zealand and the United States that had been adapted to incorporate culturally appropriate materials and processes and found reduced problem severity and enhanced self-efficacy for Indigenous participants (Leske et al., 2016).

While these studies point towards a developing evidence base for culturally driven interventions, arson research is hampered by a lack of culturally appropriate assessment tools to identify criminogenic treatment needs, and this represents an important area for future research. By taking a collectivist approach, paralleling the Indigenous worldview, arson treatment providers in this country can move forward in partnership with First Nations Australians. Lastly, as long as fire use by Indigenous Australians is viewed as separate to the cultural or socio-political context, and solely through a non-Indigenous legal or social lens, colonial discourse is likely to continue. This may lead to inappropriate labelling and perhaps misunderstanding the use and purpose of fire in Indigenous communities, giving rise to criminal charges, and poor treatment outcomes.

Strategies for Change

General risk assessments are commonly used in Australian forensic evaluations to identify the risk of further offending. This discussion has highlighted the unique factors impacting on the reoffending potential of First Nations young people who set fires, and as such, the need to develop culturally relevant risk assessment tools for this group is urged. Factors such as perceived and actual discrimination, intergenerational grief and loss, socio-economic disadvantage, and loss of cultural connections warrant further research to ascertain salience in arson offending within this group. As noted by Shepherd et al. (2016), culturally diverse groups have distinct risk and protective factors and "the identification of cultural risk markers is an essential process" (p. 264). This is also emphasised by Kendall et al. (2011), who note "to achieve culturally grounded knowledge requires that we stay informed of both the history and the present social, cultural, and political circumstances of those we hope to help" (p. 7).

Offending programs emphasising indigenous models, in conjunction with strength-based approaches such as the good lives model (Ward, 2002; Ward & Mann, 2004; Ward et al., 2007), positive youth development theory (Lerner et al., 2005) and acceptance and commitment therapy (ACT), are being endorsed across some Australian jurisdictions (Purvis et al., 2011). The good lives model prioritises social and emotional well-being (SEWB) or primary goods to emphasise the pursuit of goals and facilitate agency/autonomy. This approach to offender rehabilitation aligns well with standpoint theory and social and emotional well-being, as it focuses less on risk management and more on sustainable ways individuals can achieve prosocial goals and meaningful lives. Positive youth development theory also emphasises focusing on the strengths of young people, recognising developmental plasticity and enhancing psychosocial competence through positive community influence (Shek et al., 2019), and Bruner et al. (2016) report empowerment, connection to traditional culture, wellbeing and resiliency are important protective factors for Aboriginal youth.

Gibson et al. (2018) identify six dimensions that align SEWB within a strength-based approach to working with First Nations peoples, and these are: (a) listen respectfully to the person, (b) build genuine relationships, (c) use appropriate communications skills, (d) critically reflect on Australia's political, social and historical contexts, (e) apply a human-rights-based approach, and (f) evaluate the processes and outcomes. These strategies appear simplistic, but when unpacked, they involve considerable attention to the specific needs of Indigenous individuals. By structuring programs and interventions that directly match the needs of the target group, as opposed to generic alternatives, treatment gains can be maximised, and responsivity problems reduced for First Nations young people.

Strategies designed to enhance outcomes for Indigenous offenders have been collected over a number of years and have broad applicability for therapeutic programs (Ellis-Smith, 2016). These strategies are drawn from a range of sources reflecting good practice with Indigenous offenders, both young and old. While not firesetter program specific, they are general intervention strategies that emphasise sound cultural awareness, respect for potential responsivity barriers, and the recognition of an Indigenous standpoint:

- Awareness of acculturation/deculturation – deculturation describes the process where aspects of ones' culture are lost after contact with another more dominant culture. This can lead to acculturative stress or feelings of being marginalised, alienated or experiencing identity confusion, and this in turn can impact on therapeutic relationships and trust.
- Respect cultural paranoia – this is the fear of facing white racism and can be very real for First Nations young people.
- Understand the slow burn of intergenerational trauma from childhood – the child-rearing practices and early social learning experiences are often very different in Indigenous and non-Indigenous communities, and a tendency to view one better than the other has led to some practitioners taking a "deficit" approach to the therapeutic relationship, which is not helpful.
- Recognise a tendency for external attribution – this is often difficult for clinicians as they seek to have clients accept responsibility for their own behaviour, especially in a correctional offending behaviour program. The natural tendency is for some First Nations people to see themselves in context with their environment and their community, and it is common to attribute bad luck, ill health or negative circumstances to some external wrong doing.

- Allow time for engagement – assessment interviews conducted over several sessions are likely to yield more information and a better understanding of an Indigenous young person.
- Services and programs are also advised to be mindful of gender differences when working with clients. Research suggests that the greater the extent of cultural difference between a practitioner and a client – the less likelihood there will be successful engagement.
- Visual-spatial learning (See and Do) vs auditory – care with language and a focus on learning by watching and then doing is considered to be a better approach to skills acquisition for Indigenous peoples.
- Paraphrasing or reflective feedback disrupts the story – it is considered better to just listen, rather than interrupting or trying to translate.
- Side by side – this means no spotlighting or putting First Nations people on the spot with a direct question (particularly in a group situation). Doing so can often result in them feeling shamed. Questions need to be open-ended and encourage a narrative or a story.
- Vouching – if group facilitators are not Indigenous, it is appropriate to engage a local Elder to "vouch" for the facilitators, to introduce the program and motivate participants to contribute to their learning and insight development.
- Standpoint and assumptions – this refers to the clinician or program facilitators having recognised and thought through their assumptions or views about working with Indigenous clients. This assists insight and self-awareness and is based on standpoint theory. Co-facilitator reflexivity also provides opportunities for program facilitators to monitor and share any concerns or misunderstandings they may have while working with Indigenous clients.
- Avoidance relationships – prior to the commencement of treatment, a thorough analysis of avoidance relationships amongst group members is necessary to maximise group compatibility. Group participants who have incompatible relationships according to First Nations culture and family traditions should not be placed in the same group. If it emerges after a group has commenced that there are incompatible relationships in the group, then changes to the group mix are necessary. Group processes should include an early opportunity for participants to tell their stories (family history). This assists each participant to understand where their group colleagues are from and who they are.
- Acknowledge that there are differences across mobs of First Nations peoples and reflect the various perspectives on specific behaviours, such as the historical use of fire for cultural purposes and present-day use.
- Understand differences between those Indigenous youth who have been raised in a culturally rich environment and those who haven't – there is no shame in not having a language. Similarly, young people from the cities will have a different perspective on how they see their culture than those raised in more remote communities.
- Use of narratives or stories as tools to assist Indigenous group members to articulate their thoughts, feelings, and behaviours.

Justice Reinvestment and Elder Involvement

While the above strategies are designed for individual criminogenic interventions or programs, a broader systemic approach that guides government policy and funding, based on self-determination and community engagement, is also a necessary plank when establishing culturally sound and sustainable interventions. Recognition of the importance of community-led initiatives focused on justice reinvestment is emerging following funding by the Australian government in 2022. Justice reinvestment is "a way of working that shifts power and decision making to First Nations communities to self-determine the best way to improve justice outcomes in their community" (Justice Reinvestment Network Australia). It emphasises a place-based approach to problems, local community leadership, and collaboration across sectors and agencies. It aims to reduce the number of First Nations people coming into contact with the justice system at a young age, both juvenile and adult recidivism rates, and the failures of the interventionist approaches of the past. It is a long-term approach that invests in and supports community initiatives through leadership and capability, preventative programs, early intervention and rehabilitation and improvements to social and emotional wellbeing. Most importantly, this approach to youth crime emphasises the value of Elders and the importance of community solutions, which will, appropriately, look different across various communities.

In communities where adolescent firesetting is problematic, justice reinvestment would call upon community leaders to identify the precipitating factors and work with justice personnel to design interventions or responses to assist their youth in learning and reflecting on their offending. Understanding the impact of their behaviour on others and their wider community through the influence and guidance of local Elders can often be a very powerful way for young people to learn.

Conclusion

This discussion has attempted to outline the growing problem of juvenile firesetting in our community and provide a critique of current theory so that programs and treatments can be developed to reflect cultural relevance for First Nations youth. Whilst identifying the limits of existing theories and interventions for First Nations adolescent firesetters can highlight gaps, it is also important to recognise that detecting cultural blindness provides the opportunity for culturally appropriate responses to evolve. It is hoped that this chapter has pointed clearly to the importance of considering the historical and cultural context in which Indigenous youth offend, and that interventions go beyond addressing obvious criminogenic factors by bringing in Elders' perspectives, and Indigenist concepts such as social and emotional well-being, when developing treatment programs.

It is recommended that primary school providers consider educational programs for all students and that youth justice agencies implement culturally appropriate assessments and programs for those First Nations youth involved in setting illegal fires. Given the wealth of research on best practice interventions with First Nations young people, and the call for justice reinvestment applications by government, there is little justification for the absence of any response to this growing community problem. Adolescent firesetting is increasing and clinical failures that characterise the current juvenile detention, educational and community-based responses to adolescent firesetting can no longer be tolerated.

References

Aboriginal Corporation. (2019). *Cultural protocols*. Central Australian Aboriginal Congress.

Andrews, D. A., & Bonta, J. (2010). *The psychology of criminal conduct* (5th ed.). New Providence NJ: LexisNexis Group.

Andrews, D. A., Zinger, I., Hoge, R. D., Bonta, J., Gendreau, P., & Cullen, F. T. (1990). Does correctional treatment work? A psychologically informed meta-analysis. *Criminology*, 28, 369–404. https://doi.org/10.1111/j.1745-9125.1990.tb01330.x|

Anthony, T. (2013). *Indigenous people, crime and punishment*. Abingdon: Routledge.

Atkinson, G., & Jones, R. (2005). *An evaluation of the Koorie cognitive skills program pilots for Corrections Victoria*. http://www.healthinfonet.ecu.edu.au/key-resources/bibliography/?lid=20601

Atkinson, J. (2002). *Trauma trials, recreating song lines: The transgenerational effects of trauma in indigenous Australia*. Melbourne: Spinifex Press.

Australian Bureau of Statistics. (2021). *Estimates of Aboriginal and Torres Strait islander Australians*. https://www.abs.gov.au/statistics/people/aboriginal-and-torres-strait-islander-peoples/estimates-aboriginal-and-torres-strait-islander-australians/30-june-2021

Australian Bureau of Statistics. (2023). *Prisoners in Australia*. https://www.abs.gov.au/statistics/people/crime-and-justice/prisoners-australia/latest-release

Australian Indigenous HealthInfoNet. (2017). *Overview of Aboriginal and Torres Strait islander health status*. http://www.healthinfonet.ecu.edu.au/health-facts/overviews

Australian Institute of Health and Welfare. (2023). *Youth justice*. https://www.aihw.gov.au/reports/australias-welfare/youth-justice

Bennett-Levy, J., Richards, D., & Farrand, P. (2010). Low intensity CBT interventions: A revolution in mental health care. In J. Bennett-Levy, D. Richards, & P. Farrand (Eds.), *The Oxford guide to low intensity CBT interventions*. Oxford: Oxford University Press.

Berry, S. L., Crowe, T. P., Deane, F. P., Billingham, M., & Bhagerutty, Y. (2012). Growth and empowerment for indigenous Australians in substance use treatment. *International Journal of Mental health Addiction*, 10, 970–983. https://doi.org/10.1007/s11469-012-9393-2

Blagg, H. (2008). *Crime, aboriginality and the decolonisation of justice*. Sydney: Hawkins Press.

Bruner, M.W., Hillier, S., Baillie, C. P. T., Lavallee, L. F., Bruner, B. G., Hare, K., Lovelace, R., & Lévesque, L. (2016). Positive youth development in aboriginal physical activity and sport: A systematic review. *Adolescent Research Review*, 1, 257–269.

Bureau of Crime Statistics and Research. (2023). https://www.bocsar.nsw.gov.au/Pages/bocsar_pages/Aboriginal-over-representation.aspx

Calma, T. (2008). *Preventing crime and promoting rights for indigenous young people with cognitive disabilities and mental health issues*. Canberra: Australian Human Rights Commission.

Canter, D., & Fritzon, K. (1998). Differentiating arsonists: A model of firesetting actions and characteristics. *Legal and Criminological Psychology*, 3, 73–96. https://doi.org/10.1111/j.2044-8333.1998.tb00352.x

Crime and Misconduct Commission. (2009). *Restoring order: Crime prevention, policing and local justice in Queensland's indigenous communities*. Brisbane: Crime and Misconduct Commission. https://www.ncjrs.gov/App/AbstractDB/AbstractDBDetails.aspx?id=251154

Cunneen, C. (2011). Indigeneity, sovereignty and the law: Challenging the processes of criminalisation. *South Atlantic Quarterly*, 110(2), 309–328. https://doi.org/10.1215/00382876-1162471

Danaher, P. A. (2011). Indigenous population mobilities and school achievement: International educational research itineraries, issues and implications. *International Journal of Educational Research*, 54, 1–8. https://doi.org/10.1016/j.ijer.2011.11.001

Day, A. (2003). Reducing the risk of re-offending in Australian indigenous offenders: What works for whom? *Journal of Offender Rehabilitation*, 37(2), 1–15. https://doi.org/10.1300/J076v37n02_01

Day, A., Davey, L., Wanganeen, R., Casey, S., Howells, K., & Nakata, M. (2008). Symptoms of trauma, perceptions of discrimination and anger: A comparison between Australian indigenous and non-indigenous prisoners. *Journal of Interpersonal Violence*, 23(2), 245–258. https://doi.org/10.1177/0886260507309343

DeSorcy, D. R., Olver, M. E., & Wormith, J. S. (2016). Working alliance and its relationship with treatment outcome in a sample of aboriginal and non-aboriginal sexual offenders. *Sexual Abuse: A Journal of Research and Treatment*, 28(4), 291–313.

Dingwell, K. M., & Cairney, S. (2010). Psychological and cognitive assessment of indigenous Australians. *Australian and New Zealand Journal of Psychiatry*, 44, 20–30. https://doi.org/10.3109/00048670903393670

Dingwell, K. M., Lindeman, M. A., & Cairney, S. (2014). You've got to make it relevant: Barriers and ways forward for assessing cognition in aboriginal clients. *BMC Psychology*, 2(13), 1–11. https://doi.org/10.1186/2050-7283-2-13

Doery, E., Satyen, L., Paradies, Y., & Toumbourou, J. W. (2023). The relationship between cultural engagement and psychological well-being among indigenous adolescents: A systematic review. *Journal of Cross-Cultural Psychology*, 54(1), 90–113. https://doi.org/10.1177/00220221221128215

Dolan, K., Rodas, A., & Bode, A. (2015). Drug and alcohol use and treatment for Australian indigenous and non-indigenous prisoners: Demand reduction strategies. *International Journal of Prisoner Health*, 11(1), 30–38. https://search.proquest.com/docview/1661340992?accountid=26503

Dudgeon, P., & Kelly, K. (2014). Contextual factors for research on psychological therapies for aboriginal Australians. *Australian Psychologist*, 49, 8–13. https://doi.org/10.1111/ap.12030

Ellis-Smith, T. (2016, October). *Interventions for indigenous offenders. Closing the prison gap: Building cultural resilience*. Conference Presentation, Kingscliff, New South Wales.

Ellis-Smith, T. (2017). Firesetters: A review of theory, facts and treatment. In W. Petherick & G. Sinnamon (Eds.), *The psychology of criminal and antisocial behaviour.* London: Academic Press. https://doi.org/10.1016/B978-0-12-809287-3.00019-5

Ellis-Smith, T. (2020). *Australian arsonists: A typology, offending and sentencing trends, and theoretical adjustments for an indigenous cultural context* (Doctoral Thesis). Bond University.

Ellis-Smith, T., Watt, B., & Doley, R. M. (2019). Australian arsonists: An analysis of trends between 1990 and 2015. *Psychiatry, Psychology and Law*, 26(4). https://doi.org/10.1080/13218719.2018.1556131

Evans, R., Cronin, K., & Saunders, K. (1988). *Race relations in colonial Queensland: A history of exclusion, exploitation, and extermination.* St. Lucia, Australia: University of Queensland Press.

Ferrante, A. M. (2012). Assessing the influence of "standard" and "culturally specific" risk factors on the prevalence and frequency of offending: The case of indigenous Australians. *Race and Justice*, 3(1), 58–82. https://doi.org/10.1177/2153368712462410

Finnane, M., & Richards, J. (2010). Aboriginal Violence and State Response: Histories, Policies and Legacies in Queensland 1860–1940. *The Australian and New Zealand Journal of Criminology*, 43(2), 238–262. https://doi.org/10.1375%2Facri.43.2.238

Gannon, T. A., Ó Ciardha, C., Doley, R. M., & Alleyne, E. (2012). The multi-trajectory theory of adult firesetting (M-TTAF). Aggression and Violent Behaviour, 17(2), 107–121. https://doi.org/10.1016/j.avb.2011.08.001

Gee, G., Dudgeon, P., Schultz, C., Hart, A., & Kelly, K. (2014). Social and emotional well-being and mental health. In P. Dudgeon, R. Walker, & H. Milroy (Eds.), *Working together. Aboriginal and Torres Strait islander mental health and wellbeing principles and practice* (2nd ed., pp. 55–68). Canberra: Department of Prime Minister and Cabinet.

Gibson, C., Crocket, J., Dudgeon, P., Bernoth, M., & Lincoln, M. (2018). Sharing and valuing older aboriginal people's voices about social and emotional wellbeing services: A strength-based approach for service providers. *Aging and Mental Health*. Advance online publication. https://doi.org/10.1080/13607863.2018.1544220

Griffiths, K., Coleman, C., Lee, V., & Madden, R. (2016). How colonisation determines social justice and indigenous health: A review of the literature. *Journal of Population Research*, 33(1) 9–30. https://link.springer.com/article/10.1007/s12546-016-9164-1

Hodgetts, D., Drew, N., Sonn, C., Stolte, O., Nikora, W., & Curtis, C. (2010). *Social psychology and everyday life*. Hampshire, UK: Palgrave MacMillan.

Holland, C. (2015). *The close the gap campaign: Progress and priorities report 2015*. The Close the Gap Steering Committee. Paragon Australasia Group.

Homel, R., Lincoln, R., & Herd, B. (1999). Risk and resilience: Crime and violence prevention in aboriginal communities. *Australian and New Zealand Journal of Criminology*, 32, 182–196. https://doi.org/10.1177/000486589903200207

Hovane, V., Jones, T., & Smith, P. (2014). Aboriginal offender rehabilitation programs. In P. Dudgeon, R. Walker, & H. Milroy (Eds.), *Working together Aboriginal and Torres Strait islander mental health and wellbeing principles and practice* (2nd ed.). Canberra: Department of Prime Minister and Cabinet.

Intergovernmental Committee on Drugs. (2014). *National Aboriginal and Torres Strait islander people's drug strategy 2014–2019*. Canberra. http://www.nationaldrugstrategy.gov.au/internet/drugstrategy/Publishing.nsf/content/6EE311AA9F620C82CA257E-AC0006A8F0/$File/FINAL%20National%20Aboriginal%20and%20Torres%20Strait%20Islander%20Peoples'%20Drug%20Strategy%202014-2019.pdf

Jacobs, L. A., Ashcraft, L. E., Sewall, C. J., Folb, B. L., & Mair, C. (2020). Ecologies of juvenile reoffending: A systematic review of risk factors. *Journal of Criminal Justice*, 66. https://doi.org/10.1016/j.jcrimjus.2019.101638

Jorm, A. F., Bourchier, S. J., Cvetkovski, S., & Stewart, G. (2012). Mental health of indigenous Australians: A review of findings from community surveys. *The Medical Journal of Australia*, 196(2), 118–121. https://doi.org/10.5694/mja11.10041

Justice Reinvestment Network Australia. https://justicereinvestment.net.au

Kendall, E., Sunderland, N., Barnett, L., Nalder, G., & Matthews, C. (2011). Beyond the rhetoric of participatory research in indigenous communities: Advances in Australia over the last decade. *Qualitative Health Research*, 21(12), 1719–1728. https://doi.org/10.1177/1049732311418124

Kilcullen, M., & Day, A. (2018). Culturally informed case conceptualisation: Developing a clinical psychology approach to treatment planning for non-indigenous psychologists working with Aboriginal and Torres Strait islander clients. *Clinical Psychologist*, 22, 280–289. https://doi.org/10.1111/cp.12141

Kilcullen, M., Swinbourne, A., & Cadet-James, Y. (2016). Aboriginal and Torres Strait islander health and well-being: Implications for a cognitive behavioural therapy framework. *Australian Psychologist*, 51, 453–462. https://doi.org/10.1111/ap.12159

Kilcullen, M., Swinbourne, A., & Cadet-James, Y. (2017). Aboriginal and Torres Strait islander health and wellbeing: Social emotional wellbeing and strengths-based psychology. *Clinical Psychologist*, 22(1), 16–26. https://doi.org/10.1111/cp.12112

Kim, U., Yang, K., & Hwang, K. (2006). Contributions to indigenous and cultural psychology: Understanding people in context. In U. Kim, K. Yang, & K. Hwang (Eds.), *Indigenous and cultural psychology: Understanding people in context*. New York: Springer Science & Business Media.

Kingsley, J., Townsend, M., Henderson-Wilson, C., & Bolam, B. (2013). Developing an exploratory framework linking Australian aboriginal peoples' connection to country and concepts of wellbeing. *International Journal of Environmental Research and Public Health*, 10(2), 678–698. https://doi.org/10.3390/ijerph10020678

Lambie, I., & Randell, I. (2011). Creating a firestorm: A review of children who deliberately light fires. *Clinical Psychology Review*, 31(3), 307–327. https://doi.org/10.1016/j.cpr.2010.12.010

Lerner, R. M., Lerner, J. V., Almerigi, J. B., Theokas, C., Phelps, E., Gestsdottir, S., & von Eye, A. (2005). Positive youth development, participation in community youth development programs, and community contributions of fifth-grade adolescents: Findings from the first wave of the 4-H study of positive youth development. *The Journal of Early Adolescence*, 25(1), 17–71. https://doi.org/10.1177/0272431604272461

Leske, S., Harris, M. G., Charlson, F. J., Ferrari, A. J., Baxter, A. J., Logan, J. M., Toombs, M., & Whitefors, H. (2016). Systematic review of interventions for indigenous adults with mental and substance use disorders in Australia, Canada, New Zealand and the United States. *Australian and New Zealand Journal of Psychiatry*, 50(11), 1040–1054. https://doi.org/10.1177/0004867416662150

MacGillivray, P., & Baldry, E. (2015). Australian indigenous women's offending patterns. *Indigenous Justice Clearing House*, 19. https://www.indigenousjustice.gov.au/wp-content/uploads/mp/files/publications/files/brief019.pdf

Macklin, A., & Gilbert, R. (2011). Working with indigenous offenders to end violence. *Indigenous Justice Clearinghouse, Brief 11*, 1–8. https://www.indigenousjustice.gov.au/wpcontent/uploads/mp/files/publications/files/brief011.v2.pdf

Mals, P., Howells, K., Day, A., & Hall, G. (2008). Adapting violence rehabilitation programs for the Australian aboriginal offender. *Journal of Offender Rehabilitation*, 30, 121–153. https://doi.org/10.1300/J076v30n01_08

Marchetti, E. (2017). Nothing works? A meta-review of indigenous sentencing court evaluations. *Current Issues in Criminal Justice*, 28(3), 257–276. https://doi.org/10.1080/10345329.2017.12036074

Marshall, J. (2008). *Juvenile offending trajectories: A South Australian study*. Adelaide: Department of Justice.

McCausland, R., & Vivian, A. (2010). Why do some aboriginal communities have lower crime rates than others? A pilot study. *Australian & New Zealand Journal of Criminology*, 43(2), 301–332. https://doi.org/10.1375/acri.43.2.301

Mellor, D. (2004). Responses to racism: A taxonomy of coping styles used by aboriginal Australians. *American Journal of Orthopsychiatry*, 74(1), 56–71. https://doi.org/10.1037/00029432.74.1.56

Moreton-Robinson, A. (2004). Whiteness, epistemology and indigenous representation. In A. Moreton-Robinson (Ed.), *Whitening race: Essays in Social and Cultural Criticism*. Canberra: Aboriginal Studies Press.

Muller, D. A. (2008). *Offending and reoffending patterns of arsonists and bushfire arsonists in New South Wales*. Trends and issues no. 348. Canberra: Australian Institute of Criminology.

Muller, D., & Stebbins, A. (2008). *Offending and reoffending patterns of arsonists and bushfire arsonists in New South Wales* (1921185627). Australian Institute of Criminology Canberra.

Murrup-Stewart, C., Searle, A. K., Jobson, L., & Adams, K. (2018). Aboriginal perceptions of social and emotional wellbeing programs: A systematic review of literature assessing social and emotional wellbeing programs for Aboriginal and Torres Strait islander Australians perspective. *Australian Psychologist*, 0(0). https://doi-org.ezproxy.bond.edu.au/10.1111/ap.12367

Nakata, M. (2007). The cultural interface. *The Australian Journal of Indigenous Education*, 36(S1), 7–14. https://doi.org/10.1017/S1326011100004646Nakata
Parke, E. (2019). The Christian converts who are setting fire to sacred aboriginal objects. *ABC News*. https://www.abc.net.au/news/2019-09-20/the-christian-converts-who-are-setting-fire-to-sacred-aboriginal/11527402?utm_campaign=abc_news_web&utm_content=link&utm_medium=content_shared&utm_source=abc_news_web
Parker, R., & Milroy, H. (2014). Mental illness in Aboriginal and Torres Strait islander peoples. In P. Dudgeon, H. Milroy, & R. Walker (Eds.), *Working together: Aboriginal and Torres Strait islander mental health and wellbeing principles and practice*. Canberra: Commonwealth of Australia.
Perks, D. L. C. (2019). *The functional consistency of proximal dynamic risk factors across co-occurring behavioural problems: Do juvenile arsonists and general offenders differ?* (Doctoral Thesis). Bond University. https://research.bond.edu.au/en/studentTheses/the-functional-consistency-of-proximal-dynamic-risk-factors-acros
Perks, D. L. C., Watt, B. D., Fritzon, K., & Doley, R. M. (2019). Juvenile firesetters as multiple problem youth with particular interests in fire: A meta-analysis. *Aggression and Violent Behaviour*, 47, 189–203. https://doi.org/10.1016/j.avb.2019.04.003
Prior, D. (2007). Decolonising research: A shift toward reconciliation. *Nursing Inquiry*, 14(2), 162–168. https://doi.org/10.1111/j.1440-1800.2007.00361.x
Purvis, M., Ward, T., & Willis, G. (2011). The good lives model in practice: Offence pathways and case management. *European Journal of Probation*, 3(2), 4–28. https://doi.org/10.1177/206622031100300202
Putt, J., Payne, J., & Milner, L. (2005). *Indigenous male offending and substance abuse*. Trends & issues in crime and criminal justice no. 293. Canberra: Australian Institute of Criminology. https://www.aic.gov.au/publications/tandi/tandi293
Queensland Corrective Services, Department of Justice and Attorney General. (2015). Retrieved from www.correctiveservices.qld.gov.au.
Ryan, L., Debenham, J., Brown, M., Pascoe, W., & Smith, R. (2022). *Colonial Frontier Massacres in Australia, 1788–1930*. https://doi.org/10.26193/L0WEID, ADA Dataverse, V1 Australian Data Archive.
Schwartz, M. (2010). Building communities, not just prisons: Justice reinvestment and indigenous over-imprisonment. *Australian Indigenous Law Review*, 14(1), 2–17. http://www.austlii.edu.au/au/journals/AILRev/2010/1.pdf
Seidler, K. (2010). *Crime, culture & violence: Understanding how masculinity and identity shapes offending*. Bowen Hills: Australian Academic Press.
Shek, D. T., Dou, D., Zhu, X., & Chai, W. (2019). Positive youth development: Current perspectives. *Adolescent Health, Medicine and Therapeutics*, 10, 131–141. https://doi.org/10.2147/AHMT.S179946
Shepherd, S. M., Delgardo, R. H., Sherwood, J., & Paradies, Y. (2018). The impact of indigenous cultural identity and cultural engagement on violent offending. *BMC Public Health*, 18(50). https://doi.org/10.1186/s12889-017-4603-2
Shepherd, S. M., Ogloff, J. R. P., & Thomas, S. D. M. (2016). Are Australian prisons meeting the needs of indigenous offenders? *Health and Justice*, 4(13), 1–9. https://doi.org/10.1186/s40 352-016-0045-7
Shepherd, S. M., Ogloff, J. R. P., Paradies, Y., & Pfeifer, J. (2017). *Aboriginal prisoners with cognitive impairment: Is this the highest risk group?* Trends and issues no. 536. Canberra; Australian Institute of Criminology. https://aic.gov.au/publications/tandi/tandi536
Silburn, S., Robinson, G., Leckning, B., Henry, D., Cox, A., & Kickett, D. (2014). Preventing suicide among aboriginal Australians. In P. Dudgeon, H. Milroy, & R. Walker (Eds.), *Working together: Aboriginal and Torres Strait islander mental health and wellbeing principles and practice*. Canberra: Commonwealth of Australia.
Social Health Reference Group. (2004). *Social and emotional well being framework: A national strategic framework for Aboriginal and Torres Strait islander mental health and social and emotional well being 2004–2009*. Canberra: Australian Government.

Trotter, C., Baidawi, S., & Evans, P. (2015). Good practice in community-based supervision of aboriginal youth offenders. *Australian Social Work*, 68(1), 5–18. 10.1080/0312407X.2014.940359

Tuhiwai Smith, L. (2012). *Decolonizing methodologies: Research and indigenous peoples*. London: Zed Books.

Vickery, J., Faulkhead, S., Adams, K., & Clarke, A. (2007). Indigenous insights into oral history, social determinants and decolonisation. In I. Anderson, F. Baum, & M. Bentley (Eds.), *Beyond bandaids: Exploring underlying determinants of aboriginal health*. Darwin: Co-operative Research Centre for Aboriginal Health.

Vos, T., Barker, B., Begg, S., Stanley, L., & Lopez, A. D. (2009). Burden of disease and injury in Aboriginal and Torres Strait islander peoples: The indigenous health gap. *International Journal of Epidemiology*, 38(2), 470–477. https://doi.org/10.1093/ije/dyn240

Wanganeen, R. (2014). Seven phases to integrating loss and grief. In P. Dudgeon, H. Milroy, & R. Walker (Eds.), *Working together: Aboriginal and Torres Strait islander mental health and wellbeing principles and practice*. Canberra: Commonwealth of Australia.

Ward, T. (2002). Good lives and the rehabilitation of offenders: Promises and problems. *Aggression and Violent Behavior*, 7, 513–528. https://doi.org/10.1016/S1359-1789(01)00076-3

Ward, T., & Mann, R. (2004). Good lives and the rehabilitation of offenders: A positive approach to treatment. In A. Linley & S. Joseph (Eds.), *Positive psychology in practice* (pp. 598–616). New York, NY: John Wiley.

Ward, T., Mann, R. E., & Gannon, T. A. (2007). The good lives model of offender rehabilitation: Clinical implications. *Aggression and Violent Behavior*, 12, 87–107. https://doi.org/10.1016/j.avb.2006.03.004

Weatherburn, D. (2014). *Arresting incarceration: Pathways out of indigenous imprisonment*. Canberra: Aboriginal Studies Press.

West, R., Stewart, L., Foster, K., & Usher, K. (2012). Through a critical lens: Indigenist research and the dadirri method. *Qualitative Health Research*, 22(11), 1582–1590. https://doi.org/10.1177/1049732312457596

Willis, G. M., Yates, P. M., Gannon, T. A., & Ward, T. (2012). How to integrate the good lives model into treatment programs for sexual offending: An introduction and overview. *Sexual Abuse*, 25(2), 123–142. https://doi.org/10.1177/1079063212452618

Wundersitz, J. (2010). *Indigenous perpetrators of violence: Prevalence and risk factors for offending*. Research and public policy series no. 105. Canberra: Australian Institute of Criminology. https://search.informit.com.au/fullText;dn=613237959283630;res=IELHSS

Year Book Australia 2008. (2008). Australian Bureau of Statistics. https://www.abs.gov.au/AUSSTATS/abs@.nsf/Lookup/1301.0Main+Features12008?OpenDocument

Zubrick, S. R., Shepherd, C. C. J., Dudgeon, P., Gee, G., Paradies, Y., Scrine, C., & Walker, R. (2014). Social determinants of social and emotional wellbeing. In P. Dudgeon, H. Milroy, R. Walker (Eds.), *Working together: Aboriginal and Torres Strait islander mental health and wellbeing principles and practice* (2nd ed., pp. 93–112). Canberra: Australian Government Department of the Prime Minister and Cabinet.

8 The Gendered Pathways of Justice-Involved Girls in Australia and Aotearoa New Zealand

Lorana Bartels, Sharynne Hamilton, and Raewyn Mutch

Key objectives:

- Highlights the gendered pathways of girls in youth justice systems in Australia and **Aotearoa/New Zealand**.
- These pathways are characterised by trauma, child protection contact, poverty, discrimination and mental health issues.
- Indigenous children and families experience higher rates of justice and other state system contact, as an ongoing legacy of colonisation.
- We present examples of gender-positive pathways, with a focus on recent developments in Hawaii.

Introduction

Most adults, children and young people held in criminal justice systems in Australia and Aotearoa/New Zealand (NZ) have experienced significant disadvantage across the lifespan, including childhood trauma (Marr et al., 2023); contact with state child protection systems (Baidawi & Ball, 2023; Hamilton S. L. et al., 2020; Malvaso et al., 2017; Mutch et al., 2022; Vidal et al., 2017); poverty and discrimination (Shepherd, 2016), often arising from intergenerational and intersectional harms seeded at colonisation, including discrimination based on race, gender, sexual preferences, and/or disability (Gueta, 2020); and mental health problems (Dale et al., 2023; Marr et al., 2023; Yee et al., 2023). People in the justice system are also more likely than the general population to have lived experiences of inequitable and harmful economic and social exclusions (see Borschmann et al., 2020; Shepherd, 2016; Kinner & Young, 2018), as well as living with consequences of such adversities, including chronic psychosocial and physical morbidities (Linnane et al., 2023; Mutch et al., 2022), cognitive impairments and neurodevelopmental disabilities (Bower et al., 2018; Hamilton S. et al., 2020; McCausland & Baldry, 2023; Mutch et al., 2022); trauma and mental health conditions (Dale et al., 2023; Marr et al., 2023; Yee et al., 2023); and morbidities and social exclusion related to past or current alcohol and other drug use (Doyle et al., 2023), early school disengagement,

DOI: 10.4324/9781003298410-13

low levels of social capital, and restricted opportunities for employment that for many result in poor economic and life outcomes (Hamilton S. L. et al., 2020).

This chapter examines the issues that arise in relation to girls[1] involved in youth justice (YJ) systems, focusing on the Australian and Aotearoa/NZ contexts, with particular attention to Indigenous peoples.[2] Our discussion is underpinned by the need for a gender-responsive approach, which is trauma-informed and considers girls' gendered "pathways" into, through and away from the justice system (Gobeil et al., 2016). As will be seen, although the common experiences of justice-involved girls in Australia and Aotearoa/NZ reinforce the need for gender-responsive approaches, there is often little attention paid to them. Instead, a punitive model prevails that retraumatises girls already subjected to racial, patriarchal, and other structural systems of oppression and extortion. This punitive model amplifies the negative impacts of unmet and specific needs arising from embodied harms common to girls subject to YJ systems. We call for a restorative, comprehensive, holistic health response, within a strengths-based approach, which recognises that criminalised girls have unmet health and wellbeing needs, as well as the skills and strengths for their healing and transformation, which is both "quintessential to gender-responsive programming and is a distinct approach to correctional programming" (Fedock & Covington, 2022, p. 7). We also provide examples of this in practice.

Background

Over 200 years have passed since colonisation commenced in Australia and Aotearoa/NZ. Colonisation has brought with it a range of destructive elements, from invasion wars, massacres, poisonings, removal of children from families, and removal of entire communities from their homelands, often into imprisonment or slavery. The negative effects have reverberated across generations of Indigenous families and communities and continue to perpetrate harm, through settler-colonial institutions and laws, which continue to be imposed on Indigenous peoples. This has contributed to over-representations in criminal justice and child protection systems in both Aotearoa/NZ and in Australia (Cunneen & Tauri, 2019; Kaiwai et al., 2020). In light of this, the absence of Indigenous philosophies in mainstream global justice theorising is problematic (Watene, 2020).

Australian and Aotearoa/NZ imprisonment profiles are similar to the global profile of Western colonised countries, with evidence of discrimination based on race, gender, and disability both influencing and impacting the intergenerational transmission of trauma and inequality in society (United Nations, 2009; McCausland & Baldry, 2023; Porter & Cunneen, 2021).

In both countries, responses to criminal activity are organised, distributed, and justified, politically and socially, and delivered through a range of often punitive measures, including policing, courts, community-based interventions, and incarceration. Those most affected by these measures are likely to be already marginalised or have experienced multiple levels of marginalisation and disadvantage. Indigenous peoples are overrepresented at all junctions of their respective criminal justice system, from arrest to imprisonment (Australian Bureau of Statistics (ABS), 2024; Australian Institute of Health and Welfare (AIHW), 2023; McCausland & Baldry, 2023; New Zealand Ministry of Justice, 2019).

The harm incurred by Indigenous peoples in Australia and Aotearoa/NZ from colonisation and associated policies of forced removal from kin and country and the desecration of culture and language are well-established (Paradies, 2016; Holland et al., 2023; Fogarty et al., 2018; Hamilton et al., 2021). Criminal justice issues in both countries cannot be discussed without consideration of this history, and the complex intersections common to both countries' child protection and youth justice systems, and this is of particular concern for Indigenous people. For Indigenous families in both Australia and Aotearoa/NZ, there are much greater rates of contact with state child protection systems and "dual system" (i.e. child protection and YJ) contact (Baidawi & Ball, 2023). Aboriginal and Torres Strait Islander peoples experience child protection involvement at over 10 times the rate of their non-Aboriginal counterparts (AIHW, 2024), and this is over 15 times higher for YJ involvement (AIHW, 2023). Indigenous children involved with these dual systems experience poorer outcomes across their lifetimes than their non-Indigenous peers, for example, more convictions (Malvaso et al., 2017).

In Aotearoa/NZ, recent figures show that 92% of children (aged 10–13 years) and 88% of young people (aged 14–18) with youth justice involvement had previous notifications to Oranga Tamariki (NZ government agency responsible for the wellbeing of children and young people) (New Zealand Ministry of Justice, 2023). Concerningly, at the time of writing, the current NZ Government was actively trying to extinguish pivotal aspects of Te Tiriti o Waitangi (The Treaty of Waitangi), in full knowledge that such action would seed new and entrench existing harms to Māori tamariki (children), as well as to their whānau (extended family), hapū (community), and Iwi (tribe).

It is well-established that being male, from an ethnic or racial minority, and from a low socio-economic background, as well as poverty and early childhood maltreatment-related factors, like abuse and neglect, are prevalent in families involved with child protection services (Baidawi & Ball, 2023; Hamilton & Maslen, 2022). Children involved with these "dual systems" (Baidawi & Ball, 2023) have additional factors to consider, including trauma resulting from removal and placement instability, which can also affect education and health services, as well as a range of behavioural and mental health conditions (Baidawi & Ball, 2023; Herz et al., 2019; Hurren et al., 2017; Malvaso et al., 2017; Vidal et al., 2017).

Australian and Aotearoa/NZ Youth Justice

There are deep-rooted issues for children and young people entering the YJ systems. They have often endured physical, sexual and or emotional abuse and constant transience. Detained children and young people have also been found to have chronic sleep difficulties, including delayed onset of sleep and poor sleep quality, aggravated by mental health conditions (Mutch et al., 2022); early-onset of social difficulties and lived trauma (Hafekost et al., 2017; Indig et al., 2016; Hamilton S. L. et al.,

2020; Mutch et al., 2022); and trouble with self-regulation, attention, comprehension and communication (Mutch et al., 2022). They are commonly suspended or expelled from school and disengage from school early and engage in problematic substance use (Hamilton S. L. et al., 2020; Marr et al., 2023; Mutch et al., 2022 Hamilton et al., 2019). Children and young people in custody are also highly likely to be living with mental health and behavioural disorders, often undiagnosed, as well as suicidal ideation and self-harm (Bickel & Campbell, 2002; Marr et al., 2023; Mutch et al., 2022; Putniņš, 2005; Wasserman et al., 2005). Moreover, neurodisability is clearly understood as a risk factor for involvement in criminal activity and the criminal justice system (Bower et al., 2018; Houston & Butler, 2019). Justice-involved children and youth have been reported to have high rates of undiagnosed and unrecognised neurodevelopmental disabilities including fetal alcohol spectrum disorder, autism, attention deficit hyperactivity disorder (ADHD) and traumatic or acquired brain injuries (Bower et al., 2018; Leonard, 2016; Mutch et al., 2022; Sotiri & Simpson, 2006). Neurodisabilities can negatively impact on every aspect of a child's interaction with the youth justice systems, from arrest to imprisonment.

Youth crime has generally been falling in Australia in recent years (see ABS, 2024), despite an alleged "youth crime wave" (Goldsworthy et al., 2023). According to the most recent data from the AIHW (2023), there were about 689 young people aged 10–17 in youth detention on an average night in the June 2023 quarter (there were also an average of 42 detainees aged over 18, serving the remainder of their sentence). Of those aged 10–17 in detention, 78 (11.3%) were female. Aboriginal and Torres Strait Islander young people represent 5% of the relevant population in Australia, but 53% of the youth detention population (AIHW, 2023). Aboriginal and Torres Strait Islander girls were even more overrepresented than their male counterparts (accounting for 65% vs 52% of the respective population). Girls, especially Aboriginal and Torres Strait Islander girls, accounted for a relatively larger proportion of the younger cohort in youth detention (aged 10–13).

The use of remand is high, especially after several jurisdictions have made it more difficult for young people to obtain bail (for discussion, see, e.g. Bartels, 2022). In the March 2023 quarter, 83% of young people aged 10–17 in detention were unsentenced and this rose to 87% for girls (AIHW, 2023). Disaggregated by gender and Aboriginal status, it emerged that 90% of non-Aboriginal girls were on remand, as were 86% Aboriginal girls, compared with 83% of Aboriginal boys and 82% of non-Aboriginal boys (AIHW, 2023).

Offending by children aged 10–13 years in Aotearoa/NZ from 2010 to 2013 had dropped for both genders, across all ethnic groups and ages, across almost all offence types, and in all regions. An estimated 1 in 20 Aotearoa/NZ children were known to Police for offending before reaching 14 years of age. Boys are twice as likely as girls to offend as children. In 2013, Māori tamariki were approximately three times more likely than non-Māori children to become known to the Police as an offender by 14 years of age (New Zealand Ministry of Social Development, 2024). Data from Aotearoa/NZ (New Zealand Ministry of Justice, 2024) in 2023/2024 reveal that females accounted for 20% of matters finalised in the Youth Court, and 60% of these were Māori, with a further 6% identifying as Pacific

Islander (as of June 2023, Aotearoa/NZ's estimated Māori population was 17 of the total national population). However, the proportion of Māori girls in Youth Court has been falling in recent years, down from 65% and 64% in 2020/2021 and 2021/2022, respectively.

The total daily custody numbers averaged 161 in early March 2020 to an average of 175 in April 2023. Across 2022/2023, there were 949 children and young people in custody, the highest recorded since 2016/2017. In September 2024, 89% of adolescents remanded in youth justice custody were Māori youth, who also accounted for 81% of all adolescents in custody each day. As most young people in custody are on remand, this is also likely to apply to girls, but the overall numbers are small, ranging from three to 22 and averaging 14 over the last seven years (Oranga Tamariki, 2024). Accordingly, further disaggregation by gender and legal status is not possible.

There are several differences between girls' and boys' experiences of the YJ and related systems. For example, Silva et al. (2014) found that boys with ADHD were two-and-a-half times more likely to have a community correction or incarceration record than their non-ADHD peers. However, girls with ADHD were nearly three times and seven times, respectively, more likely to have a community correction record and/or incarceration record. Unfortunately, the authors did not reflect on these gender differences or their implications. It is also worth noting that the children in this study were being treated with stimulants for ADHD, whereas many people with this condition are undiagnosed and untreated. Crucially, girls (and women) are less likely to be diagnosed with ADHD, even when they experience serious impairment, including increased risk of self-harm (Hinshaw et al., 2022). Even with a pre-existing neurodiverse diagnosis, such as ADHD, and a pre-existing and registered stimulant prescription, there may be failure to continue this medication, once a child or adolescent is engaged in YJ services. One of the authors (RM) was told by a medical practitioner employed in the Australian YJ system that their reasoning to discontinue stimulant medication for detained children and young people was that "stimulant medication did not prevent them from getting into trouble and coming into detention, so there's no point continuing the medication while they are here".

Gendered Pathways to Youth Justice for Girls

A recent study published by the Australian Institute of Criminology (Baidawi et al., 2024) found that girls comprised a greater proportion of young people aged 10–13 proceeded against by police, compared with those aged 14 years and older (33.5% vs 29.2%; this difference was statistically significant). In the youth custody context, girls were nearly 10 times more likely than boys to have experienced three or more incidents of severe child maltreatment (Moore et al., 2013). In related research, Baidawi et al. (2023) found that justice-involved girls in Australia experienced higher rates of maltreatment than boys, especially sexual abuse and multi-type maltreatment. However, they suggested that justice-involved boys may be more likely to under-report or minimise abuse and neglect, compared with girls. Earlier research showed that girls in custody had experienced significant traumatic life experiences and were more likely than boys in custody to develop posttraumatic stress disorder (PTSD) and report self-harm (Kerig & Becker, 2012; Nooner et al., 2012; Best et al., 2021).

Case Study

Amy is 14 years old, and currently in detention. She has lost count of how many places she has lived in her short life. Amy was removed from her family and taken into child protection when she was three, because her mum, a single parent, had mental health issues and was unable to provide for her care. Amy has never met her father, as her mother left him due to violence during her pregnancy. Professionals and her teachers, have constantly labelled Amy as a 'bad' kid. As a result, Amy only attended high school for the first six months and has not returned to school. She has trouble with reading and sitting still and suffers from extreme mood swings. Amy left her care arrangement, and has been living on the streets, or couch-surfing with friends. She uses alcohol and drugs to cope with her thoughts and emotions. She has been on remand for six months, waiting for some property damage and shoplifting charges to come to court. She was recently placed in isolation, following an episode of self-harm. During that isolation period, Amy disclosed for the first time to a prison psychologist she had built trust with, that she had been sexually abused numerous times in her foster care placement.

Amy's situation is a common story for girls in the YJ systems in both Australia and Aotearoa/NZ. Growing up in child protection care arrangements, histories of childhood sexual abuse, mental health problems and self-medicating behaviours are all well-established characteristics (DeHart et al., 2013). This is unsurprising, given that the long-term effects of child sexual abuse include depression, anxiety, low self-esteem, isolation, stigma, low trust, and substance use (Browne & Finkelhor, 1986). Mental health problems among justice-involved females are also strongly correlated with different types and volumes of female offending. For example, Dixon et al.'s (2004) research showed that 83% of the offending cohort of girls had been diagnosed with two to eight mental health conditions, compared with only 17% of the non-offending cohort. In the United States, DeHart et al. (2013) found that those who had experienced serious mental illness were at higher risk for substance use and drug offending, while substance use disorder was a significant contributor to driving under the influence and commercial sex work.

Experiences of family dysfunction, physical, emotional, and sexual abuse and domestic and family violence are also more prevalent among girls and women who offend and among the drivers of criminal activity (Conrad et al., 2014; Hubbard & Pratt, 2002). For girls like Amy, pathways are then forged through truancy, emotional dysregulation, alcohol and other drug use, mental health problems and untreated trauma (Blum et al., 2003; Piquero et al., 2005; Shepherd et al., 2013). There is a need for programmes and responses that reflect girls' experiences of care, domestic and family violence, and homelessness. They also reinforce the need for early intervention and support strategies for girls, to prevent them from ultimately progressing into the adult justice system.

Research from Victoria has found that girls had more child protection involvement than boys and experienced more carers. In addition, Aboriginal and Torres Strait Islander girls who entered the YJ system early had the highest level of welfare involvement (Victorian Sentencing Advisory Council, 2020). Similarly, in Tasmania, 52% of legally aided girls aged under 14 when first charged were involved with both the YJ and welfare systems, compared with 38% of boys (Tasmania Legal Aid, 2021). This again highlights that the relationship between these systems, which is already well-established, is particularly pronounced for girls. Similar findings have emerged in Aotearoa/NZ, with Best et al. (2021) citing government data indicating that 94% of young females referred for a youth justice family group conference had previously been the subject of a care and protection report, compared with 88% of males. According to Matthews, an Australian juvenile justice specialist:

> The abuse-to-prison pipeline is a real phenomenon where girls who experience sexual or physical abuse are then routed into the juvenile justice system. The offences committed are an externalisation of untreated trauma and are rarely violent or threaten public safety. Abuse and neglect suffered by children can disrupt the emotional, cognitive and interpersonal development processes throughout adolescence, which in turn impedes emotion and behaviour regulation, interpersonal trust and complex problem-solving abilities. As a result, girls resort to coping strategies and self-preserving behaviour, such as relational aggression, running away and substance use. The juvenile justice system is then used as a response for their "uncontrollable" behaviour, often for relatively minor crimes.
>
> (2018, p. 15)

Matthews has also noted:

> The combination of high rates of prior abuse and overly punitive responses to low-level offending leads too many girls to incarceration, where the system offers more harm than help. . . . Numerous reports into Australian juvenile detention centres have exposed how girls, being a small minority of the detained population, are wedged into facilities designed for boys, where their needs are deprioritised.
>
> (2018, p. 15)

Toward Positive Gender Pathways for Girls

The first step for Indigenous justice-involved youth is decolonisation of justice systems. This includes cultivating an understanding of ancestral histories of place, resilience, perseverance, survival, family, and community, via intergenerational learning. Intergenerational learning is needed to transmit Indigenous knowledges, values, practices, and customs, to hold up culturally grounded initiatives and, in so doing, feed forward into preventive interventions. Indigenous governance and leadership should provide strong guidance to the revision of systems; Indigenous ways of knowing and being are required, along with Indigenous decision-making and self-determination, as well as Indigenous professionals working with the children and young people for effective change. For Indigenous peoples, social and emotional wellbeing and identity is inextricably linked to connection to family, culture, community and country (Dudgeon et al., 2014). System redesign needs be place-based "as, by, for and with Indigenous peoples" with Indigenous ways of being and doing informing all aspects. Given the colonial history and ongoing harms common to Australia and Aotearoa/NZ and the overrepresentation of justice-involved Indigenous children and young people, there is an urgent need among the non-Indigenous majority for cultural competence and capacity-building, together with a willingness to relinquish power and the paternalistic assumption that the authorities know what is best for Indigenous communities. Being Indigenous-led in all areas of the justice system may provide a much-needed solution to the issues faced by Indigenous girls in and at risk of becoming enmeshed in YJ systems.

Diversion from the justice system plays an important role, particularly for young people involved in low-risk offending. Diversion provides an opportunity for positive change and personal development, improving community safety and reducing the costs associated with imprisonment (Bagaric & Begg, 2023). Successful community interventions are more than activities, requiring significant efforts at community engagement in crime responses and expanding ideas of social and community justice (Stout, 2017). This requires a broader understanding of the concept of what constitutes the criminal justice field, including institutions, programmes, practices, language, and relationships (Cunneen et al., 2013). Systems containing children and young people must be responsive to their individual needs, as articulated and understood by the children and young people, together with their families and communities. Providing a structured framework to effectively respond to adversity, distress and health problems can inform how justice practitioners help justice-involved children and young people.

Ward (2020) has identified the following "pillars" to improve justice outcomes for children and young people:

1. Treat young people differently to adults.
2. Keep young people away from the criminal justice system.
3. Privilege engagement and relationships.
4. Collaborate with family and community.
5. Partner with education.
6. Address trauma and complexity therapeutically.
7. Connect service systems.
8. Invest in restorative approaches.

9. Tailor responses to different cohorts.
10. Provide safe, structured custodial environments.

For justice-involved girls, a recent review by Impact Justice (2021) emphasised that programmes should include the following core elements:

- **Relational approaches:** adolescence is a time of significant change and growth, requiring an emphasis on supporting healthy social contexts. This includes building and supporting healthy romantic and non-romantic relationships and supporting girls' continuous, positive relationships with older women, family, and peers.
- **Restorative**: helping girls navigate the justice system, paying attention to their trauma and victimisation histories.
- **Socio-culturally relevant and intersectional**: anchored in girls' multiple marginalities by virtue of their gender, as well as, for example, sexual orientation, age, race, immigration status and socio-economic class.
- **Multilevel**: design approaches that target girls' individual, peer, family, community and multiple system involvements (e.g. welfare, school, and juvenile justice).
- **Community-based**: provide flexible services to girls in their natural communities and foster healthy family relationships and sustainable community connections.
- **Strength-based/empowering**: move away from deficit-oriented approaches and instead promote developmental assets, while encouraging leadership and developing strengths.
- **Safe**: promote healing from traumas caused by physical and psychological abuse.
- **Individualised**: tailor responses to meet the individual needs of a heterogeneous group of young women.

The intersection of race/ethnicity and gender matters, when considering justice involvement. As discussed above, there are typically gendered pathways into the justice system and, as such, girls' needs driving their behaviours are also specific to these gendered needs and experiences and require gender-responsive activities, education, programmes, and practice (Chesney-Lind & Pasko, 2013; DeHart & Lynch, 2021; Belisle et al., 2022).

Pillars and Practice

There have been promising evaluations of justice interventions that are therapeutic, where youth are remanded to low-level security, community-based facilities, with organised education and/or work. Under these models, the young people are expected to take responsibility for their pathways; autonomy and individual agency are strongly promoted (see, e.g. Spain: Diagrama Foundation, 2019; Netherlands:

Souverein et al., 2022; Sweden, Finland, Norway: Lappi-Seppälä, 2011). In this section, we discuss one example of a programme that significantly influenced the lives of justice-involved females. In 2022, Hawai'i made headlines around the world because there were no girls in long-term incarceration at the Hawai'i Youth Correctional Facility, in a state of 1.4 million. Just over a decade earlier, the number of girls at the facility had been 30–40 (Kelsey-Sugg & Arnold, 2022). Several steps went into making this a reality.

In 2004, Hawai'i established a dedicated "Girls' Court" in Honolulu, whose objectives were to: reduce recidivism, particularly runaway offences; detention and commitment to custody for girls; and address risk factors in girls' lives that may entrench their pathways to criminal behaviours (Davidson et al., 2011). The programme's core values include honouring female experience; nurturing strengths; building relationships and connecting with community, instilling hope, healing and adopting a holistic view, and accountability (Hawai'i Girls' Court, n.d.).

One unusual feature of the programme is a monthly "Girl Circle", where:

> each girl tak[es] turns talking and listening to one another respectfully about their respective concerns and interests at that moment in their lives. In a purposely developed safe environment, the girls use role playing, drama, journaling, poetry, dance, drawing, collage, and other activities as a means of self-expression. Staff (including the probation officers) introduce gender-specific topics that relate to the girls' lives, such as being a girl, trusting themselves and friendships, developing healthy body images, setting goals, understanding healthy sexuality, understanding addiction, and learning skills to make good life decisions
>
> (Davidson et al., 2011, p. 312).

Davidson et al.'s (2011) evaluation found that reoffending and absconding ("runaways") were both reduced by 90%. Participants also had 252% fewer days on the run and reduced drug use. In addition, they experienced improved academic achievement, awareness of healthy relationships and family relationships. However, they had more shelter admissions and shelter days, as well as admissions to and days in detention than their non-Girls' Court peers (a matched comparison group consisting of female offenders referred to family court and adjudicated in the same years as the Girls Court participants). The authors concluded that the programme:

> yield[ed] positive results . . . reduce[d] girls' overall recidivism in comparison to the matched group [and] . . . particularly impressive is the fact that Girls Court was able to successfully foster an environment in which similarly situated girls openly encouraged one another to avoid making harmful choices.
>
> (2011, p. 324)

Girls' Court was made permanent in 2017 and informed the development of Project Kealahou ("the new pathway", in Hawai'ian) (Cicchiello, 2022). In this programme, participants ("PK girls") and their families:

> receive gender-responsive, trauma-informed, culturally responsive, community-based services, including: intensive case management; community supports by paraprofessionals (i.e. peer support for youth and caregivers); structured group activities; and evidence-based treatments (e.g., Trauma-Focused Cognitive Behavioral Therapy and Girls Circle psychoeducational support groups). PK seeks to help girls who have experienced psychological trauma find "a new pathway" (*kealahou*) to a better future by healing past hurts and taking constructive steps toward a more hopeful future.
>
> (Suarez et al., 2014, p. 388)

Other aspects of the programme include hula dance groups and paddling classes (Cicchiello, 2022). Suarez et al.'s (2014) research on this programme found that PK girls were ethnically diverse (e.g. 57% identified as Native Hawaiian) and had experienced a high level of trauma (e.g. 77% had experienced substance use in the family and 35% were survivors of sexual assault). The most common mental health issues were mood (42%), substance use (32%), and conduct (29%) disorders, followed by PTSD (21%).

After six months in the programme, there were statistically significant improvements in youth strengths, competence, depression, impairment, behavioural and emotional problems and caregiver strain. PK girls reported satisfaction levels of 75–90% on a range of measures, while their caregivers reported levels of 71–100%. For both, the measure with the highest score was cultural sensitivity. PK participants and their families received more services in the programme than before enrolment, but the cost for mental health services in the programme was only slightly higher than the cost of their mental health services *prior* to PK enrolment ($365,803 vs $344,141). As Suarez et al. also noted, "these figures do not account for expected cost savings from decreased service usage and costs for PK girls in juvenile justice, child welfare, and educational settings" (2014, p. 390).

Of note, one type of service changed: only 2.4% of PK girls received community support services (e.g. peer support for young people and their caregivers) in the six months before enrolling in the programme, compared with 68.3% of PK girls during the first six months of enrolment in the programme, and this was achieved at minimal cost. Some limitations were acknowledged, namely, the low proportion of participants who completed the follow-up data. However, there was very little attrition from the programme, at only 7%.

Perhaps the most surprising prong has been the changes to the Hawaiian youth justice centre, led by Mark Patterson, "a native Hawaiian man [who has] long wanted 'to be a positive influence' for his community" (Kelsey-Sugg & Arnold, 2022, n.p.). Some of the steps he took have included rebranding the Hawai'i Youth Correctional Facility as the Kawailoa Youth and Family Wellness Center

(Cicchiello, 2022). Buildings have been converted into less threatening and more welcoming spaces for at-risk young people. This now includes a homeless shelter, a residential vocational training programme and a high school. In addition, youth services have been encouraged to develop programmes and settings for young people who are not able to safely stay with their families. The model focuses on helping to heal and rehabilitate often traumatised young women, many of whom are Indigenous Hawaiian (Kelsey-Sugg & Arnold, 2022).

This approach has seen the addition of on-site vocational training, a homeless shelter, opportunities for young people to farm and tend cattle and an assessment centre for victims of sex trafficking (Cicchiello, 2022; Kelsey-Sugg & Arnold, 2022). The assessment centre has wooden doors and rooms, instead of cells. The residents can leave and initially 90% did, but they did so with safety plans, money, and service contacts. Over the next two weeks:

> 80 per cent of the girls who'd left, returned. They voluntarily sought out the therapeutic environment that had been established. Having choice and not being held against their will led to more success in the treatment. "They wanted to stay, they wanted to come back . . .[and they] would continue to come back whenever they needed help," [Mr Paterson] says.
>
> (cited in Kelsey-Sugg & Arnold, 2022, n.p.)

Conclusion

The consequences of colonisation for Indigenous children and young people are evident in their overrepresentation in the Australian and Aotearoa/NZ justice systems. There are deep-rooted issues and profound concerns with the way in which our YJ systems respond to children and young people. This chapter has explored the gendered pathways for justice-involved girls, particularly Indigenous girls. This intersectional focus on Indigeneity and gender has allowed for exploration of ways for change, when considering programmes and service delivery for girls.

Notwithstanding the overrepresentation of Indigenous young people, the case study of Amy's life and journey into and through the justice system is not uncommon, regardless of ethnicity. Children and young people who are removed from their families and taken into care routinely travel on to the YJ system and have long-term poor health and wellbeing outcomes (Baidawi & Ball, 2023; Malvaso et al., 2017). Amy's experiences of being removed from her mother, who experienced unsupported mental health issues that impacted on her parenting ability, not knowing her father and multiple placements and sexual abuse in foster care are all too common (Hamilton S. L. et al., 2020). Her trauma and resultant alcohol and other drug use (Doyle et al., 2023) are symptomatic of her experiences and highlight the gendered pathways to her justice involvement. At 14, Amy was finally able to disclose her abuse to an adult who listened to her. But this was not until after experiences of self-harm, running away, homelessness, all underpinned by a lack of care. Amy needed very specific support to deal with her identity and family loss, behavioural needs (Bower et al., 2018; Mutch et al., 2022), and abuse needs

(Dale et al., 2023; Marr et al., 2023; Yee et al., 2023), which undoubtedly contributed to the multiple placements she experienced (Hamilton S. L. et al., 2020). To spend extended time on remand for petty offences and spend time in isolation for self-harm is not conducive to healing or recovery. If this trajectory continues, there is no doubt Amy is destined for adult incarceration.

Consistent with Ward's (2020) pillars discussed earlier, and the core elements described by Impact Justice (2021), there is a need to treat the unique gender-specific needs of justice-involved girls, to divert them from the criminal justice system. This incorporates the need to build trust and relationships and provide therapeutic interventions and environments which are restorative and specifically tailored to the needs of justice-involved girls (Ward, 2020). Building trust and using relational and restorative approaches (Braithwaite, 2002) is critical for girls like Amy, who have not had positive trusting relationships. Understanding what is or is not violence will be difficult and require significant support from positive peers and role models (Impact Justice, 2021). Building safe community connections where services are provided locally and, in the case of Indigenous children and young people, with Indigenous leadership and control and Indigenous ways of being and doing, will be critical to successfully assisting justice-involved girls. Individualised and tailored responses to abuse, particularly sexual abuse, will require commitment to culturally safe, strength-based psychological therapies and spaces (Impact Justice, 2021).

Approaches such as these have been the basis for YJ reforms in several countries, including the United States (McCarthy et al., 2016; Muhammad, 2019), Scandinavia (Lappi-Seppälä, 2011), the Netherlands (Souverein et al., 2022), Spain (Diagrama, 2019), and the United Kingdom (Welsh Government, 2019). Commonly, these are small, community-integrated facilities that emphasise education, achievement, positive relationships, engagement with family members, and social connections. They include a focus on therapeutic, tailored approaches that build and strengthen the development and trajectories of young people. Our discussion of the Hawai'i Girls Court provides an exemplary model for changing the trajectory and gendered pathways for girls heading to incarceration and addressing criminogenic risk factors (Davidson et al., 2011). Providing safe forums such as the Girl Circle, where respectful dialogue and listening are facilitated, using a variety of activities with trusted adults, and learning skills – such as goal setting, building friendships, understanding health and sexuality, addictions, and learning how to make positive life decisions – along with providing shelter (Davidson et al., 2011), is invaluable. The programme evaluation outcomes speak to the effectiveness of adopting and investing in such approaches.

In Māori tradition, the whole community is involved, which gave rise to the processes understood through the Family Group Conference (FGC). The way forward needs to continue to be decolonised and honour the principles of Te Tiriti o Waitangi. Voices of our Tamariki, Rangatahi, and their Whānau, together with Kaumātua and Ahorangi, can inform immediate and long-term change, ensuring the right ways of building up our Tamariki, shaping and healing our Rangatahi and communities from persistent colonial harms, including displacement from whenua, obstruction of Te Reo Māori and ignoring Tikanga. Key concepts for Māori health and wellbeing require YJ services to fund space and time for Iwi-led solutions that allow for more than Taha Tinana (physical wellbeing), funding Iwi-led solutions to nourish Taha Hinengaro (mental and emotional wellbeing), Taha Wairua (spiritual wellbeing), Taha Whānau (family and social wellbeing) on tūrangawaewae (place to stand), and on whenua (land and whakapapa). The Aotearoa/NZ Government needs to sustainably fund Iwi-based solutions, removing the spectre of detention or prison.

The evidence about the gendered pathways of justice-involved girls is now overwhelmingly clear. There are also ample practice examples that have successfully addressed the underlying issues. It is now incumbent on governments and communities in Australia and Aotearoa/New Zealand to implement such models. Doing so will provide the opportunity for justice-involved girls, who are disproportionately Indigenous, to heal and thrive.

Notes

1 It is beyond the scope of this chapter to consider the specific needs of transgender and gender-diverse people.
2 We use the term "Indigenous" collectively to refer collectively to Aboriginal and Torres Strait Islander peoples in Australia and Māori people in Aotearoa/NZ. However, we recognise this term is contested by some.

References

Australian Bureau of Statistics. (2024). *Recorded crime – Offenders, 2022–23*. Australian Bureau of Statistics.
Australian Institute of Health and Welfare. (2023). *Youth justice in Australia 2021–22*. Australian Institute of Health and Welfare.
Australian Institute of Health and Welfare. (2024). *Child protection Australia 2021–22*. Australian Institute of Health and Welfare.
Bagaric, M., & Begg, M. (2023). *Let them work: How criminal justice reform can help address Australia's worker shortage*. Institute of Public Affairs.
Baidawi, S., & Ball, R. (2023). Child protection and youth offending: Differences in youth criminal court-involved children by dual system involvement. *Children and Youth Services Review*. https://doi.org/10.1016/j.childyouth.2022.106736
Baidawi, S., Ball, R., Sheehan, R., & Papalia, N. (2024). *Police and children's court outcomes for children aged 10 to 13*. Australian Institute of Criminology.
Baidawi, S., Papalia, N., & Featherston, R. (2023). Gender differences in the maltreatment-youth offending relationship: A scoping review. *Trauma, Violence & Abuse*, 24, 1140–1156.
Bartels, L. (2022). Sentencing review 2020–21. *Criminal Law Journal*, 46, 44–66.
Belisle, L., Salisbury, E., & Keen, J. (2022). Did they move on? An outcome evaluation of the gender-responsive program, girls . . . moving on. *Feminist Criminology*, 17, 223–251.
Best, C., Ioane, J., & Lambie, I. (2021). Young female offenders and the New Zealand youth justice system: The need for a gender-specific response. *Psychiatry, Psychology & Law*, 28, 867–884.
Bickel, R., & Campbell, A. (2002). Mental health of adolescents in custody: The use of the 'Adolescent Psychopathology Scale' in a Tasmanian context. *Australian and New Zealand Journal of Psychiatry*, 36, 603–609.

Blum, J., Ireland, M., & Blum, R. (2003). Gender differences in juvenile violence: A report from Add Health. *Journal of Adolescent Health*, 32, 234–240.

Borschmann, R., Janca, E., Carter, A., Willoughby, M., Hughes, N., Snow, K., et al. (2020). The health of adolescents in detention: A global scoping review. *The Lancet: Public Health*, 5, E114–E126.

Bower, C., Watkins, R., Mutch, R., Marriott, R., Freeman, J., Kippin, N., Safe, B., Pestell, C., Cheung, C., & Shield, H. (2018). Fetal alcohol spectrum disorder and youth justice: A prevalence study among young people sentenced to detention in Western Australia. *BMJ Open*, 8(2), e019605. https://doi.org/10.1136/bmjopen-2017-019605

Braithwaite, J. (2002). *Restorative justice and responsive regulation*. Oxford University Press.

Browne, A., & Finkelhor, D. (1986). Impact of child sexual abuse: A review of the research. *Psychological Bulletin*, 99, 66–77.

Chesney-Lind, M., & Pasko, L. (2013). *The female offender: Girls, women, and crime* (3rd ed.). Sage.

Cicchiello, C. (2022, October 1). How Hawaii brought its population of girls in prison to zero. *NBC News*. https://www.nbcnews.com/politics/politics-news/hawaii-brought-population-girls-prison-zero-rcna41532

Conrad, S., Tolou-Shams, M., Rizzo, C., Placella, N., & Brown, L. (2014). Gender differences in recidivism rates for juvenile justice youth: The impact of sexual abuse. *Law and Human Behavior*, 38, 305–314.

Cunneen, C., Baldry, E., Brown, D., Schwartz, M., Steel, A., & Brown, M. (2013). *Penal culture and hyperincarceration: The revival of the prison*. Routledge.

Cunneen, C., & Tauri, J. (2019). Indigenous peoples, criminology, and criminal justice. *Annual Review of Criminology*, 2, 359–381.

Dale, P. R., Meurk, C., Williams, M., Watson, M., Steele, M. L., Wittenhagen, L., Harden, S., Stathis, S., Scott, J. G., & Kinner, S. (2023). Our ways, your ways, both ways–a multi-disciplinary collaboration to develop, embed and evaluate a model of social and emotional wellbeing care for Aboriginal and Torres Strait islander young people who experience detention–phase 1. *Frontiers in Psychiatry*, 14.

Davidson, J., Pasko, L., & Chesney-Lind, M. (2011). 'She's way too good to lose': An evaluation of Honolulu's Girls Court. *Women & Criminal Justice*, 21, 308–327.

DeHart, D., & Lynch, S. (Eds.) (2021). *Women's and girls' pathways through the criminal legal system: Addressing trauma, mental health, and marginalization*. Cognella Academic Publishing.

DeHart, D., Lynch, S., Belknap, J., Dass-Brailsford, P., & Green, B. (2013). Life history models of female offending: The roles of serious mental illness and trauma in women's pathways to jail. *Psychology of Women Quarterly*, 38, 138–151.

Diagrama Foundation. (2019). *A blueprint for change: Adapting the lessons of the Spanish youth justice system to the Northern Territory – Report of Diagrama visit*. Diagrama Foundation.

Dixon, A., Howie, P., & Starling, J. (2004). Psychopathology in female juvenile offenders. *Journal of Child Psychology and Psychiatry*, 45, 1150–1158.

Doyle, M. F., Al-Ansari, F., Kaye, S., Williams, M., Conigrave, K., & Bowman, J. (2023). Alcohol and other drug use before custody among aboriginal and non aboriginal people in New South Wales, Australia. *Australian and New Zealand Journal of Public Health*, 47(3), 100052.

Dudgeon, P., Milroy, H., & Walker, R. (2014). *Working together: Aboriginal and Torres Strait islander mental health and wellbeing principles and practice*. (2nd ed.). Commonwealth of Australia.

Fedock, G., & Covington, S. (2022). Strength-based approaches to the treatment of incarcerated women and girls. In C. Langton & J. Worling (Eds.), *Facilitating desistance from aggression and crime: Theory, research, and strength-based practices* (pp. 378–396). John Wiley & Sons.

Fogarty, W., Bulloch, H., McDonnell, S., & Davis, M. (2018). *Deficit discourse and indigenous health: How narrative framings of Aboriginal and Torres Strait islander people are reproduced in policy*. The Lowitja Institute & National Centre for Indigenous Studies.

Gobeil, R., Blanchette, K., & Stewart, L. (2016). A meta-analytic review of correctional interventions for women offenders: Gender-neutral versus gender-informed approaches. *Criminal Justice and Behaviour*, 43, 301–322.

Goldsworthy, T., Brotto, G., & Cawthray, T. (2023, October 29). Is Australia in the grips of a youth crime crisis? This is what the data says. *The Conversation*.

Gueta, K. (2020). Exploring the promise of intersectionality for promoting justice-involved women's health research and policy. *Health Justice*, 8(1), 19. https://doi.org/10.1186/s40352-020-00120-8

Hafekost, K., Lawrence, D., O'Leary, C., Bower, C., Semmens, J., & Zubrick, S. (2017). Maternal alcohol use disorder and child school attendance outcomes for non-indigenous and indigenous children in Western Australia: A population cohort record linkage study. *BMJ*, 7, e015650. https://doi.org/10.1136/bmjopen-2016-015650

Hamilton, S., Doyle, M., & Bower, C. (2021). Review of fetal alcohol spectrum disorder (FASD) among Aboriginal and Torres Strait Islander people. *Australian Indigenous Health Bulletin*, 2(1). http://dx.doi.org/10.14221/aihjournal.v2n1.1

Hamilton, S., Reibel, T., Maslen, S., Watkins, R., Jacinta, F., Passmore, H., Mutch, R., O'Donnell, M., Braithwaite, V., & Bower, C. (2020). Disability "in-justice": The benefits and challenges of "yarning" with young people undergoing diagnostic assessment for fetal alcohol spectrum disorder in a youth detention center. *Qualitative Health Research*, 30(2), 314–327.

Hamilton, S. L., & Maslen, S. (2022). Redressing 'unwinnable battles': Towards institutional justice capital in Australian child protection. *Journal of Sociology*, 58, 535–553. https://doi.org/10.1177/14407833211010220

Hamilton, S. L., Maslen, S., Best, D., Freeman, J., O'Donnell, M., Reibel, T., Mutch, R. C., & Watkins, R. (2020). Putting 'justice' in recovery capital: Yarning about hopes and futures with young people in detention. *International Journal for Crime, Justice and Social Democracy*, 9(2), 20–36.

Hamilton, S. L., Reibel, T., Watkins, R., Mutch, R. C., Kippin, N. R., Freeman, J., Passmore, H. M., Safe, B., O'Donnell, M., & Bower, C. (2019). 'He has problems; he is not the problem . . .' A qualitative study of non-custodial staff providing services for young offenders assessed for foetal alcohol spectrum disorder in an Australian Youth Detention Centre. *Youth Justice*, 19(2), 137–157.

Hawai'i Girls' Court. (n.d.). *About*. https://www.girlscourthawaii.org/about.

Herz, D., Dierkhising, C., Raithel, J., Schretzman, M., Guiltinan, S., George, R., Cho, Y., Coulton, C., & Abbott, S. (2019). Dual system youth and their pathways: A comparison of incidence, characteristics and system experiences using linked administrative data. *Journal of Youth and Adolescence*, 48, 2432–2450.

Hinshaw, S., Nguyen, P., O'Grady, S., & Rosenthal, E. (2022). Attention-deficit/hyperactivity disorder in girls and women: Underrepresentation, longitudinal processes, and key directions. *Journal of Child Psychology and Psychiatry*, 63, 484–496.

Holland, L., Reid, N., Hewlett, N., Toombs, M., Elisara, T., Thomson, A., et al. (2023). Alcohol use in Australia: Countering harm with healing. *The Lancet Regional Health–Western Pacific*, 37.

Houston, S., & Butler, M. (2019). More than just a number: Meeting the needs of those with mental illness, learning, speech and language difficulties in the criminal justice system. *Irish Probation Journal*, 16, 22–41.

Hubbard, D., & Pratt, T. C. (2002). A meta-analysis of the predictors of delinquency among girls. *Journal of Rehabilitation*, 34, 1–13.

Hurren, E., Stewart, A., & Dennison, S. (2017). Transitions and turning points revisited: A replication to explore child maltreatment and youth offending links within and across Australian cohorts. *Child Abuse and Neglect*, 65, 24–36.

Impact Justice. (2021). *Gender-responsive programming for girls involved in the juvenile justice system.* Impact Justice.
Indig, D., Frewen, A., & Moore, E. (2016). Predictors and correlates of re-incarceration among Australian young people in custody. *Australian & New Zealand Journal of Criminology*, 49, 73–89.
Kaiwai, H., Allport, T., Herd, R., Mane, J., Ford, K., Leahy, H., & Kipa, M. (2020). *Ko te whakwhiti it's time for change: A Māori inquiry into Oranga Tamariki.* Whānau Ora Commissioning Agency.
Kelsey-Sugg, A., & Arnold, A. (2022, July 28). Girls in Hawaii were once jailed for 'offences' like fleeing unsafe homes. Now they're not locked up at all. *ABC News.* https://www.abc.net.au/news/2022-07-28/hawaii-reduced-incarceration-to-zero-girls-imprisoned-here-show/101237740
Kerig, P., & Becker, S. (2012). Trauma and girls' delinquency. In S. Miller, L. D. Leve, & P. K. Kerig (Eds.), *Delinquent girls: Contexts, relationships and adaptation* (pp. 119–143). Springer.
Kinner, S., & Young, J. (2018). Understanding and improving the health of people who experience incarceration: An overview and synthesis *Epidemiologic Reviews*, 40, 4–11.
Lappi-Seppälä, T. (2011). Nordic youth justice. In M. Tonry & T. Lappi-Seppälä (Eds.), *Crime and justice in scandinavia* (pp. 199–264). University of Chicago Press.
Leonard, M. (2016). *The sociology of children, childhood and generation.* Sage.
Linnane, D., McNamara, D., & Toohey, L. (2023). Ensuring universal access: The case for Medicare in prison. *Alternative Law Journal*, 48, 102–109.
Malvaso, C., Delfabbro, P., & Day, A. (2017). The child protection and juvenile justice nexus in Australia: A longitudinal examination of the relationship between maltreatment and offending. *Child Abuse and Neglect*, 64, 32–46.
Marr, M., Gaskin, C., Kasinathan, J., Kaye, S., Singh, Y., & Dean, K. (2023). The prevalence of mental illness in young people in custody over time: A comparison of three surveys in New South Wales, *Psychiatry, Psychology and Law.* https://doi.org/10.1080/13218719.2023.2192257
Matthews, S. (2018). Girls in juvenile detention: Deprioritised and retraumatised. *Precedent*, 147, 14–18.
McCarthy, P., Schiraldi, V., & Shark, M. (2016). The future of youth justice: A community-based alternative to the youth prison model. *New Thinking in Community Corrections Bulletin.* https://www.ojp.gov/pdffiles1/nij/250142.pdf
McCausland, R., & Baldry, E. (2023). Who does Australia lock up? The social determinants of justice. *International Journal for Crime, Justice and Social Democracy*, 12, 37–53.
Moore, E., Gaskin, C., & Indig, D. (2013). Childhood maltreatment and post-traumatic stress disorder among incarcerated young offenders. *Child Abuse and Neglect*, 37, 861–870.
Muhammad, D. (2019). *A positive youth justice system.* National Institute for Criminal Justice Reform.
Mutch, R., Freeman, J., Kippin, N., Safe, B., Pestell, C., Passmore, H. M., Hamilton, S., Shield, H., Argiro, E., Rainsford, C., Condon, C., Giglia, R., Watkins, R., Marriott, R., & Bower, C. (2022). Comprehensive clinical paediatric assessment of children and adolescents sentenced to detention in Western Australia. *Journal of Fetal Alcohol Spectrum Disorder*, 3, e16–e31.
New Zealand Ministry of Justice. (2019). *Children and young people in court.* https://www.justice.govt.nz/assets/i1zasc-Children-and-young-people-data-highlights-jun2019-v1.0.pdf
New Zealand Ministry of Justice. (2023). *Youth justice indicators summary report.* https://www.justice.govt.nz/assets/Documents/Publications/Youth-Justice-Indicators-Summary-Report-April-2023.pdf

New Zealand Ministry of Justice. (2024). *Research and data – Children and young people with finalised charges in the Youth Court*. https://www.justice.govt.nz/justice-sector-policy/research-data/justice-statistics/data-tables/#cyp

New Zealand Ministry of Social Development. (2024). *Child and youth offending patterns – Research reports*. https://www.msd.govt.nz/about-msd-and-our-work/publications-resources/research/child-and-youth-offending-patterns/index.html.

Nooner, K., Linares, L., Batinjane, J., Kramer, R., Silva, R., & Cloitre, M. (2012). Factors related to posttraumatic stress disorder in adolescence. *Trauma, Violence & Abuse*, 13, 153–166.

Oranga Tamariki. (2024). *Youth justice custody: Updated trends and outlook.*

Paradies, Y. (2016). Colonisation, racism and indigenous health. *Journal of Population Research*, 33, 83–96.

Piquero, N., Gover, A., MacDonald, J., & Piquero, A. (2005). The influence of delinquent peers on delinquency: Does gender matter? *Youth & Society*, 36, 251–275.

Porter, A., & Cunneen, C. (2021). Policing settler colonial societies. In P. Birch, M. Kennedy, & E. Kruger (Eds.), *Australian policing: Critical issues in 21st century practice* (pp. 397–411). Routledge.

Putniņš, A. (2005). Assessing recidivism risk among young offenders. *Australian & New Zealand Journal of Criminology*, 38, 324–339.

Shepherd, S. (2016). Violence risk instruments may be culturally unsafe for use with indigenous patients. *Australasian Psychiatry*, 24, 565–567.

Shepherd, S., Luebbers, S., & Dolan, M. (2013). Identifying gender differences in an Australian youth offender population. *SAGE Open*, 3, 1–12.

Silva, D., Colvin, L., Glauert, R., & Bower, C. (2014). Contact with the juvenile justice system in children treated with stimulant medication for attention deficit disorder: A population study. *The Lancet Psychiatry*, 1, 278–285.

Sotiri, M., & Simpson, J. (2006). Indigenous people and cognitive disability: An introduction to issues in police stations. *Current Issues in Criminal Justice*, 17, 431–443.

Souverein, F., Mulder, E., van Domburg, L., Adriaanse, M., & Popma, A. (2022). Toward a tailored model of youth justice: A qualitative analysis of the factors associated with successful placement in a community-integrated facility. *International Journal of Offender Therapy and Comparative Criminology*, 66, 147–167.

Stout, B. (2017). Community justice in Australia: Developing knowledge, skills and values for working with offenders in the community. *Aotearoa New Zealand Social Work*, 29, 135–136.

Suarez, E., Jackson, D., Slavin, L., Michels, S., & McGeehan, K. (2014). Project Kealahou: Improving Hawai'i's system of care for at-risk girls and young women through gender-responsive, trauma-informed care. *Hawai'i Journal of Medicine and Public Health*, 73, 387–392.

Tasmania Legal Aid. (2021). *Children first: Children in the child safety and youth justice system*. Tasmania Legal Aid.

United Nations (2009). *State of the world's Indigenous peoples*. United Nations.

Victorian Sentencing Advisory Council. (2020). *'Crossover kids': Vulnerable children in the youth justice system – Report 2: Children at the intersection of child protection and youth justice across Victoria*. Victorian Sentencing Advisory Council.

Vidal, S., Prince, D., Connell, C., Caron, C., Kaufman, J., & Tebes, J. (2017). Maltreatment, family environment, and social risk factors: Determinants of the child welfare to juvenile justice transition among maltreated children and adolescents. *Child Abuse and Neglect*, 63, 7–18.

Ward, L. (2020). *Ten pillars of youth justice*. Australia and New Zealand School of Government.

Wasserman, G., Larkin, S., McReynolds, S., Ko, L., Katz, J., & Carpenter, R. (2005). Gender differences in psychiatric disorders at juvenile probation intake. *American Journal of Public Health*, 95(1), 131–137. https://doi.org/10.2105/AJPH.2003.024737

Watene, L. (2020). Transforming global justice theorizing: Indigenous philosophies. In T. Brooks (Ed.), *The Oxford handbook of global justice* (pp. 163–180). Oxford University Press.

Welsh Government. (2019). *Youth justice blueprint for Wales*. Welsh Government.

Yee, N., Chemjong, P., Korobanova, D., Scade, S., Large, M., Nielssen, O., Carr, V., & Dean, K. (2023). The full spectrum of clinical stages of psychosis among mentally ill prisoners in New South Wales (NSW), Australia. *Psychiatry, Psychology and Law*, 30(5), 600–617.

9 The Forgotten Children

Child Offending

Kate Perry, Ian Lambie, Susan Baidawi, Amanda Jones, Negar Panahi, Chris Garrod, and Nina Papalia

CHILDREN WITH OFFENDING BEHAVIOURS

Introduction

Although child offending rates have been declining globally, and most offending behaviour in children is of minor to moderate seriousness, a small proportion of children do commit serious and violent crimes (Reil & Lambie, 2022). This chapter reviews the responses to offending behaviours in children under the age of 14 across Aotearoa New Zealand and Australia and the unique challenges presented. Traditional youth justice interventions, which are designed for older adolescents, are typically unsuited to this group as they often fail to address the unique developmental, emotional and social needs of younger children (Office of the Children's Commissioner, 2020). Understanding the demographics, underlying drivers, and effective responses for young people with offending behaviours is crucial for developing strategies that prevent the progression of these behaviours, avert children's pathways from criminal justice systems, and promote their positive life trajectories.

Children with Offending Behaviours

For the past two decades, international justice research, policy, and clinical practice have predominantly focused on offending behaviours that have their origins during adolescence. Consequently, our understanding of the offending behaviours of children who continue to offend into adolescence and beyond is very limited. Whilst not all children who display disruptive behaviour or conduct-related concerns in early childhood go on to experience police or criminal justice contact, earlier studies indicated that one-quarter to a half of children with behavioural difficulties faced an increased risk of these outcomes (Reil & Lambie, 2022). Yet these studies should be read with a critical eye, as many rely on samples of more disadvantaged children (e.g kindergartners in low socio-economic areas or child psychiatric inpatient samples), increasing the likelihood of these children's offending relative to the general population. The longitudinal Christchurch Health and Developmental Study, however, found that certain behavioural problems in early

DOI: 10.4324/9781003298410-14

childhood (e.g. conduct-related problems such as aggression, defiance, and impulsivity) were associated with a five times increased likelihood of self-reported adolescent and adult offending behaviour (Fergusson et al., 2000; Fergusson et al., 2015). Indeed, for a small proportion of children, serious and chronic offending behaviours may evolve from a steady progression of increasingly severe and persistent difficulties during childhood (Slot et al., 2016). An important distinction to note is that these characteristics are not taken to be "inherent" in the child, leading to an inevitable "predictable" outcome of offending behaviour or criminal justice involvement. Indeed, language, models and frameworks that locate "risk" within children tend to replicate the structural violence and systemic neglect which have been shown to contribute to the criminalisation of children who live with experiences of victimisation, disability and disadvantage (Baidawi et al., 2022; Baidawi & Sheehan, 2020).

Clinical and child psychologists argue that offending behaviour in younger children warrants particular concern, as children who offend before the age of 13 are two to three times more likely to engage in persistent, violent and chronic offending relative to those who start to offend in adolescence (Loeber & Farrington, 2000; Moffitt et al., 2002; Reil et al., 2022). To be sure, studies have shown that the younger a child is at the first noted offence, the higher the chances of their engaging in serious and chronic offending behaviours or criminal justice system involvement. However, rather than being solely indicative of greater inherent "risk" of a child, several scholars have identified the criminogenic or "iatrogenic" effect of criminal justice system contact during childhood and adolescence that significantly contributes to these outcomes (Gatti et al., 2009; Robertson, 2018). As a result, children with early offending behaviours are more vulnerable to what has been coined the "prison pipeline" which follows a negative trajectory: from child welfare involvement to childhood offending behaviours, entry into the youth justice system, and involvement with the adult criminal justice system (Lambie, 2018b).

Whilst it may be easy to attribute offending-related behaviours in children to youthful or impulsive behaviour, there is an indisputable body of scientific evidence and literature indicating that serious child offending behaviours do not occur in a vacuum (Reil et al., 2021). A theory of life-course persistent offending proposed by Terrie Moffitt over 30 years ago (using data from the Dunedin longitudinal study in New Zealand) suggested that across a given population, some individuals will begin engaging in antisocial behaviour in early life and continue to offend into adulthood. This pattern is understood to be linked to neurological, psychological, family and environmental factors that shape behaviour from a young age, leading to a more persistent and stable trajectory of offending over the life course (Moffitt & Caspi, 2001; Moffitt, 2015). Research has consistently shown high levels of maltreatment (e.g. physical, sexual, and emotional abuse), neglect and family violence, stand-downs/suspensions from school and indicators of social deprivation among children who offend (Reil et al., 2022; Reil & Lambie, 2022). The adverse effect of exposure to traumatic experiences is also shown to be cumulative, emphasising that children and young people who commit serious and violent offences were first and foremost victims themselves (Lambie, 2018a). In addition, the impact of various systems, policies and practices that result in school exclusion, entry to out-of-home care, and early criminal justice system contact, forms a critical component of facilitating these trajectories (Baidawi et al., 2022; Baidawi & Sheehan, 2020).

Offending behaviours in children cannot be fully understood without also recognising the profound influence of the developing brain and the impact of neurodevelopmental disorders. The prefrontal cortex, responsible for decision-making, impulse control, and consequential thinking, undergoes a long period of development, taking over two decades to reach full maturity. The prefrontal cortex is generally not considered "fully developed" until the age of 25, with this neurological immaturity likely limiting a child's capacity for foresight, self-regulation and moral reasoning (Lambie, 2018c). For children with neurodevelopmental disorders such as attention deficit disorder (ADHD), autism spectrum disorder (ASD), fetal alcohol spectrum disorder (FASD), traumatic brain injury (TBI), cognitive impairment/intellectual disability and learning difficulties, the risk of contact with the criminal justice system is even greater. Research indicates that neurodevelopmental conditions are vastly overrepresented in child and youth justice populations, yet these children are rarely identified or treated appropriately. Additionally, children with neurodevelopmental disorders may not understand the consequences of their actions, legal processes, or their rights, leaving them vulnerable to unfair treatment and inappropriately punitive justice responses (Reddy, 2025).

We must also ask ourselves, why are the long-term psychosocial impacts of childhood offending not being addressed in the same way as physical and public health concerns for children are, when the adverse outcomes across the lifespan are in many ways comparable? To many, physical and public health concerns are considered more measurable, visible, and politically neutral, making them easier to fund and address through the available mainstream services. In contrast, addressing the causes and impact of childhood offending requires transformative, long-term, and culturally grounded responses. Such complexities appear to have made governments reluctant to act decisively and effectively. To provide quality and targeted services that strengthen families and divert children away from justice systems, a comprehensive public health approach towards early intervention and prevention of childhood offending behaviours must be applied (He et al., 2025).

The impact on Indigenous populations must also be acknowledged, with Indigenous and ethnically diverse children continuing to face significant inequities within the justice system often through differential processing and poorer psychosocial outcomes (Cunneen & Porter, 2017; Lambie & Ioane, 2024). These disparities stem from a complex interplay of factors that include poverty and social disadvantage, a failure to address the root causes of offending, and a lack of access to culturally appropriate support services. The enduring impact of colonisation on Indigenous populations and embedded institutional and systemic racism further compound these disparities (He et al., 2025).

Considering that offending onset in childhood is associated with a greater likelihood of persistent criminal justice system involvement across the life course and attendant adverse life outcomes, a monumental shift towards preventative methods through early intervention is required. Increased focus on addressing the underlying needs contributing to childhood offending behaviours is crucial to support our children, families and communities. These efforts must also be accompanied by meaningful changes in governmental policies that prioritise prevention, allocation of resources towards early support services and promotion of cross-sector collaboration.

Legal Responses to Children with Offending Behaviours Across Aotearoa New Zealand and Australia

Age of Criminal Responsibility – Aotearoa New Zealand

Aotearoa New Zealand's criminal justice system takes a graduated approach towards age-related responsibility and liability. Under the Oranga Tamariki Act 1989, a child is defined as being under the age of 14 years, whilst a young person is defined as being between the ages of 14 and 17 years (Oranga Tamariki Act, 1989). Whilst a child of any age can be apprehended by the New Zealand Police, the actions taken in response to an alleged crime differ across age brackets.

The current minimum age of criminal responsibility (MACR) in Aotearoa New Zealand is 10 years old, meaning no child under the age of 10 can be held criminally responsible for any type of offence even through informal processes such as a warning, restorative justice or police diversion (Spier, 2016). All children aged 10 to 13 years who are charged with an offence benefit from the legal presumption "*doli incapax*" whereby:

> "No person shall be convicted of an offence by reason of any act done of omitted by him or her when of the age of 10 but under the age of 14 years, unless he or she knew that the act or omission was wrong or contrary to law" (Crimes Act, 1961).

The Crown must prove that a child knew what they were doing was wrong or against the law. "*Doli incapax*" is a rebuttable presumption, meaning that all children aged under 14 years are presumed to be incapable of such understanding, unless the prosecution can provide evidence refuting this presumption. Evidence can include observations or admissions of the child during arrest and interview processes, previous dealings with police, the circumstances of the alleged offending, or formal psychological or psychiatric assessments, which may include an assessment of a child's level of sociomoral reasoning and intellectual ability (Lynch et al., 2021). Numerous academic, legal, and family organisations have advocated for an urgent increase in the minimum age of criminal responsibility (to a minimum age of 14 years) across Aotearoa New Zealand to meet international human rights recommendations and our obligations under Te Tiriti o Waitangi. Concerns have been raised that Aotearoa New Zealand is noticeably out of step with its international peers, with many feeling children's interests are not centred within the current system and that there is a lack of consideration for age-appropriate outcomes (Amnesty International, 2022).

Responses to Children with Offending Behaviours – A Focus on Aotearoa New Zealand

In Aotearoa New Zealand children who display offending behaviours are a group who are significantly under-researched and underserved by specialist therapeutic services. In recent years, however, children and young people who display offending-related behaviours have dominated social, scientific and political arenas. Nationwide, children as young as seven are being implicated in serious and violent offences, coming to the attention of the public through "ram raids and violent robberies" of a variety of businesses from high-end stores to corner dairies. The pressure of the collective conscience of both government officials and the public has prompted several to question whether sufficient action is being taken to identify and support this group of individuals. Many have argued that Aotearoa's response to childhood offending reflects a concerning shift toward the criminalisation of care and protection matters, an approach that is particularly troubling in light of the inherent developmental vulnerabilities' children possess (Werry, 2022).

Childhood offending in Aotearoa New Zealand often results in involvement with the Care and Protection and Youth Justice systems. Within legislation, a child or young person in need of care and protection falls under Section 14(1) of the Oranga Tamariki Act 1989, formally known as the Children, Young Persons, and Their Families Act 1989 (Oranga Tamariki Act, 1989). Section 14(1) outlines the duty to assist children and young people who are at risk of harm, neglect or abuse, including those who display a risk to themselves or others in the context of offending. In Aotearoa New Zealand, outcomes of young people who come into contact with the care and protection system before the age of 14 are shown to be worse than those of the general population. Figures show that by the age of 21, these individuals are more likely to have left school without a National Certificate of Educational Achievement (NCEA), to be on a benefit, and to have had contact with Youth Justice or have received a custodial or community-based sentence in the adult correctional system (Chrichton et al., 2015).

Most criminal offences committed by children aged 10 to 13 years are minor and are dealt with by Police through "alternative action plans" and the use of strategies such as warnings, restorative justice or diversion programmes. There are, however, exceptions for where a child aged 10 to 13 years can appear before the criminal courts (Office of the Children's Commissioner, 2020). These include when a child is formally charged with murder or manslaughter, or when they have allegedly committed very serious offences (carrying a maximum term of imprisonment of 14 years or more) or are serious repeat offenders (have previously been charged with an offence carrying a maximum sentence of at least 10 years imprisonment). Should a child be formally charged with an offence in criminal court, a "push-back" mechanism can be applied by a Youth Court Judge. This mechanism is used where a Youth Court Judge feels the matter can be resolved by the care and protection system and if it is in the public interest to do so. Any other criminal offending is dealt with as a care and protection matter, whereby the "number, nature, or magnitude" of the child's offending may give rise to a formal order granted by the Family Court (Lynch et al., 2021; Oranga Tamariki Act, 1989).

Māori, as the Indigenous population of Aotearoa New Zealand, are disproportionally represented among child and youth offending statistics. The disproportionate criminalisation of tamariki and rangatahi Māori reflects deep-rooted structural inequities and ongoing institutional bias that is heavily influenced by the profound and enduring impact of colonisation. In 2024, 61% of young people aged 10–16 years with finalised charges before any court were identified as Māori. Young Māori were also more likely to have Police proceedings taken against them and have offending that leads to a Family Group Conference (FGC) or court action, whilst being less likely to receive a diversionary sentence compared to European/Other populations (Ministry of Justice, 2024). These disparities have lasted well over a decade and continue to undermine Māori autonomy and well-being. Previously, Oranga Tamariki had a responsibility under Section 7AA of the Oranga Tamariki Act to ensure their policies and practices had the objective of reducing disparities and improving outcomes for tamariki and rangatahi Māori who came to their attention. Whilst this section of the Act was repealed in April 2025, Oranga Tamariki are still obligated to provide a practical commitment to the principles of Te Tiriti o Waitangi/the Treaty of Waitangi (Dickson, 2025). To date, there is little evidence regarding the implementation of culturally specific evidence-based youth justice interventions aimed at prevention, reducing reoffending and inequities, and the promoting of tamariki and rangatahi well-being (Oranga Tamariki, 2019). Further discussion regarding the importance of culturally specific and safe interventions for Māori is provided later in this chapter.

Age of Criminal Responsibility – Australia

In Australia, responses to children under 14 years with offending behaviours have become a subject of considerable recent debate, with most Australian states and territories continuing to criminalise children as young as 10 years (Baidawi et al., 2024a). Like Aotearoa New Zealand, two major legislative provisions currently direct Australian criminal justice system responses to younger children. The first is the minimum age of criminal responsibility, which is currently 10 years of age across all but two Australian jurisdictions (Victoria and the Australian Capital Territory), where the minimum age of criminal responsibility is set at 12 and 14 years, respectively (Baidawi et al., 2026). The second is the legal provision of *doli incapax* (Fitz-Gibbon & O'Brien, 2019). Whilst some in Australia argue that the existence of the *doli incapax* principle acts as a safeguard against the inappropriate criminalisation of younger children, numerous concerns have been raised about its inconsistent application in practice (Armstrong, 2019; Attorney General's Department, 2020; Australian Human Rights Commission, 2020). For example, concerns have been raised regarding:

- the challenges of retrospectively assessing a child's understanding of their actions at the time they were committed, especially noting the dynamic nature of children's development;

- the frequency with which the onus of proof is reversed, such that defence lawyers seek to prove a child lacked capacity rather than prosecutors having to rebut the presumed incapacity;
- the vagueness of the principle in legislation, leaving much to the discretion of police, courts, and assessors (United Nations Committee on the Rights of the Child, 2019); and
- regional variations in service provision and specialisation that affect access to *doli incapax* assessments (Fitz-Gibbon & O'Brien, 2019).

A further concern is that children may become criminalised by their contact with the justice system (e.g. police, lawyers, courts, and remand) while waiting on the outcome of *doli incapax* assessments (Fitz-Gibbon & O'Brien, 2019). This contact occurs at a crucial point in their development, putting them at risk of assuming a criminal identity, particularly if they are ultimately found to be *incap*able of being held criminally responsible. Third, clinical, legal and judicial professionals are concerned that, in seeking to avoid unnecessary criminalisation, *doli incapax* might still lead to children not receiving the support necessary to meet their needs and divert them from future justice system involvement. This lack of targeted support can result in more entrenched behavioural challenges and a lack of timely access to key therapeutic interventions.

Similar to Aotearoa New Zealand, research shows that most 10- to 13-year-old children coming to police attention in Australia are dealt with by way of cautions and warnings (55–57%), with only 20–36% of these children's matters proceeding to court (Baidawi et al., 2024a; Freeman & Donnelly, 2024). Of matters that proceed to court, approximately half (45–50%) are dealt with via diversions or youth justice conferences, while 36–53% of matters are withdrawn by the prosecutors (often the *doli incapax* principle was not successfully rebutted). Only in around 20% of 10- to 13-year-old children's matters that proceed to court are children found guilty of at least one charge, and statutory youth justice sentences in the community or custody are very rarely made – in fact these account for only 2–3% of 10- to 13-year-old children with police involvement, and only 8–10% of those matters that proceeded to court (Baidawi et al., 2024a; Freeman & Donnelly, 2024).

Demographic Profile of Children with Offending Behaviours Across Aotearoa New Zealand and Australia

Aotearoa New Zealand – Ministry of Justice, 2024

Recent statistics indicate a nuanced picture of offending behaviours among children in Aotearoa New Zealand. Although offending rates of New Zealander's aged 10 to 17 are 54% lower than they were a decade ago, trends for the 2022/2023 year (ending June 2023) showed an increase on the year prior. The rate of children aged 10–14 entering the youth justice system increased by 14% (relative to the population), marking the first rise in over a decade. Figures for the 2023/2024 year (ending June 2024) showed that the number of children charged with an offence, and the nature of their offending, was similar to the previous year. The rate of children reported to the police in the 2023/2024 year was 75 per 10,000 children, compared to 250 per 10,000 young people.

As mentioned, tamariki Māori (and rangatahi Māori) continue to be overrepresented in the youth justice system, with such disparities persisting over the past decade. Although the rate of tamariki Māori proceeded against declined by 4% from the 2022/2023 to 2023/2024 year, tamariki Māori are still more likely to be proceeded against compared to the total population. For example, the rate of tamariki Māori proceeded against was 175 per 10,000, compared with 75 per 10,000 for the total population, as shown below in Figure 9.1.

Theft was the most common offence for police proceedings in the 2023/2024 year, making up 34% of all police proceedings among children, followed by injury causing (assault) which made up 14%. The number of children with serious and persistent offending, however, showed an 8% decrease from the year prior, with serious offences being defined as those which hold a maximum penalty of greater than or equal to seven years imprisonment. Whilst the overall number of child offenders has declined over the years, gender imbalances remain a consistent feature. The group of children and young people who offend in Aotearoa New Zealand are predominantly male. In 2024, for example, 81% of all children and young people aged 10 to 16 years with finalised charges in any court were male.

Although regional variation has reduced, regional differences in the justice system continue to exist. Offending rates for children per 10,000 population were highest in the Bay of Plenty (130), Eastern (122), and Tasman (121) Police Districts. The proportion of children proceeded against who had a FGC or court action

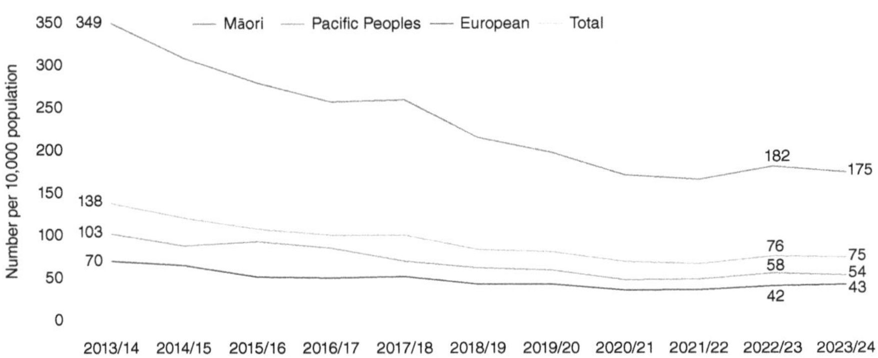

Figure 9.1 Total number of children and young people against whom the police take action per 10,000 population

Note: Total number of children and young people against whom the police take action per 10,000 population. This indicator shows the proportion of children coming into contact with the youth justice system. It measures the number of children against whom the police proceed for allegedly breaking the law, compared to all children. Police action includes warnings, alternative actions, FGCs, and prosecution (Ministry of Justice, 2024).

was highest in the Waitemata (14%), Counties Manukau (14%), Auckland City (12%), and Bay of Plenty (12%) Police Districts.

Most children prosecuted by the police are managed outside of the formal justice system, with only a small proportion of children being referred to Oranga Tamariki for an FGC or being dealt with directly by the Youth Court. Although not all children who are involved in the care and protection system go on to offend, 93% of children in the 2023/2024 year who were referred for an FGC had previously been the subject of a report of concern to Oranga Tamariki about their care and protection. The data highlights that children who offend are often those who have the most complex needs, which can be among the underlying causes of their offending.

Australia

In Australia, children aged 10–13 years comprised 18.5% of the 46,798 children aged 10 to 17 years proceeded against by police in 2023–2024 (Australian Bureau of Statistics (ABS), 2025). Since 2008, this figure has remained relatively stable, with 10–13-year-olds comprising between 15.3% (2013–14) and 19.5% (2022–23) of 10–17-year-olds charged with offending during this period (ABS, 2025).

As outlined above, most younger children in Australia who come to police attention in relation to offending behaviours will be diverted from further criminal justice system processing, however, a small number do receive criminal justice sentences. Children aged 10 to 13 years comprised 7.4% of all children aged 10–17 years under statutory youth justice supervision (764 of 9,924 children under supervision) in 2023–2024. However, the proportion of youth justice clients who were aged 10–13 years varied considerably between Australian jurisdictions, from 1.9% in Victoria to 14.4% in Western Australia (Australian Institute of Health and Welfare (AIHW), 2025). Even after accounting for recent fluctuations in the minimum age of criminal responsibility across Australia, these differences suggest a concerning level of variation in police practices towards younger children.

One area of particular concern is the variability in the overrepresentation in police and youth justice system involvement of First Nations children across Australian states and territories. Data indicate that First Nations children are particularly overrepresented among younger children with police and youth justice system contact in Australia (Baidawi et al., 2024a; Baidawi, 2020). Further, the proportion of 10- to 13-year-old children under youth justice supervision who are Aboriginal and Torres Strait Islanders varies considerably across Australian jurisdictions, from 18.2% in Victoria to 92.6% in the Northern Territory (AIHW, 2025), suggestive of variation in policing and prosecution practices nationwide. Aside from national variations, research has also identified racial bias in the criminal justice system processing of Indigenous young people. For example, one New South Wales (NSW) study demonstrated that Indigenous young people were more likely to receive a court summons (rather than diversionary alternative) following their first offence compared with non-Indigenous offenders when controlling for gender, age, and the nature and number of charges processed at first offence (Papalia et al., 2019). Other NSW research similarly found that after adjusting for the effects of legally relevant factors, Indigenous juvenile offenders (regardless of sex) were more likely to be prosecuted than cautioned, compared with their non-Indigenous counterparts (Weatherburn & Thomas, 2022).

Australian research has repeatedly shown that offending behaviour among younger children under 14 years tends to be non-violent in nature, most commonly minor offences such as shoplifting and trespassing (Baidawi et al., 2024b; Freeman & Donnelly, 2024). At the same time, a minority of 10- to 13-year-old children appear to engage in more serious or persistent offending behaviour consistent with international evidence. For example, one Australian study found that only a small number of children (less than 2% of those charged with offences) accounted for one-quarter of all youth offending over an eight-year period (Sutherland & Millsteed, 2016).

Overall, the above figures show that younger children are involved with a small proportion of the offending behaviour that comes to police and youth justice attention in Australia, and that most of the offending behaviour seen among this cohort is non-violent and time-limited.

Systemic Gaps and Systemic Failures

Systemic gaps and failures for responding to younger children with offending behaviours are evident across both Aotearoa New Zealand and Australia's youth justice systems, with similar experiences observed between the two nations. A recent study conducted by Reil et al. (2024) highlighted the experiences of key stakeholders regarding the systemic issues present for children who had offended in Aotearoa New Zealand. Key stakeholders included family members, lawyers, police officers, social workers, psychologists, and school and cultural leaders. Barriers to effectively responding to childhood offending were identified through the following themes:

- **Child-welfare engagement that was delayed and ineffective** – a unanimous theme whereby children and families received support far too late in a child's life (despite various welfare concerns being made prior).
- **Deficit-focused engagement with families and children** – engagement with child-welfare systems was often perceived as deficit-based (compared to strengths-focused), punitive towards the child and family, and lacking respect.
- **Under-resourced Family Court systems that delayed court proceedings and further hindered effective child-welfare intervention** – with the Family Court being the busiest court in Aotearoa New Zealand, unanimous frustration was expressed regarding significant delays. These delays were seen to negatively affect children and families, with concerns raised regarding the increased risk of offending within communities.
- **System shortfalls that continued once a child had offended** – concern regarding children "falling through the cracks" due to ineffective practices which continued once children had offending. This included a lack of comprehensive need assessments and subsequent assistance from the involved agencies.
- **All of which occurred within the context** of widespread uncertainty as to how to best respond or access appropriate and culturally safe interventions.

A recent Australian study which sought the views of a range of professionals who work with children aged 10–13 years displaying offending behaviours, identified similar systemic gaps and failures. Professional parties interviewed included judicial officers, defence lawyers, police prosecutors and officers, psychologists and mental health clinicians, youth justice and youth support and advocacy professionals (Baidawi et al., 2024a). The participants' collective experience identified the following key concerns in the Australian context:

- **Limitations of child protection system responses:** Child protection seen to withdraw support from children with early offending behaviours, deferring to a youth justice system response instead; out-of-home care providers were seen to be overly reliant on punitive criminal justice responses to younger children's challenging behaviours (i.e. calling police), in lieu of more therapeutic approaches; the placement of children in out-of-home care settings with older peers who were already engaged in offending behaviours was also seen to inflate younger children's risk.
- **Limitations of education system responses:** Children charged with early offending were seen to be excluded from, or unsupported by educational systems. Additionally, a lack of flexible education options for younger children aged 10–13 years was identified, with the available programmes seen to target older adolescents.
- **Limitations of overall system responses:** Systems' differing ideologies and practices in responding to younger children with offending behaviours were problematic (e.g. viewing these through a criminal justice vs mental health, vs therapeutic welfare lens); a lack of available services targeting younger children with offending behaviours was also observed, alongside stigmatised responses to racialised minority children and their families (including New Zealand citizens living in Australia who are often ineligible for various government-funded services).
- **Limitations of system responses for Aboriginal and/or Torres Strait Islander children:** Insufficient culturally responsive programmes and services outside of Aboriginal Community Controlled Organisations (ACCOs); despite the acknowledged overrepresentation of Aboriginal and Torres Strait Islander children in these systems, there remained insufficient funding for ACCOs to deliver culturally safe services to families and communities. Additionally, more punitive policing approaches (over-policing and other harsher responses), and police racism were observed towards Aboriginal and Torres Strait Islander children.

A Current Lack of Specialist Responses

It is important to highlight that Youth Justice is not synonymous with early intervention. Notably, there remains a deafening silence present across literature as to what feeds the youth justice system and the outcomes for children who engage in offending behaviours. Various reports and inquires having been completed which have emphasised the importance of early intervention to reduce future crime and improve life outcomes in Aotearoa New Zealand [AGCP, 2009; New Zealand Parliament, 2012; Youth Crime Action Plan (Ministry of Justice, 2013)]. Despite this, literature remains limited on how to identify and intervene with children who may be at risk of escalating to offending behaviours and few coordinated efforts to translate these views into action have been taken. The limited focus on childhood offending behaviours has also contributed to a lack of understanding regarding the extent to which our legal processes effectively respond to children who offend (Reil et al., 2021).

As discussed, in Aotearoa New Zealand, childhood offending behaviours are often considered to be a result of underlying welfare issues and are handled as care and protection matters. Care and protection matters, however, do not always result in applications to the Family Court or Family Court Orders, leading to various missed opportunities to provide effective intervention services to children in need (Reil et al., 2021). Furthermore, no specialised child court division has been developed to date to hear, determine and respond to criminal cases involving children. Whilst the diversionary efforts applied by the child justice system in Aotearoa New Zealand can be commended for their restorative (versus punitive) approach, it is evident that this has inadvertently led to children and families in need of support falling through the gaps. In addition to the lack of specialised child courts, overworked staff and under-resourced organisations may mean those who are involved with the care and protection system do not receive the extent of support they need (Reil et al., 2021).

Whilst initiatives like the "cross-over" courts have been implemented in Aotearoa New Zealand, which aim to deliver more effective service delivery to children who experience involvement with both care and protection and youth justice systems, some have raised concerns that such initiatives are a reactive solution to an ever-growing concern (FitzGerald, 2018). What is clear is that to effectively block entry into the "prison pipeline", increased attention must be directed towards child welfare concerns and conduct-related behaviours in children at the earliest opportunity, before an offence is committed (Baidawi, 2020; Baidawi & Sheehan, 2020).

In Australia, there are likewise minimal specialist responses to younger children's offending behaviour (Baidawi et al., 2024a). While specialist Children's Courts exist in all Australian states and territories, these do not differentiate in their responses to younger and older children. However, some jurisdictions (including Victoria and the Australian Capital Territory [ACT]) have recently increased their MACR, and are consequently developing or implementing alternative service models to respond to harmful behaviours in younger children. For example, from mid-2025, the ACT Government raised its MACR to 14 years of age (with exceptions for very serious offences). The alternative service model implemented in 2024 is one of a legislated Therapeutic Panel (TSP), comprised of a Chair and 10 to 12 other members with qualifications, experience and expertise in areas including psychology, criminology, education, social work, or working with Aboriginal and Torres Strait Islander children and young people, among others (Barker, 2024). The panel also has four government-appointed positions from the community services, education, health and policing sectors. The TSP coordinates multidisciplinary therapeutic services and supports for referred children. This involves reviewing referrals, supporting assessments, developing therapeutic plans, and recommending when more intensive options should be sought (e.g. mandated therapeutic orders). Additionally, the TSP has a broader role in identifying systemic barriers (e.g. lack of services) that prevent effective responses to younger children with harmful behaviours (Barker, 2024). While the state of Victoria has also recently increased its MACR to 12 years of age, it is yet to finalise its Alternative Service Model to better support 10- and 11-year-olds with harmful behaviours.

The Imperative for Focusing on Offending Behaviours in Children

Early offending behaviours are often indicative of complex unmet needs related to social learning and attachment difficulties, ongoing experiences of colonisation, and other cultural and historical trauma, leading to family challenges, exposure to violence, and socio-economic challenges. Intervening during childhood with appropriate supports is essential for addressing these root causes and preventing the entrenchment of offending behaviours and criminal justice system involvement. Research suggests that without timely and appropriate interventions, children with offending behaviours may be at a higher risk of continuing on a trajectory that leads to more serious offences in adolescence and adulthood. However, the support required need not come through a criminal justice system response. Indeed, many of the required supports are inherently best provided outside of the criminal justice system.

Important Considerations for Early Intervention

Despite compelling scientific evidence across the literature demonstrating the impact of early-onset offending behaviours, our understanding of how to best identify and intervene with children who may be at risk of entering this pathway remains limited. It is apparent within developmental literature that the factors underlying childhood offending behaviours are complex, and that interventions need to be equally well-considered and targeted in order to be effective.

To date, available interventions have largely focused on the treatment and management of conduct problems in children. Such programmes include parent management training/social learning programmes, classroom and school-based interventions, and individual child therapies that centre around intervention in preschool years. The overall body of evidence indicates that well-designed and effectively implemented interventions can significantly reduce the long-term risk of conduct problems and further antisocial behaviour. Several key cautions, however, must be emphasised. For interventions to be effective, they must be carefully planned, properly delivered, culturally responsive, and thoroughly evaluated. Programmes that lack these essential components are often ineffective and may result in wasted resources (AGCP, 2009).

Promising Interventions

Current responses to children with early offending behaviours result in substantial missed opportunities to better support this group, while continuing to criminalise such children – directly and indirectly – with little therapeutic or developmental benefit. Recommended reforms for better supporting this group centre on mental health and disability assessment and support, educational engagement, referral to diversion programmes, supporting families and parents, and development of the child's network of prosocial and culturally supportive activities and relationships (Lambie & Ioane, 2024). Service reforms recommended to better support younger children with offending behaviours should focus on justice reinvestment into culture and trauma-informed approaches that centre child wellbeing and engage the child within the context of their family and community (Baidawi et al., 2024a). Given the overrepresentation of Indigenous and ethnic minorities across Aotearoa New Zealand and Australia's youth justice systems, there is a clear need for culturally responsive and safe interventions. The following section looks to examine promising intervention strategies tailored to Indigenous and ethnic minority children and their families.

Balit Ngulu Service (Victorian Aboriginal Legal Service – VALS) – Australia

Balit Ngulu, which means "Strong Voice" in Woiwurrung, is a specialist youth legal service for Aboriginal and Torres Strait Islander children and young people with matters in the Melbourne metropolitan, Greater Shepparton areas (including Echuca) and Hume region in north-central Victoria, Australia. The services' primary area of practice is criminal law. Balit Ngulu was first established in 2017 for Aboriginal children and young people who came into contact with the justice system and/or child protection to receive high-quality legal advice and representation from dedicated youth lawyers and holistic support and case management from Aboriginal Community Engagement (ACE) workers. The service re-launched in September 2021, with a primary focus in youth justice.

The purpose of Balit Ngulu is to give clients high-quality legal advice and representation, address the drivers of their contact with the justice system and/or child protection services and support positive pathways for their longer-term recovery and resilience. In this way, the programme works to contribute to reducing the overrepresentation of Indigenous people in the justice system and child protection, and to contribute to creating conditions in which Aboriginal and Torres Strait Islander children and young people are empowered and thrive.

The Critical Design Features of the Balit Ngulu Service Model Include:

- Highly accessible legal advice, support and representation (as active outreach response).
- Provision of culturally safe, empowering wraparound support and case work with Aboriginal children and young people.
- Development of trauma-informed client plans to address drivers and impacts of Child Protection, family violence and justice involvement, and other non-legal needs, to facilitate positive pathways.

- Advocacy and active referral and linkage for Aboriginal Children and young people (CYP) ongoing case load, and family where appropriate, to a range of community justice, SEWB, healing, cultural and other supports and services.
- Collaboration with key ACCO's and other services to develop and deliver tailored support for each Aboriginal CYP.

The Model Consists of the Following Staffing:

- A Principle Managing Lawyer with accredited specialisation in Children's Law.
- Across Preston and Shepparton, four full-time youth specialist lawyers equipped to represent CYP in respect of their criminal matters, with a caseload of 15–20 CYP depending on level of complexity.
- One Senior Lawyer secondee from Victoria Legal Aid.
- Two part-time legal secretaries equivalent to 1 FTE.
- Across Shepparton and Preston, two full-time Aboriginal community engagement (ACE) workers with a caseload of 10–15 CYP depending on level of complexity.

Evaluation of Balit Ngulu: In mid-2019, VALS, in collaboration with the National Aboriginal and Torres Strait Islander Legal Services (NATSILS), engaged Nous Group (Nous) to evaluate Balit Ngulu. VALS wanted to understand and document the benefits that Balit Ngulu may have had for its clients and identify, through facilitated reflection and assessment, what matters for the delivery of effective, culturally safe legal services and holistic support for young Aboriginal and Torres Strait Islander people. The feedback the evaluation received on Balit Ngulu's service quality and outcomes was overwhelmingly positive. Young people who participated in the programme said they felt supported by experienced staff who demonstrated they cared about them and whom they could trust. They said this support helped them manage stress, participate in court, feel stronger in their family and community, and start re-establishing their lives. These outcomes were very valuable to clients.

Wraparound Model – Aotearoa New Zealand

The high-fidelity wraparound model, developed by the National Wraparound Initiative (NWI) in the United States, provides a comprehensive, culturally responsive framework for supporting children, adolescents, and their families with emotional, social, and behavioural challenges (Lightfoot et al., 2023). It is based on holistic, strengths-based principles, aligning closely with Māori wellbeing models, and has demonstrated effectiveness in improving life outcomes and therefore reducing youth offending (Bruns et al., 2010).

Wraparound is a personalised, theory-of-change-driven care planning process. The approach is for a collaborative team of professionals, family members, and community supports to discover the underlying needs of the family, which may have developed into behaviours of concern, and to create a coordinated plan to meet the needs of tamariki, whānau, and their community (Bruns & Walker, 2010). The model focuses on the family system, prioritising cultural values, strengths, and aspirations as the team work towards intervening and changing current behaviours. The models' adaptability is particularly suited to tamariki with complex behavioural, mental health, developmental, and cultural needs across multiple domains (Burchard et al., 2002).

Research from the United States has shown that high-fidelity wraparound services significantly reduce out-of-home placements, improve educational engagement, and decrease justice system involvement (Bruns et al., 2014; Olsen et al., 2021). Internal evaluations showed improved academic engagement and social-emotional well-being, protective factors against later offending (Hill, 2020). Although programme designs vary, there is strong evidence to support wraparound as a promising approach for disrupting offending trajectories in children and young people.

The NWI defines ten core principles underpinning the wraparound philosophy: family voice and choice; team-based planning; natural supports; collaboration; community-based delivery; cultural competence; individual approach; strengths-based focus; persistence; and outcome-driven practice (Bruns et al., 2010). The wraparound process follows four dynamic phases: engagement, plan development, implementation, and transition (Walker et al., 2004):

- Engagement involves whakawhanaungatanga (relationship-building), culturally humble and safe practices, comprehensive needs assessment, and gathering the whānau story, cultural identity, and trauma/neurodiversity considerations.
- Plan Development centres on collaboratively designing a concise, systemic plan informed by the whānau vision and the team's mission.
- Implementation requires regular team meetings to monitor progress, adjust interventions, and ensure fidelity to wraparound principles, while integrating community and natural supports.
- Transition focuses on sustainability, gradually moving from professional-led supports to naturally occurring community and whānau systems.

Adaptations of the Wraparound Model Internationally and for Aotearoa New Zealand

Originally developed in the USA, the wraparound model has also been adapted internationally. Agencies exist in these territories that have implemented the Wraparound Model; however, peer-reviewed evidence is limited. In Canada, Henderson and van den Heuvel (2008) discussed how high-fidelity wraparound was developed across Ontario and demonstrated improvements in young people's social and emotional needs and cost savings due to less demand for residential placements. In Australia, Smith et al. (2018) discussed a case study supporting at-risk young people and improved clinical outcomes and cost savings over time. Furthermore, Aboriginal and Torres Strait Islander organisations have emphasised trauma-informed, kinship, and cultural continuity approaches within wraparound frameworks are preferred options for working with their Indigenous peoples (Higgins & Davis, 2019).

In Aotearoa, early pilot initiatives demonstrated the potential for integrated wraparound responses to reduce school exclusion, family dysfunction, and social disconnection (Robertson et al., 2015). Several agencies in Aotearoa have adapted the wraparound model, although fidelity and target populations have varied. Currently, no agency specialises in applying wraparound specifically for tamariki aged 5–12 at risk of offending. Nevertheless, the model's flexibility suits the bicultural context of Aotearoa, particularly when working with neurodiverse tamariki and their whānau (Shailer et al., 2018).

Tamariki Māori are disproportionately overrepresented in child protection and youth justice systems (Lambie, 2018c), reflecting systemic, historical, and social inequities. Many tamariki present with in the care of social services may have developmental trauma, Fetal Alcohol Spectrum Disorder (FASD), ADHD, and executive functioning challenges, which heighten vulnerability to adverse life outcomes (McLachlan et al., 2020). Standard interventions often rely on verbal engagement, potentially disadvantaging tamariki Māori with neurodevelopmental differences and cultural communication styles, highlighting the need for adapted, multisensory, strengths-based approaches (Maitland et al., 2025). Essential adaptations for effective wraparound practice in Aotearoa include whānau-focused psychoeducation, integrated specialist planning across health, education, and social sectors, sensory-informed interventions, and positive behavioural support frameworks.

Culturally Aligned Wraparound Practice in Aotearoa New Zealand: The wraparound model aligns with Māori wellbeing frameworks such as Te Whare Tapa Whā and Te Waka Oranga (Durie, 2004; Elder, 2017). These models emphasise relational, holistic, and culturally anchored approaches to healing and development. Te Waka Oranga specifically integrates neurodevelopmental science with Māori healing traditions to address trauma and adversity among tamariki Māori. The waka metaphor provides a culturally resonant narrative, affirming identity, facilitating intergenerational healing, and promoting collective whānau empowerment. Wellbeing is conceptualised as a shared journey, supported by tūpuna (ancestors), whānau, hapū, and iwi. Embedding Te Waka Oranga within the wraparound process supports dual epistemologies of Western neurodevelopmental science and Mātauranga Māori, therefore upholding kaupapa Māori values such as manaakitanga (care and compassion), whanaungatanga (relationships and connectedness), and rangatiratanga (self-determination and agency).

Evaluating the Effectiveness of Wraparound in Aotearoa: While international evidence for the effectiveness of the wraparound model is positive, especially in the United States, in Aotearoa, specific research remains limited primarily due to the years it has been in existence and the resources allotted towards research. Internal agency reports and small-scale studies suggest positive impacts, but further peer-reviewed evaluation is needed. Successful implementation for tamariki aged 5–12 at risk of offending would require attention to several factors:

- Building a skilled, culturally competent workforce.
- Establishing enduring partnerships across government, iwi, and NGO sectors.
- Securing sustainable funding mechanisms.
- Utilising robust fidelity measures and outcome monitoring tools (Attell et al., 2023).

Future programmes should embed rigorous evaluation frameworks to strengthen the evidence base, ensuring that culturally adapted, high-fidelity wraparound practice can drive transformative outcomes for tamariki and their whānau. The high-fidelity wraparound model can be a useful vehicle for change in the Aotearoa context, with appropriately skilled practitioners and in combination with other evidence-based interventions.

Wraparound in Practice – Mana Tamariki: Mana Tamariki is a service set up within Oranga Tamariki to work preventatively with whānau and tamariki (aged 6–10.5 years) across Tāmaki Makaurau (Auckland) to address their underlying needs, reduce future poor life outcomes and youth justice involvement. Mana Tamariki utilises the wraparound framework, which includes an individualised plan to support behavioural issues, non-compliance, school refusal, emotional regulation and parenting skills. Mana Tamariki employs an intensive social work team whose aim is to build trust with the whānau, collectively problem solve and support the whānau, increase natural supports which will endure past the programme end, and improve life outcomes for tamariki through a reduction in youth justice involvement (Oranga Tamariki, 2022). Outcomes for tamariki involved with the Mana Tamariki Programme have included:

- Re-engagement with school, a safe return to parents/whānau.
- Greater parental success in managing and subsequently reducing challenging behaviour.
- Increased involvement of supportive wider whānau.
- Increased tamariki engagement in prosocial community engagements and therapeutic supports.

Long-Term Benefits of Early Intervention

Addressing offending behaviours in children yields significant long-term benefits across individual, societal and economic domains. By intervening early, we are able to support the development of healthier children whilst also fostering safer communities.

- **Reduced Recidivism**: Early, targeted interventions disrupt the cycle of reoffending by addressing the root causes of problematic behaviour, leading to fewer interactions with the justice system over time. Providing children with the appropriate support in early childhood assists with the development of prosocial behaviours and works to decrease their likelihood of re-entering the justice system in adolescence or adulthood.
- **Enhanced Well-being**: Children who exhibit offending behaviours can struggle with unaddressed trauma, emotional regulation difficulties or mental health challenges. Early intervention can provide therapeutic support, stable mentorship and positive role models that aims to improve overall well-being.
- **Economic Advantages**: Investing in prevention and early support is significantly more cost effective than responding to offending behaviour after is has

occurred. Decreasing offending behaviours in children reduces the financial burden on the justice system and fosters a more productive, contributing citizen. Fewer court proceedings and reduced reliance on incarceration allows for substantial public savings that can be diverted to further rehabilitation and intervention initiatives.

- **Improved Life Outcomes:** Early intervention plays a crucial role in shaping the life trajectories of children who exhibit offending behaviours. By addressing the underlying causes of these behaviours through effective intervention, children are provided better opportunities to develop the social, emotional and cognitive skills necessary for long term success and a healthier lifestyle.
- **Reduce Prison Populations:** Effective early intervention reduces the number of young people who progress into the "prison pipeline", easing pressure on the prison system. This shift allows for justice resources to be directed toward proactive rehabilitation compared to reactive rehabilitation.
- **Fewer Victims:** By preventing offending behaviour before it escalates, early intervention strategies reduce the number of people affected by crime. This leads to safer communities, reduced emotional and physical harm to individuals, and lower societal costs related to victim support services.
- **Thriving Communities:** Communities benefit when young people are supported. A culture of early intervention and support fosters increased trust in public services and encourages civic engagement. Ultimately, early intervention helps to promote social stability and long-term prosperity for our communities.

Key Relevant Points and Integration of Theory and Practice

12.10.1 Cultural Integration: Incorporating Indigenous cultural practices into intervention programmes enhances their relevance and effectiveness for Indigenous and ethnic minority children. Internationally, there is significant recognition and appreciation of the important role culture plays in generating and supporting individual and community wellbeing. Such appreciation has driven the need for dual clinical and cultural competencies and the development of a workforce that is committed to attaining the best outcomes for Indigenous peoples. In developing culturally informed interventions for conduct concerns and offending related behaviours in children, the following must be considered;

- Whilst the use of evidence-based approaches remains the gold standard for psychological intervention, approaches must also recognise Indigenous knowledge and experience as valid and work to incorporate them into practice (AGCP, 2009).
- At all stages of development, cultural consultation and participation must be included to effectively design, implement and deliver culturally appropriate and responsive interventions (AGCP, 2009).
- Practitioners working with conduct problems and offending related behaviours in children must be competent in delivering inclusive practices that extend beyond behaviour management and encompass both the broader family system and the wider ecology of the child (Barker & Hawes, 2024).

Community Involvement**:** Engaging families and communities in rehabilitation ensures that support systems are in place, facilitating sustainable positive outcomes. Removal of a young person from their community can impact both social and psychological development, in turn creating challenges for their successful transition into adolescence and adulthood (Lambie & Randell, 2013; Lambie & Ioane, 2024). Effective intervention and rehabilitation do not occur in isolation and require families and communities to be actively engaged in the process. Community engagement builds a sense of shared responsibility for child outcomes and works to encourage cross-agency collaboration between social services and law enforcement. The aim of an inclusive and wraparound approach is to ensure that progress for children is sustained over time and is maintained even after the formal intervention has ended.

Holistic Approaches**:** Children who display offending behaviours often face multiple interconnected challenges. A one-dimensional or traditional Western approach in these cases is unlikely to create lasting change. Addressing the multifaceted needs of children with offending behaviours, including education, mental health, and social support, leads to more comprehensive and lasting solutions. Holistic approaches recognise the complexity of a child's individual situation and look to address the full spectrum of their needs. For Indigenous and ethnic minority populations, this requires the delivery of interventions which consider and promote collective ownership, shared beliefs or world views, and reinforcement of community values. By tackling the root causes of offending behaviour, rather than just individual symptoms, holistic and culturally minded approaches offer a greater chance of long-term success across populations (Advisory Group on Conduct Problems, 2009).

Where to From Here?

To sustain and build on the successes of existing programmes, a strategic and inclusive approach is required. This involves expanding accessibility, ensuring programme quality through evaluation, and emphasising the need for strong policy support.

Expand Access: Ensure culturally responsive interventions are available to all children who display offending behaviours, particularly in underserved regions such as rural, remote, and marginalised communities. Expanding access will mean that every child who exhibits early signs of offending behaviour will have the opportunity to benefit from support – preventing potential entry into the "prison pipeline". A particular emphasis must be placed on culturally responsive interventions given the overrepresentation of Indigenous children to ensure programmes are designed in consultation with the communities they aim to serve. Without equitable access, the cycle of disadvantage and offending behaviours within our communities with persist, likely undermining the broader success of early intervention strategies.

Continuous Evaluation**:** Intervention effectiveness must not be assumed but measured and continually improved through evaluation. To do so, we must implement robust monitoring and evaluation frameworks to assess programme effectiveness and inform ongoing improvements. Continuous evaluation allows for stakeholders to assess whether interventions are achieving the desired outcomes (i.e. behavioural changes), identify areas for improvement, and ensure child well-being remains at the forefront. Qualitative feedback from families, children, and practitioners is equally as important to understand how the intervention is experienced and received. High-quality outcomes are closely tied to those delivering the intervention, emphasising the importance of having well-trained, competent practitioners delivering such evidence-based interventions. Practitioner skill, adherence to treatment protocols and ongoing professional development and cultural competency must also be evaluated across intervention implementation (Barker & Hawes, 2024). In development and implementation stages, consideration must also be given to the scalability and sustainability of programmes. This is to ensure programmes are not limited to isolated pilot initiatives scattered across regions without long-term funding and strategic integration into broader social systems.

Policy Support: For early intervention to be achievable and sustainable, we must advocate for policies that prioritise child and family welfare. This requires long-term investment and political commitment to prevention over and above intervention. The gaps evident between policy and practice, as well as between evidence and implementation, must be closed. Policies must prioritise early intervention as a core strategy across justice, health, and education systems. Particularly, we must advocate for policies that prioritise early intervention and allocate resources toward programmes that address the specific needs of Indigenous and ethnic minority children to reduce the disproportionate overrepresentation of these communities within the justice system. Advocacy efforts must aim to reduce clear systemic barriers, promote equity, and create communities in which all children are provided a fair chance to thrive.

References

Advisory Group on Conduct Problems (AGCP). (2009). *Conduct problems: Best practice*. Conduct Problems: Best Practice Report – conduct-problems.pdf – University of Otago.

Amnesty International. (2022). *NZ Government must raise the age of criminal responsibility.* Amnesty International Aotearoa. Government must raise the age of criminal responsibility in Aotearoa New Zealand.

Armstrong, B. (2019). Why the presumption of doli incapax should be the first consideration in youth court matters. *Law Society of South Australia Bulletin*, 41(7), 8–9.

Attell, B., Singleton, A., McLaren, S., & Moses, G. (2023). Measurement characteristics of the Wraparound Fidelity Index Short Form: Results from a statewide implementation. *Evaluation & the Health Professions*, 46(1), 50–70.

Attorney-General's Department. (2020). *Draft final report to Council of Attorneys-General: Age of Criminal Responsibility Working Group*. https://www.ag.gov.au/about-us/publications/standingcouncil-attorneys-general-communiques

Australian Bureau of Statistics (ABS). (2025). *Recorded crime – Offenders, 2023–24.* ABS cat. no. 4519.0. Canberra: Australian Bureau of Statistics.

Australian Human Rights Commission. (2020). *Review of the age of criminal responsibility. Submission to the Council of Attorneys-General Age of Criminal Responsibility Working Group.* Sydney: Australian Human Rights Commission

Australian Institute of Health and Welfare (AIHW). (2025). *Youth justice in Australia 2023–24.* AIHW cat. no. JUV 138. Canberra: Australian Institute of Health and Welfare.
Baidawi, S. (2020). Crossover children: Examining initial criminal justice system contact among child protection-involved youth. *Australian Social Work*, 73(3), 280–295. https://doi.org/10.1080/0312407X.2019.1686765
Baidawi, S., Ball, R., Newitt, R., Turnbull, L., Kembhavi-Tam, G., Avery, S., & Sheehan, R. (2022). *Research report – Care criminalisation of children with disability in child protection systems.* Royal Commission into Violence, Abuse, Neglect and Exploitation of People with Disability.
Baidawi, S., Ball, R., Sheehan, R., & Papalia, N. (2024a). *Children aged 10 to 13 in the justice system: Characteristics, alleged offending and legal outcomes. Report to the Criminology Research Advisory Council.* Canberra: AIC. https://www.aic.gov.au/sites/default/files/2024-01/crg_41_20_21_children_aged_10_to_13_in_the_justice_system.pdf
Baidawi, S., Ball, R., Sheehan, R., & Papalia, N. (2024b). *Police and children's court outcomes for children aged 10 to 13.* Trends & issues in crime and criminal justice no. 679. Canberra: Australian Institute of Criminology. https://doi.org/10.52922/ti77192
Baidawi, S., Huggins, L., Forrester, L., Sheehan, R., Ogloff, J. R. P., & Papalia, N. (2026). Expert assessment of children's criminal capacity: An analysis of doli incapax psychological reports in Australia. *Psychiatry, Psychology & Law*, 679, 1–23.
Baidawi, S., & Sheehan, R. (2020). *"Crossover" children in the youth justice and child protection systems.* Routledge.
Barker, J. M. (2024). *Therapeutic support panel for children and young people report.* Canberra: ACT Government. https://www.act.gov.au/data/assets/pdf_file/0010/2834983/Therapeutic-support-panel-for-children-and-young-people-2024-report.pdf
Barker, J. M., & Hawes, D. J. (2024). Practitioner review: A core competencies perspective on the evidence-based treatment of child conduct problems. *Journal of Child Psychology and Psychiatry*, 65(2), 124–136.
Bruns, E. J., Pullmann, M. D., Sather, A., Brinson, R., & Ramey, M. (2014). Effectiveness of wraparound versus case management for children and adolescents: Results of a randomized study. *Administration and Policy in Mental Health and Mental Health Services Research*, 42(3), 309–322.
Bruns, E. J., & Walker, J. S. (2010). The wraparound process: Individualized, community-based care for children and adolescents with intensive needs. In C. A. Heflinger & C. T. Nixon (Eds.), *Families and the mental health system for children and adolescents* (pp. 135–154). SAGE.
Bruns, E. J., Walker, J. S., Zabel, M., Matarese, M., Estep, K., Harburger, D., & Pires, S. A. (2010). Ten principles of the wraparound process. National Wraparound Initiative.
Burchard, J. D., Bruns, E. J., & Burchard, S. N. (2002). The wraparound approach. In B. J. Burns & K. Hoagwood (Eds.), *Community treatment for youth: Evidence-based interventions for severe emotional and behavioral disorders* (pp. 69–90). Oxford University Press.
Chrichton, S., Templeton, R., Tumen, S., Otta, R., Small, D., Wilson, M., & Rea, D. (2015). *New findings on outcomes for children and young people who have contact with Child, Youth and Family.* Wellington, NZ: Ministry of Social Development.
Crimes Act. (1961). Crimes Act 1961 No 43 (as at 14 March 2025), Public Act 22 Children between 10 and 14 – New Zealand Legislation.
Cunneen, C., & Porter, A. (2017). Indigenous Peoples and Criminal Justice in Australia. In A. Deckert & R. Sarre (Eds.), *The Palgrave handbook of Australian and New Zealand criminology, crime and justice*. Cham: Palgrave Macmillan.
Dickson, N. (2025, April). *Chief social worker practice note: Understanding what the repeal of section 7AA means for our practice.* Oranga Tamariki. https://practice.orangatamariki.govt.nz/assets/practice/Practice-notes/practice-note-understanding-what-the-repeal-of-section-7aa-means-for-our-practice.pdf
Durie, M. (2004). Understanding health and illness: Research at the interface between science and indigenous knowledge. *International Journal of Epidemiology*, 33, 1138–1143.

Elder, H. (2017). *Te Waka Oranga: A model for bicultural neurodevelopmental assessment.* Te Pou o te Whakaaro Nui.

Fergusson, D. M., Boden, J. M., & Horwood, L. J. (2015). From evidence to policy: Findings from the Christchurch health and development study. *Australian and New Zealand Journal of Criminology*, 48(3), 386–408.

Fergusson, D. M., Horwood, L. J., & Nagin, D. S. (2000). *Offending trajectories in a New Zealand birth cohort. Criminology*, 38(2), 525–552.

FitzGerald, A. (2018). Children in both youth and family courts: New Zealand. *Court in the Act: The Youth Court of New Zealand*, 81, 16–20.

Fitz-Gibbon & O'Brien. (2019). A child's capacity to commit crime: Examining the operation of doli incapax in Victoria (Australia). *International Journal for Crime, Justice, and Social Democracy*, 8(1), 18–33.

Freeman, K., & Donnelly, N. (2024). *The involvement of young people aged 10 to 13 years in the NSW criminal justice system.* Bureau brief no. 171. Sydney: NSW Bureau of Crime Statistics and Research.

Gatti, U., Tremblay, R. E., & Vitaro, F. (2009). Iatrogenic effect of juvenile justice. *Journal of Child Psychology and Psychiatry*, 50(8), 991–998.

He, V. Y., Roche, S., Williams, J., Williams, T., & Guthridge, S. (2025). Prevalence and factors associated with alleged offending among children aged 10–13 years in the Northern Territory of Australia. *Australian Journal of Social Sciences*, 1–14.

Henderson, D. J., & van den Heuvel, M. (2008). The Canadian High Fidelity Wraparound model: A community-based approach for children and youth with complex needs and their families. *Ontario Association of Children's Aid Societies Journal*, 52(1), 16–22.

Higgins, D., & Davis, K. (2019). Law and policy frameworks supporting Aboriginal and Torres Strait islander child and family services. *Australian Social Work*, 72(3), 331–344.

Hill, R. A. (2020). Wraparound: A key component of school-wide culture competence to support academics and socio-emotional well-being. *Peabody Journal of Education*, 95(1), 66–72.

Lambie, I. (2018a). *It's never too early, never too late: A discussion paper on preventing youth offending in New Zealand.* Wellington, New Zealand: Office of the Prime Minister's Chief Science Advisor.

Lambie, I. (2018b). *Using evidence to build a better justice system: The challenge of rising prison costs.* Wellington, New Zealand: Office of the Prime Minister's Chief Science Advisor.

Lambie, I. (2018c). *What were they thinking? A discussion paper on brain and behaviour in relation to the justice system in New Zealand.* Office of the Prime Minister's Chief Science Advisor.

Lambie, I., & Ioane, J. (2024). Youth offending interventions. In L. A. Craig., L. Dixon, & T. A. Gannon (Eds.), *In the Wiley handbook of what works in correctional rehabilitation: An evidence-based approach to theory, assessment and treatment* (pp. 273–286). John Wiley & Sons, Inc.

Lambie, I., & Randell, I. (2013). The impact of incarceration on juvenile offenders. *Clinical Psychology Review*, 33(3), 448–459.

Lightfoot, L. R., de Terte, I., Ross, K., Etheredge, R., & Gammon, R. (2023). Wraparound: An adaptable, promising intervention to support isolated youth or those at risk of stress, social support, and the buffering. In S. Mozes & M. Israelashvili (Eds.), *Youth without family to lean on: Global challenges and local interventions* (pp. 259–277). Routledge.

Loeber, R., & Farrington, D. P. (2000). Young children who commit crime: Epidemiology, developmental origins, risk factors, early interventions, and policy implications. *Development and Psychopathology*, 12(4), 737–762.

Lynch, N., Lambie, I., Becroft, A., & Wilson-Tasi, T. (2021). *Four urgent law changes for the youth justice system.* Te Herenga Waka – Victoria University of Welling. Four-Urgent-Law-Changes-for-the-Youth-Justice-System.pdf

Maitland, R., Smith, J., Gillon, G., & Hyter, Y. (2025). *Culturally responsive practices for supporting youth in the youth justice system.* Routledge.

McLachlan, A., MacMillan, H. L., & Wekerle, C. (2020). Developmental trauma and its correlates: Implications for child welfare. *Child Abuse & Neglect*, 110, 104437.
Ministry of Justice. (2013). *Youth crime action plan 2013–2023.* 41110_YCAP_full_report_0.pdf
Ministry of Justice. (2024, December). *Youth justice indicators summary report.* Wellington: Ministry of Justice.
Moffitt, T. E. (2015). Life-course-persistent versus adolescent-limited antisocial behaviour. In D. Cicchetti & D. Cohen (Eds.), *Developmental psychopathology* (pp. 570–598). John Wiley & Sons, Inc.
Moffitt, T. E., & Caspi, A. (2001). Childhood predictors differentiate life-course persistent and adolescent-limited antisocial pathways among males and females. *Development and Psychopathology*, 13, 355–375.
Moffitt, T. E., Caspi, A., Harrington, H., & Milne, B. J. (2002). Males on the life-course-persistent and adolescent-limited antisocial pathways: Follow-up at age 26 years. *Development and Psychopathology*, 14(1), 179–207.
New Zealand Parliament. (2012). *Inquiry into the identification, rehabilitation, and care and protection of child offenders.* Reports – Inquiry into the Identification, Rehabilitation, and Care and Protection of Child Offenders – New Zealand Parliament.
Office of the Children's Commissioner. (2020). *Children with offending behaviour: Supporting children, 10–13 year olds who seriously offend and are referred under s14(1)(e) of the Oranga Tamariki Act 1989. State of Care: Children with Offending Behaviour | Mana Mokopuna.* Office of the Children's Commissioner.
Olsen, A., Cook, B. G., & Hirsch, S. E. (2021). Fidelity of wraparound implementation and outcomes: A meta-analysis. *Journal of Emotional and Behavioral Disorders*, 29(3), 183–195.
Oranga Tamariki. (2019, November 22). *Kaupapa Māori approaches in contexts related to youth offending.* https://www.orangatamariki.govt.nz/assets/Uploads/About-us/Research/Latest-research/Kaupapa-Maori-approaches-in-contexts-related-to-youth-offending/Kaupapa-Maori-approaches-in-contexts-related-to-youth-offending-final.pdf
Oranga Tamariki. (2022, August 30). *Children who offend receive more support.* Oranga Tamariki – Ministry for Children.
Oranga Tamariki Act. (1989). www.legislation.govt.nz/act/public/1989/0024/65.0/DLM147088.html
Papalia, N., Shepherd, S. M., Spivak, B., Luebbers, S., Shea, D. E., & Fullam, R. (2019). Disparities in criminal justice system responses to first-time juvenile offenders according to indigenous status. *Criminal Justice and Behavior*, 46(8), 1067–1087.
Reddy, K. J. (2025). Neurodevelopmental disorders and criminal behaviour. In *Foundations of criminal forensic neuropsychology*. Cham: Springer.
Reil, J., & Lambie, I. (2022). Profiles of Children and Young Persons Who Commit Serious Offences. In N. Lynch, Y. van den Brink, & L. Forde (Eds.), *Responses to serious offending by children: Principles, practice and global perspectives* (pp. 41–54). Routledge.
Reil, J., Lambie, I., & Allen, R. (2022). 'Offending doesn't happen in a vacuum': The backgrounds and experiences of children under the age of 14 years who offend. *Journal of Criminology*, 1–19.
Reil, J., Lambie, I., & Allen, R. (2024). Systemic failures in New Zealand's child-welfare and Family Court proceedings underlie and perpetuate child offending. *Journal of Criminology*, 1–22.
Reil, J., Lambie, I., Horwood, J., & Becroft, A. (2021). Children who offend: Why are prevention and intervention efforts to reduce persistent criminality so seldom applied? *Psychology, Public Policy and Law*, 27, 65–78.
Robertson, E. L. (2018). *The potential iatrogenic effects of formal vs. informal juvenile justice system processing: The moderating influence of callous-unemotional traits* (LSU Master's Theses), 4747. Louisiana State University.

Robertson, J., Chamberlain, P., & Roberts, L. (2015). Enhancing the implementation of evidence-based interventions in New Zealand through wraparound support. *Journal of Child and Family Studies*, 24(7), 2097–2105.
Shailer, J., Gammon, R, de Tertel. (2018). Multiple perspectives of teams' experiences of a New Zealand wraparound process. *Australian and New Zealand Journal of Family Therapy*, 39(1), 67–89.
Slot, N., Hoeve, M., & Loeber, R. (2016). *Tomorrow's criminals: The development of child delinquency and effective interventions.* New York: Routledge.
Smith, S, Sitas, M, Rao, P, Nicholls, C, McCann, P, Jonikis, T, Julian, J, Cohen, S, Ellis, J, Waters, F. (2018). Intensive community treatment and support "Youth Wraparound" service in Western Australia: A case and feasibility study. *Early Intervention in Psychiatry*, 13. 10.1111/eip.12734.
Spier, P. (2016). *Offending by children in New Zealand* (Report no. 978-0-947513-29-0). Ministry of Social Development. http://www.msd.govt.nz/documents/about-msd-and-our-work/publications-resources/research/child-and-youth-offending-patterns/offending-by-children-in-new-zealand-sept-2016-publication.docx
Sutherland, P., & Millsteed, M. (2016). *Patterns of recorded offending behaviour amongst young Victorian offenders* (In brief no. 6). Melbourne: Crime Statistics Agency. https://www.crimestatistics.vic.gov.au/research-and-evaluation/publications/patterns-of-recordedoffending-behaviour-amongst-young
United Nations Committee on the Rights of the Child (UNCORC). (2019, September 18). *General comment no 24 (2019) on children's rights in the child justice system*, UN Doc CRC/C/GC/24. https://undocs.org/en/CRC/C/GC/24
Walker, J. S., Koroloff, N., Schutte, K., & Bruns, E. J. (2004). *The practice and process of wraparound: Community-based approaches for children and families*. National Wraparound Initiative.
Weatherburn, D., & Thomas, B. (2022). The influence of indigenous status on the issue of police cautions. *Journal of Criminology*, 56(2–3), 253–277. https://doi.org/10.1177/26338076221146326. (Original work published 2023)
Werry, K. (2022, April). *Criminalising care and protection issues – Child offenders in Aotearoa New Zealand.* Māori Law Review. Criminalising care and protection issues – child offenders in Aotearoa New Zealand – Māori Law Review.

Section Four

Our Final Gift

10 Sparking the Fire for Global Change – A New Beginning

Victoria Nazari, Karmyn Billing, Edmond Fehoko, Therese Ellis-Smith, Logan Hamley, Ian Lambie, Rochelle Nafatali, and Julia Ioane

"Holo pe tu'u he ko e ngalu e fasi" – "Stand firm and the waves will break".[1]

(Tongan)

"I orea te tuatara ka puta ki waho" – "A problem is solved by continuing to find solutions[2]*".*

(Māori)

On March 21, 2025, authors of this book were invited to attend a hui/fono/meeting to discuss what this book could share and teach the rest of the world. The key focus of this book was to prioritise and promote Indigenous[3] worldviews on youth offending. We hope we have done that. Indigenous worldviews are typically collective and therefore, it was important that we conclude our journey with an opinion that reflects us all – our collective identity as authors. The meeting was held online and it was a conversation about what we could share with the rest of the world; and more importantly what can we do about the ongoing overrepresentation of our Indigenous youth in the justice sector.

Two questions were asked:

What do we know about youth offending across the South Pacific?
What can we share with the rest of the world?

The conversation was recorded, and an independent researcher was asked to analyse and draft the data. For ease, the data was analysed thematically and a draft was shared with authors for their input and response. To start, we discussed and explored the structural and intergenerational forces that shaped pathways for our youth into the justice system. Secondly, we highlighted key points that we wanted to share with the rest of the world about youth offending across the south pacific. We then ended our hui with an exploration of Indigenous communities drawing on cultural knowledge and practices to support youth, resist colonial systems, and build meaningful, community-driven responses to harm. The quotes provided in this chapter will not be identified as it is the collective voice of the authors.

DOI: 10.4324/9781003298410-16

What Do We Know About Youth Offending Across the South Pacific?

"It's Bigger than that" – Colonial Legacies and Globalisation

The ongoing, enduring and lasting impact of colonisation on Indigenous peoples remains. A variety of complex, interrelated factors that contribute to youth offending were named throughout our talanoa (conversation). Factors included the legacy of colonial legal systems through the erosion of cultural frameworks, the breakdown of protective community structures, and the persistent marginalisation of Indigenous and Pacific peoples within current Australian and New Zealand state systems. The underlying and most prevalent narrative in our discussion was that offending in the South Pacific, including Australia, Aotearoa New Zealand, and the Pacific Islands, cannot be understood in isolation from the enduring impact of colonisation. Broadly, colonisation was framed by participants as a continuing structure that systematically undermines Indigenous autonomy, identity, and wellbeing, with one participant highlighting:

> colonisation and settler colonial state . . . impact . . . of policies and practices . . . are continuing to this day . . . we see the effects of that including land loss, language loss, oppression, cultural spiritual oppression and the effects that has on our Indigenous communities . . . [the] law has been used to disadvantage Indigenous peoples.

Here, attention is being drawn to how the law has historically been used as a tool of oppression and continues to do so, particularly in its role in facilitating state contact with Indigenous youth, whānau (family) and hapori (community). Laws are derived from the belief systems of cultures and tend to reflect the values, history, and reality of a society (Jackson, 1988). Traditional Māori communities had an underlying set of beliefs and principles referred to as Tikanga, that guided, prescribed, and controlled behaviours as well as protocols for interactions between individuals and groups (Jackson, 1988; Mead, 2003). Te Tiriti o Waitangi, or the Treaty of Waitangi, signed in 1840, created a unique partnership between Māori (the Tangata Whenua or Indigenous people) and the Crown, represented by the New Zealand government. However, successive governments of Aotearoa New Zealand have failed to honour Te Tiriti o Waitangi. The process of colonisation in New Zealand meant that the balance and system of social order within Māori society was disrupted. Examples of laws in Aotearoa New Zealand that have harmed Māori include the Native Lands Act, the Tohunga Suppression Act, and the 1880 Māori Prisoners Act, where it was stated that ". . . it is not necessary to try the . . . natives in order to inflict punishment" (Jackson, 1988). These laws contributed to the loss of collectively held land for Māori, suppressed cultural practices and the passing down of cultural knowledge, resulted in unjust detention and punishment, and further served to undermine the belief system and social structure of Māori. Several laws denied Māori their traditional beliefs and rights both as Māori and as British subjects as agreed to in Te Tiriti o Waitangi.

As of completing this chapter in June 2025, the current government of Aotearoa New Zealand has introduced several bills that arguably undermine Te Tiriti o Waitangi or even attempt to redefine the principles (e.g. Treaty Principles Bill, defeated in its second reading in April 2025) and made decisions that will further marginalise and hurt Māori. Relevant to rangatahi (youth) involved in offending behaviour, this includes the Oranga Tamariki (Responding to Serious Youth Offending) Amendment Bill, which introduces a young serious offender category and reintroduces military style academies for youth offending despite lack of evidence-based effectiveness of such programmes. These initiatives have potential to cause harm to youth by focusing on punitive and more restrictive measures rather than trauma-informed, culturally safe and responsive, and developmentally appropriate responses. Māori, Pasifika, and youth affected by trauma and neurodevelopmental conditions who have offended will be disproportionately affected by these measures.

In the state of Victoria, Australia, a decision was made to strengthen bail laws, with more people expected to be held on remand with the proposed Victoria bail law amendments (Office of the Premier, 2025). This was passed in March 2025, with the first stage focusing on the principle of remand as no longer "a last resort" for youth offending. As it is well-known, it is our Aboriginal Youth who will continue to be affected. Data from 2024 has shown First Nations young people (10–17 years old) are more likely to be in detention than non-Indigenous young people across states and territories (Australian Institute of Health and Welfare, 2024). Unsurprisingly, Pasifika youth remain overrepresented in youth justice statistics in Aotearoa New Zealand and Australia (Ravulo, 2016; Ioane & Lambie, 2016). Therefore, legislative acts that impact on Indigenous communities in Aotearoa New Zealand and Australia also affect our wider Polynesian communities.

The ongoing impact of colonisation was reflected in one participant's observation of "the massive overrepresentation of Aboriginal people, adults and juveniles in the criminal justice system and the appalling incarceration rates". They also noted "the disconnect between the criminal justice system responses to offending behaviour and sentencing." This reflection brings institutional discrimination and structural harm embedded within legal and policy frameworks into focus. Other participants also named specific examples of the law being used to unfairly target and harm Indigenous people today:

> They suspended the laws around racism so they can be as racist as they like. People are going to jail for taking in 1/2 a six pack of beer. Because the intervention [says] they . . . can't take any kind of alcohol into any of the communities, there are over 350 communities.

This example refers to alcohol restrictions imposed under the Northern Territory (Australia) Emergency Response (also known as "the Intervention"), a federal policy enacted in 2007. The policy was introduced under the guise of "child protection" but involved suspending parts of the Racial Discrimination Act and enforcing blanket restrictions that disproportionately targeted Aboriginal communities (Proudfoot &

Habibis, 2015). The quote underscores how such punitive laws, framed as "protective," function to increase surveillance and incarceration of Indigenous peoples. It highlights the intergenerational and structural nature of youth offending, where the "legacy" of colonisation is actively reproduced in colonial systems like justice and child protection systems.

Reflections about an overrepresentation connects closely to another major concern raised by participants: The systemic trajectory that funnels Indigenous children from out of home care into the criminal justice system. One participant detailed that:

> a lot of aboriginal kids . . . come in after being removed from their families, no fault of their own, . . . there's been neglect or abuse . . . sometimes kids are just removed because . . . in Australia, they're targeted . . . So, anything that happens to that young person, even if the parents are doing their best, they're red flagged and . . . they end up in their criminal justice system. It seems to be the trajectory as soon as they're in. . . . The abuse and neglect that happens in the out of home care system is a lot of the reason why . . . a lot of kids on the street who've run away from out of home care agencies or families that are abusive, and so they . . . do end up through that [criminal justice] system.

The structural bias and systemic harm rather than individual behaviour are named as setting Indigenous youth on a path toward criminalisation from an early age (Cunneen, 2000; O'Brien, 2021). The removal of children from their families is highlighted as not necessarily due to anything the child has done, but broader systemic issues including intergenerational surveillance (i.e. "*red flagged*"). Once in the out-of-home care system, many children experience further trauma, neglect, or abuse, which can drive them to seek safety elsewhere, and is observed to be associated with eventual engagement with the justice system.

Structural deprivation caused by colonisation also deeply impacts the physical and mental health of Indigenous communities (Paradies, 2016). These health disparities are shaped by intergenerational trauma and adverse childhood experiences, which remain prevalent due to ongoing systemic inequalities. As one participant explained:

> because of the childhood adverse experiences and the intergenerational trauma that Aboriginal people have experienced, they live less longer. They have more mental health issues; they have more chronic health issues.

This quote highlights the ongoing health impacts of colonisation and the failure of mainstream systems to address their structural causes. Experiences of structural racism and a fear of discrimination also deter Indigenous people from help-seeking. One participant stated, "*a lot of Indigenous people with mental health issues, . . . didn't put their hand up for treatment, didn't seek agency support because they expected to be discriminated against*". There is a fear among Indigenous peoples that they will be misdiagnosed, expecting as one participant highlighted, their "concerns and worries to be written off, as you know, alcohol related". The risks of racial profiling for Indigenous people were highlighted in examples of being misidentified as intoxicated, rather than being assessed for underlying medical conditions:

> people who are being arrested, they're put in jail for whatever or overnight, incarcerated. . . . They've assumed that they're drunk or on drugs, and they're actually having a physical issue. And so, they're left to die in the prison systems. And the next day, they're dead,. . . The fear of people actually being incarcerated is huge.

The profound mistrust and fear that Indigenous and ethnic minority communities have towards state systems is long-term and intergenerational. The ongoing and systemic failures in duty of care, where racial profiling and stereotyping continue to override appropriate access to, and relevance of intervention (Herring et al., 2013).

Building on the recognition of various systemic issues, participants also highlighted how colonisation has disrupted Indigenous systems of care. Families are left with fewer resources, impacting the choices young people make:

> Part of the damage of what colonisation has done . . . is dismantling lots of those systems and really severing our ways of being that kept us well, that kept children . . . safe. . . . when I look at where we are today, a lot of people um, don't have access to things that they would have normally had, had colonisation happened. So, you know, they go and seek out things that they need because they're not available in ways that are not pro social. . . . I mean just if we look at all the factors that contribute to offending, we are more exposed to more risk, as Māori due to colonisation.

Participants agreed that the loss of culturally grounded resources and supports, as a direct result of colonisation, caused harm. Indigenous people today are not always able to access the systems, relationships, and cultural foundations that would have been present had colonisation not disrupted them. As described in the quote above, in the absence of these protective factors, youth may seek to meet their needs such as searching for identity, connection and belonging, through unhelpful and at times antisocial means.

The effects of colonisation in the Pacific are now intersecting with globalisation, creating new challenges for communities, particularly in relation to youth offending (Tauri, 2014). Participants described how the introduction of foreign influences, such as drug trafficking, has exacerbated social harm in ways that local systems are struggling to manage. One participant explained:

> introduction of the . . . Western influence into the Pacific has somewhat been quite significant and in particularly with the . . . drug importation into Tonga, Fiji most recently has created unnecessary youth offending . . . as a result of drug dealing And importation into the Pacific, we see all these other social

issues that now arise, which has got a lot of our Pacific elders and churches and communities and villages in the region scrambling to try address this foreign concept or idea.

The **impact of Western influence in the Pacific**, particularly through the **recent rise in drug importation into countries like Tonga and Fiji** is highlighted above. The influx of drugs, introduced from outside the region, has led to a surge in **youth offending in the Pacific Islands**. It is a **foreign and disruptive force** within traditionally close-knit communities, leaving Pacific elders, churches, and local leaders **struggling to respond to social problems which are unfamiliar and externally driven**. Participants thus highlight how **globalisation and transnational influences** are reshaping local realities and placing significant strain on Pacific justice and social systems that were not designed to deal with these imported issues. This is an area that is currently being explored among Police in Aotearoa New Zealand – to address international drug trafficking in the Pacific Islands (Pacific Community, 2024).

In the context of migration and its effects on Indigenous families, participants also highlighted the challenges that arise when traditional communal structures are disrupted. One participant discussed how migration often leads to families working multiple jobs to support themselves, which reduces the level of supervision over children (see recent Pacific Child Wellbeing Summit in March 2025). As they explained, "*often in terms of kind of the migration story, often families are working overtime two to three jobs and so the supervision isn't there as much as it would be in the kind of village or communal societal structures.*" This lack of supervision potentially leaves children more vulnerable to external influences and can lead them to assume significant caregiving roles, impacting their education and overall development (Fuligni & Fuligni, 2007). The participant continued, noting that "*children having less supervision . . . means that other influences can come in or they [are] taking on significant caregiving roles, which impacts on things like education and things like that.*" The consequences of this shift are particularly profound in the context of migration, where families may be displaced from their communities and their cultural support systems. This migration-driven disruption is a direct consequence of the broader forces of globalisation (Anae, 2019; Prevoo & Tamis-LeMonda, 2017). As global mobility increases, these structural changes place a strain on family dynamics, further perpetuating the challenges faced by young people in Pasifika communities.

What Can We Share with the Rest of the World About?

"Lift Them Up as Opposed to Push Them Down" – Reclaiming Indigenous Strength

The resilience of Indigenous communities across the South Pacific was emphasised by participants. Indigenous communities continue to draw on cultural knowledge systems to support their youth, despite the lasting impacts of colonisation.

The theme highlights areas that participants felt were important to teach and share with the rest of the world about youth offending. Part of this was the need for reviving culturally grounded approaches to wellbeing, healing, and accountability. Participants highlighted the importance of practices like tikanga, and collective decision-making as protective factors for youth. They also critiqued the current justice, care, health and educational systems for being misaligned with Indigenous values, calling for culturally safe, community-led models that prioritise connection, identity, and relational support over punishment.

A shared primary narrative present in participants' kōrero (shared discussion) was the importance of identity. Knowing of where you come from and who you are was named as a crucial foundation for navigating adversity, consistent with previous Indigenous research (Chandler & Lalonde, 2008; Chua et al., 2019). One participant stated, "Everyone should have the access to . . . their whakapapa, to know who they are and . . .[their] identity. You can do all these other interventions, but until you have that part, it's never going to be complete". It was acknowledged that people can be at varying stages in terms of security in their cultural identity. For example, it was discussed that Indigenous and ethnic minority communities who experience racism from the dominant culture may sadly come to internalise those negative views about themselves.

Language trauma was discussed as an example of how Māori may feel ashamed for not being able to speak Te Reo, attributing this as an individual fault. However, they may be unaware that state systems, particularly schools, actively deterred and physically punished children for speaking Te Reo, leading to a significant decline in fluent Te Reo speakers. Fortunately, Māori have fought for regeneration of Te Reo Māori, significantly through the Kohanga Reo movement and advocating for the recognition of Te Reo as a taonga (treasure) and official language of Aotearoa New Zealand requiring active protection. There was a consensus across participants' accounts were that reconnection to whakapapa (kinship, ancestry) is central to healing and growth. Without this connection, interventions may fall short of addressing the deeper layers of disconnection and trauma experienced by Indigenous youth (Lincoln, 2023).

Reclaiming identity through cultural practices was seen not only as a form of restoration but also as a vital mechanism for resilience. One participant highlighted cultural rituals, such as kava circles, as providing "a social and cultural space where young people feel at home, a sense of belonging, and also fostering identity". Such interventions gave youth a sense of belonging, purpose, and direction in the face of structural challenges. Another participant noted what cultural activities could involve, such as taking "[our] tamariki (children) out, like climbing up a maunga (mountain), or getting them to play touch or waka ama (outrigger canoeing), or kapa haka (Māori performing arts). Our rangatahi (youth) and our whānau (extended family) need to be able to access that." These practices were framed as helping youth navigate contemporary challenges by grounding them in culture. As one participant concluded, "Revitalising cultural practices to address social issues that exist in our societies is critical to the future of our young people and the next generation to come". These practices offer healing, guidance, and resilience for our

Indigenous youth harmed from the systems that have contributed to the significant stressors and conflict they continue to face in our society.

Building on this, participants described the need to embed Indigenous frameworks within mainstream systems, what one interviewee referred to as the "importance of colouring in white spaces." This phrase captured a call to centre tikanga and Indigenous values in interventions and services that have historically excluded or marginalised them. The interweaving of Indigenous knowledge and perspectives in interventions was seen as essential to healing. One participant highlighted the need for all "Māori to have access to interventions and strategies that come from within our own culture . . . [as] our families have a real yearning for that, so we need to be able to have that as part of what we're providing." This quote underscores both the right to culturally appropriate services and the current gap in access. The reference to "yearning" suggests that our Indigenous youth remain underserved in this area.

A lack of cultural knowledge and tikanga being used to support youth was a common area of concern identified by participants. They connected this absence to broader political contexts. One participant reflected, "If we just look at the political situation in Aotearoa right now, there's so many. There's quite a strong kind of attack on Māori and kind of taking away things that have been really hard fought for". This absence of cultural integration was therefore not viewed as coincidental, but as reflective of ongoing political and social dynamics that actively undermine Indigenous self-determination and visibility. In response, participants called for the reclamation of space and voice within dominant systems.

Frustration with institutional responses to youth offending was expressed by many participants. They referred to systemic issues such as marginalisation and institutional racism. One participant noted the presence of "throw away policies and procedures that are supposed to look good, that really have no impact that are unfunded or they're funded for a period of time and then the funding is withdrawn so they fall over". This view was echoed by others who saw government actions as performative rather than transformative. "Youth offending is used as a political football, but there's not a willingness to come together around the table and look at long-term prevention." The prevailing sentiment was that current responses lack the depth, sustainability, and collaboration needed to address the root causes of youth offending and marginalisation.

Participants also reflected on the role of practitioners in achieving justice and care for Indigenous youth. They emphasised the need for a culturally safe and humble workforce, alongside government commitment to real systemic change. This included not only hiring more Māori and Pacific professionals but ensuring that non-Indigenous staff take responsibility for cultural upskilling. There was a discussion about the use of the terms: cultural competence versus cultural safety. While cultural competence is a core competency for many professions including psychology, some participants raised that "competency" can only be held by people from that group, with participant reflecting: "In Australia . . . the language is changing quite a bit and we're moving from cultural competency because non-aboriginal or non-indigenous people will never be competent because they can't ever walk in our shoes . . . the language is going to culturally safe and responsiveness." Professionals who are not from that culture must still prioritise learning and practicing in a culturally safe way, accept what they do not know and be humble about this. One interviewee stated: ". . . we do need to bring our Pākeha[4] colleagues along with us . . ., in upskilling so that they are able to give an intervention that's . . . just as effective as if one of us were in the room. . . . We need everyone on board." A strengths-based approach, centred in humility and respect, was seen as foundational. Participants called for a shift in institutional culture, moving away from top-down, expert-driven models toward shared, community-embedded approaches. This collaborative stance challenges traditional power hierarchies and underscores the importance of recognising Indigenous communities as knowledge holders and leaders in the design and delivery of youth justice interventions.

Participants also highlighted the importance of the youth voice. One participant talked about the need for youth-led solutions, sharing:

> there is a Samoan proverb that goes "e fofo le alamea le alamea," which means the "youth will create the issues. The youth will also have the solutions." Not in that similar translation but in context . . . but I think that's an opportunity for the globe [to understand] that our young people are also intelligent enough to give us the solutions to how they're offending.

This proverb and point challenge deficit-based models and instead recognise the agency and lived experience of young people (Alefaio-Tugia, 2022; Pitanoe et al., 2018). If supported to lead and co-design solutions, particularly within culturally grounded frameworks, youth can offer insights that adults and institutions may inadvertently overlook.

Indigenous approaches were seen not only as more effective but as fundamentally more humanising. Participants emphasised the need to move beyond punitive responses and toward culturally relevant, strengths-based approaches. As one participant explained:

> Culturally relevant risk assessment tools are really, really important and the other thing is encouraging a strength-based approach to treatment and behavioural change. All too easily, we can become very focused on punishment. And I think you know, a number of jurisdictions in Australia are particularly focused on punishment at the moment . . . it's . . . not just about punishment, but it's about understanding why the behaviour occurred, where it's come from, the factors that have contributed to it and addressing those . . . that involves connection to family and community. . . . you can't do this just with the individual young person in in the room it's . . . a holistic approach [is needed].

This highlights how punitive legal frameworks often ignore root causes such as trauma, disconnection, and structural disadvantage. Further conducting risk assessments (e.g. risk to self, to others, from others, and recidivism) with Indigenous youth may result in inaccurate estimates and conclusions, particularly if the cultural and social context is not well understood (Shepherd & Lewis-Fernandez, 2016). Culturally informed practices were framed as both more just and more effective in supporting long-term transformation and wellbeing. **Understanding the "why," that is emotional and environmental factors contributing to offending behaviour, was seen as essential for healing and change.**

Youth offending was seen not as isolated acts of bad behaviour, but as symptoms of broader failures. As one participant said "the young person is part of a collective, if something's going wrong with them, then that's a problem for everyone in their collective, not just them on their own. They're not the problem". Understanding a young person within their context is part of a holistic approach. Another participant reflected:

> across the interventions that have been successful, I think there's a few . . . commonalities . . . They see . . . risk or offending behaviour . . . a marker of something else that's going on . . . the symptom, rather than these young people are "bad" and we need to label them. . . . successful interventions . . . actually get at some of the issues around the young person which could be family disconnection, it could be all sorts of things, social issues . . . and [try] to help out with some of those on a more on a longer-term basis rather than just addressing the offending behaviour in [an] in a quick program.

Effective interventions were described as those that are long-term, relational, and culturally grounded, aligned with Indigenous models of health and wellbeing that centre cultural values, connection, and a holistic understanding of youth experience (e.g. Fonofale model) (see chapter on Pasifika youth: Identity and Belonging).

Participants drew attention to justice innovations like the Rangatahi Courts and Pasifika Youth Courts, or "Koori" court in Australia, describing them as examples of how culturally grounded approaches can work within existing systems. These Courts are seen as formally part of the Justice system, though it is delivered in a culturally responsive way that prioritises Indigenous worldviews, practice and protocols:

> [t]he rangatahi courts and the Pasifika youth courts things like that. Those have been really innovative and New Zealand's approach to youth offending, all together has tried to be innovative and it's largely been driven by people who are coming from more Indigenous ways of being and knowing . . . a return to kind of the ways that we . . . have always known how to . . . deal with behaviour within our own societies.

These courts were seen as offering an important alternative to punitive systems, by creating spaces that feel relational and safe for youth. As one participant noted, "we kind of create space for different ways of bringing people through a system that often feels very unfamiliar or . . . familiar in really awful ways in that." However, concerns remained about the limitations of such models. One participant critiqued the Youth Koori Court's effectiveness, stating, "they have Koori court, but it really isn't effective here". They highlighted resource gaps: "they do have some Aboriginal people who support our young people in the system, but not enough". They also pointed to service disparity, stating, "there are only two Aboriginal liaison officers in our police stations in one police station for the whole of the Sydney metro area." It is inferred that the presence of culturally safe spaces alone is not sufficient; they must be matched by investment in community-led infrastructure and culturally responsive staff. Without this, even well-intentioned reforms risk becoming symbolic rather than transformative.

Conclusion

Ultimately, colonisation is understood by participants as an ongoing systemic force that has not only disrupted Indigenous lives historically but continues to influence youth offending today through intergenerational trauma, structural exclusion, racism, and cultural disconnection. These colonial frameworks remain embedded in modern legal, political, and social systems, perpetuating marginalisation. For Māori, Aboriginal, Torres Strait Islander, and Pacific communities, this has resulted in increased exposure to risk factors and the erosion of traditional protective supports such as kinship networks, cultural practices, and community-led systems of care. The overrepresentation of Indigenous youth in the justice system cannot be explained solely by a disconnect between youth behaviour and legal responses; rather, it is the product of a deeper legacy of harm that spans generations and intersects with multiple systems from child protection to health and education.

Participants emphasised the importance of cultural identity, connection, and community in addressing youth offending, with reclaiming whakapapa and embedding culturally grounded practices seen as essential to healing. They pointed to the need for long-term, sustainable interventions that go beyond performative solutions, highlighting the importance of relational, strengths-based approaches rooted in Indigenous knowledge systems. The call for greater inclusion of youth voices and community leadership in service design *and* delivery further underscores that justice reform must prioritise cultural restoration, genuine collaboration, and structural change.

As we end this journey, we wanted to leave you with a Fire Blessing – an ancient prayer that is 40,000 years old. It was handed down through the Aboriginal culture and translated to English:

Fire Blessing

May the fire be in our thoughts
Making them true, good and just, may it protect us from the evil one
May the fire be in our eyes
May it open our eyes to share what is good in life.
We ask that the fire may protect us from what is not rightfully ours
May the fire be on our lips,

So that we may speak the truth in kindness;
That we may serve and encourage others.
May it protect us from speaking evil
May the fire be in our ears
We pray that we may hear with a deep, deep listening,
So that we may hear the flow of water, and of all creation and the dreaming.
May we be protected from gossip and from things that harm and break down our family
May the fire be in our arms and hands
So that we may be of service and build up love.
May the fire protect us from all violence.
May the fire be in our whole being –
In our legs and in our feet, enable us to walk the earth with reverence and care;
So that we may walk in the ways of goodness and truth,
And be protected from walking away from what is truth
By Burnum Burnum
Australian Aboriginal elder
40,000 Year-old Australian Aboriginal Prayer | The Blessing Files

Notes

1 This proverb emphasizes the importance of perseverance and resilience in the face of adversity. It encourages individuals to remain steadfast during challenging times, trusting that difficulties will eventually pass.
2 A problem is solved by continuing to find solutions. The need for dynamic solutions and ongoing creativity in what we could do.
3 Indigenous refers to Maori (Aotearoa New Zealand), First Nations (Australia) and Pacific Island communities in Aotearoa New Zealand, Australia and the Pacific Islands.
4 New Zealanders of European descent (Thomas & Nikora, 1996).

References

Alefaio-Tugia, S. (2022). Collaborators for change: Community-village leaders. In S. R. Vaioleti (Ed.), *Pacific-indigenous psychology: Galuola, a NIU-wave of psychological practices* (pp. 123–146). Springer International Publishing. https://doi.org/10.1007/978-3-031-14432-5_7

Anae, M. (2019). Faamatai: A globalized pacific identity. In S. Ratuva (Ed.), *The Palgrave handbook of ethnicity* (pp. 1–15). Palgrave Macmillan. https://doi.org/10.1007/978-981-13-0242-8_85-3

Australian Institute of Health and Welfare. (2024, December 13). *Youth detention population in Australia 2024*. Retrieved June 20, 2025, from https://www.aihw.gov.au/reports/youth-justice/youth-detention-population-in-australia-2024

Burnum, B. (n.d.). *40,000 Year-old Australian aboriginal prayer*. Retrieved February 20, 2026, from 40,000 Year-old Australian Aboriginal Prayer | The Blessing Files

Chandler, M. J., & Lalonde, C. E. (2008). Cultural continuity as a protective factor against suicide in First Nations youth. *Horizons*, 10(1), 68–72.

Chua, R. Y., Kadirvelu, A., Yasin, S., Choudhry, F. R., & Park, M. S. A. (2019). The cultural, family and community factors for resilience in Southeast Asian indigenous communities: A systematic review. *Journal of Community Psychology*, 47(7), 1750–1771.

Cunneen, C. (2020). Youth justice and racialization: Comparative reflections. *Theoretical Criminology*, 24(3), 521–539.

Fuligni, A. J., & Fuligni, A. S. (2007). Immigrant families and the educational development of their children. In J. E. Lansford, K. D. Deater-Deckard, & M. H. Bornstein (Eds.), *Immigrant families in contemporary society* (pp. 231–249). Guilford Press

Herring, S., Spangaro, J., Lauw, M., & McNamara, L. (2013). The intersection of trauma, racism, and cultural competence in effective work with aboriginal people: Waiting for trust. *Australian Social Work*, 66(1), 104–117.

Ioane, J., & Lambie, I. (2016). Pacific youth and violent offending in Aotearoa New Zealand. *New Zealand Journal of Psychology*, 45(3), 23–29.

Jackson, M. (1988). *The Māori and the criminal justice system: A new perspective = He Whaipaanga Hou*. Wellington, New Zealand: Department of Justice.

Lincoln, E. M. (2023). Going home: The importance of reconnecting to Māori culture through whakapapa. *Te Tira: A Journal of Māori and Indigenous Leadership*, 1(3), 1–12.

Mead, H. M. (2003). *Tikanga Maori: Living by Maori values*. Wellington, New Zealand: Huia Publishers.

O'Brien, G. (2021). Racial profiling, surveillance and over-policing: The over-incarceration of young First Nations males in Australia. *Social Sciences*, 10(2), 68.

Office of the Premier. (2025, March 12). *Tough bail laws to keep Victorians safe* [Press release]. Victorian Government. https://www.premier.vic.gov.au/tough-bail-laws-keep-victorians-safe

Pacific Community. (2024). *Director-general's report 2024*. Noumea, New Caledonia: SPC. https://www.spc.int/digitallibrary/get/w5ybz

Paradies, Y. (2016). Colonisation, racism and indigenous health. *Journal of Population Research*, 33(1), 83–96.

Pitanoe, E., Korocowiri, S., Martin, L., & Davidson, J. (2018). *YES (Youth Empowerment Strategy) Pasifika: The formation of a model for Pasifika youth development* (Unpublished report). DevNet. https://devnet.org.nz/wp-content/uploads/2018/07/Davidson,%20Joy%20and%20Pitanoe,%20Elisha.%20Yes%20Pasifika%20%5Bpaper%7D_0.pdf

Prevoo, M. J., & Tamis-LeMonda, C. S. (2017). Parenting and globalization in western countries: Explaining differences in parent–child interactions. *Current Opinion in Psychology*, 15, 33–39.

Proudfoot, F., & Habibis, D. (2015). Separate worlds: A discourse analysis of mainstream and aboriginal populist media accounts of the Northern Territory Emergency Response in 2007. *Journal of Sociology*, 51(2), 170–188.

Ravulo, J. (2016). Pacific youth offending within an Australian context. *Youth Justice*, 16(1), 34–48.

Shepherd, S. M., & Lewis-Fernandez, R. (2016). Forensic risk assessment and cultural diversity: Contemporary challenges and future directions. *Psychology, Public Policy, and Law*, 22(4), 427.

Tauri, J. M. (2014). An indigenous commentary on the globalisation of restorative justice. British *Journal of Community Justice*, 12(2), 35–55.

Thomas, D. R., & Nikora, L. W. (1996). Māori, Pakeha and New Zealander: Ethnic and national identity among New Zealand students. *Journal of Intercultural Studies*, 17(1–2), 29–40.

Index

Note: page numbers in *italics* indicate a figure on the corresponding page.

For Product Safety Concerns and Information please contact our EU
representative GPSR@taylorandfrancis.com
Taylor & Francis Verlag GmbH, Kaufingerstraße 24, 80331 München, Germany

www.ingramcontent.com/pod-product-compliance
Ingram Content Group UK Ltd.
Pitfield, Milton Keynes, MK11 3LW, UK
UKHW020007200926
475702UK00015B/2514

* 9 7 8 1 0 3 2 2 8 7 6 7 6 *